THE OFFICIAL

ebaY ™

Guide

to Buying,

Selling, and

Collecting

Just About

Anything

Laura Fisher Kaiser & Michael Kaiser

with an Introduction by Pierre Omidyar, Founder and Chairman of eBay Inc.

A Fireside Book
Published by Simon & Schuster

FIRESIDE
Rockefeller Center
1230 Avenue of the Americas
New York, NY 10020

FIRST EDITION

FIRESIDE and colophon are registered trademarks
of Simon & Schuster, Inc.

eBay™ and the eBay Logo are trademarks of eBay Inc.

Designed by Bonni Leon Berman

Interior illustrations by Stephen Schudlich

Manufactured in the United States of America

20 19 18 17 16 15 14

Library of Congress Cataloging-in-Publication Data is available.

ISBN-13: 978-0-684-87372-5
ISBN-10:   0-684-87372-9
ISBN-13: 978-0-684-86954-4 (Pbk)
ISBN-10:   0-684-86954-3 (Pbk)

The joy of writing this book has been the collaborative effort that brought it to life. While we may have hammered away at the keys, the voices in this book come from many arenas.

We are most grateful to the staff of eBay, who shared so much about this online phenomenon: Chris Agarpao, Karin Bauer, Arlene J. Brenner, Scott S. Barnum, Bruce Brownstein, Barry Boone, Randy Ching, Chris Curtis, John Dex, Mark Flaa, Tiffaney Fox, Pam Goncalves, Jim Griffith (AKA Uncle Griff), Brad Handler, Brian Jones, Tim Kunihiro, Maria S. Lee, Jay Monahan, Buffy Poon, Kristie Reed, Rockin' Robin Rosaaen, Simon Rothman, Cathy Siciliano, Kristin Seuell, Jeff Skoll, Mary Lou Song, Karin Stahl, Brian Swette, Tom Walter, and Meg Whitman. Among all the standouts at eBay, George H. Koster II merits a special salute for his coordination of the whole project. We would have been lost without him. Steve Westly also provided important information and support.

Many thanks to John Gallo at Butterfield & Butterfield for sharing plans for the Great Collections. The eBay Ambassadors and PowerSellers featured in these pages provided insightful comments and wonderful anecdotes. To Ed Greenberg, Alan Wilensky, and the staff of the Guild Agency, many thanks for straightening us out on the issues of insurance. Cynthia Stern provided invaluable advice about the world of photography. We thank them all for their wisdom.

This Old House Magazine editor in chief Donna Sapolin and president Eric Thorkilsen deserve special thanks for being so understanding about Laura's extracurricular pursuits.

acknowledgments

Nothing is possible without family. Our cousin Charles Kaiser reminded us that writing a book has its own rewards. Sarah, Bob, Tess, and Ethan Hyams; Tema, Mark, Abraham, Ezra, and Isaac Silk; and Robert Morgan Fisher, Rebeca Goalby Fisher, and Grant William Fisher (welcome) have been remarkable throughout the entire process. Thanks especially to our parents, who touch and support everything we do: Roslyn Kaiser (who can never pass up an antiques store); George Fisher (a happy hunter in his own right), and Loretta Fisher (whom we forgive for long ago selling Laura's Barbies, Trolls, *Mad* magazines, etc., at her numerous garage sales).

To Bernice Silk, we are eternally grateful for allowing us the use of Sow's Ear in Hulls Cove, Maine, where many fine volumes have been crafted. All writers should be as lucky as we were to be able to gaze up from their laptops out at Frenchman Bay.

Besides being a cherished friend, Rebecca Cabaza at Simon & Schuster is a terrifically supportive and talented editor who had the good sense to call us first and ask if we knew anyone who was "really into eBay." Carrie D. Thornton, her assistant, is also a joy to work with. Mark Reiter, our agent at IMG, encouraged us at every turn. Thanks, also, to the hardworking managing editorial, copyediting, design, art, and production staffs at S&S, who made this book happen in record time.

Finally, we are deeply indebted to Pierre Omidyar, without whom none of this would be possible. His stewardship of eBay and his belief that common decency can prevail inspire us all. We think we speak for eBaysians everywhere when we say thank you for following your dream, which has enabled so many to pursue their own.

Laura Fisher Kaiser & Michael Kaiser
New York City
1999

Acknowledgments   v
Introduction by Pierre Omidyar, Founder
    and Chairman of eBay Inc.   xv
How to Use This Book   xix

Part I
The Thrill of the Hunt

Chapter 1
Welcome to the World's Largest Person-to-Person Online Trading Community   3

The eBay Revolution: The Mouse That
    Roared   4
The Four Pillars of eBay   4
Who Makes Up the eBay Community?   6
Before eBay/After eBay   7
Meet Our Extended Family   8
Mastering the eBay Way in Five Easy
    Steps   9
Why Buying on eBay is Safe   11
A Nickel Tour of the Site   12
What Makes eBay Auctions Unique?   14
Traditional Auction vs. eBay Auction   15

contents

Chapter 2
The Perfect Setup   17

You Gotta Be in It to Win It: Technical
    Stuff   17
The Need for Speed: Bits and Band-
    width   17
Registering to Become Part of the eBay
    Community   20
What's in a Name?   22
What eBay Charges Per Item   23

Contents

Going Dutch   25

Who You Are: Picking a Handle and Password   26

How eBay Keeps You in the Loop   30

Community Customs   30

Why Spam Ain't Kosher   35

Chapter 3
The Quest for Amazing Stuff   37

Homing In, Category by Category   37

The Big List at a Glance   38

What You Won't Find   39

Finding What You're Looking For   41

The No-Frills Search   46

Follow the Leader: Tracking Like-minded Bidders and Sellers 48

Personal Shopper   49

Gallery Hopping and Shopping   51

Beyond Collectibles: Everyday Wonders   51

Real Estate Reality Check   53

The "Great Collections" Connection   54

Kruse Control   55

Chapter 4
Let the Bidding Begin   57

Demystifying the Bidding Process   57

What It Means to Bid   60

Retracting a Bid   61

You Absolutely Positively Have to Have It: Bidding to Win   61

Capitalism for the Rest of Us   62

Up and Up: Bidding Increments   67

Cracking the Bid Code   68

Understanding Reserves   69

Dutch Auctions   70

Do Your Due Diligence   71

Good Questions to Ask   71

Part II
Parting Is Such Sweet Sorrow

Chapter 5
Putting It on the Block   77

    Details, Please: Listing Your Item for Sale   78

    The Key to Winning Titles   83

    Some Like Plain Vanilla   85

    The Great Listing Checklist   89

    Files with Style: Using HTML   89

    Say It with Pictures   92

    A Host of Options   93

    Off-the-Shelf Software   101

Chapter 6
Taking Care of Bidness   103

    Name Your Price   103

    Is It Really What You Think It Is?   104

    To Reserve or Not to Reserve?   106

    Establishing Payment Methods and Terms   108

    Perfect Timing   109

    Payments Made Easy   110

    Sorry, You Can't Bid on Your Own Auction   111

    Getting the Shipping Straight   111

    Happy Returns   112

    Final Touches   113

    Forget Something?   114

    Sellers, Please Stand By   115

    Knocking Off Early   116

    Canceling Bids   117

    Your Item Didn't Sell   117

    Building a Business on eBay   119

Contents

Part III:
Making Contact

Chapter 7
The Bidding Is Closed—Now What?   125

Buyer Meet Seller, Seller Meet Buyer   125
You've Got Mail   126
Tracking Down Email Addresses   127
I Want a Cookie   127
Temporary Parking: Escrow Services   128
Shipping News: Getting Out the Goods   131
Ordering Supplies on the Net   132
Stamp Me—I Must Be Dreaming   134
Closing the Loop: Leaving Feedback   136

Chapter 8
SafeHarbor and Happy Trading   137

Heading for SafeHarbor   138
Suspicious Minds: Identifying and Reporting Bad Behavior   138
Stake Your Claim: Insurance Against Fraud   142
Violations eBay Responds to Automatically   144
It's the Law: Prohibited, Questionable, and Infringing Items   144
Protecting Your Privacy   146
eBay's Privacy Policy   146
Making Your Experience More Positive   147
When a Deal Goes South   148
Best Remedy Prevention   151
Escrow Services   152
Who Was That Masked Man? Reaching Out to People
     Beyond Email   152

Chapter 9
When You Need a Friend   153

For Do-It-Yourselfers   154
By the Boards   155

eBay Customer Service Boards   158

Peer-to-Peer Support Boards   159

Talk the Talk   162

Giving Back   164

Part IV
You Are What You Collect

Chapter 10
Collecting Your Thoughts   173

Why Do People Collect?   173

Collecting vs. Accumulating   176

When Does a Collection Start? When Does It End?   176

Kids' Kollections   177

Getting Picky: Building and Upgrading   180

Chapter 11
The Mystery of Value   181

Separated at Birth: No Two Collectibles Are Exactly Alike   181

Eight Is Enough: The Collectibles Checklist   183

Mint to Be   186

Consult Before You Clean   188

Distinguishing Price from Value   189

Car Collecting Caveats   190

Where Passion Meets Price: Collecting as an Investment   193

Ready, "Set," Go: Collectors' Series   196

How Limited Is a Limited Edition?   197

Chapter 12
Becoming an Expert   199

Mastering the Details   199

Training Your Eye—and Ear, Nose, and Fingers   200

Immersing Yourself in the Market   203

Research, Research, Research   203

Chapter 13
Where the Action Is   211

Making the Rounds   211

Collector Connections on the Web   219

Special Sources for Established Dealers   220

Chapter 14
Out In the Field   223

Marketplace 101   223

Dealing with Dealers   224

Haggling with the Best of Them   224

Price Check, Aisle Six   226

Everything's Negotiable   226

A Tax Break for Dealers   230

Mood Breakers   230

Maximizing Your Auction Action   231

Beyond Negotiating: The Law of Averages   233

Finders Keepers: Shopping Etiquette   234

Tricks of Trading   236

It Happens to Everyone: Buying Mistakes   237

Part V
Putting It All Together
Chapter 15
My eBay and Other Ways to Keep Track
of It All   241

My eBay   241

Simple Spreadsheets You Can Create   248

Chapter 16
Documenting the Goods   251

Creating an Inventory   251

Insurance   255

Appraisals   259

Questions for the Appraiser   259
Collector, Appraise Thyself   260
Coming to Your Town: The *Antiques Road Show*   261
You Can't Take It With You   261
Going Public: Donating to an Institution   262
Trailblazing a Library   262

APPENDICES

eBay Site Map   263
eBay Category Overview   267

INDEX   289

First, a confession: I'm not a real collector. But I like to consider myself a collector by proxy—someone who's interested in other people's collections. As many people know, my wife, Pam, collects

by Pierre

Omidyar,

Founder and

Chairman of

eBay Inc.

Pez dispensers, and it's become part of the eBay legend that I invented the Web site just so she could pursue this hobby. The truth is, long before I clued in to her Pezmania, I had been thinking about how to create an efficient marketplace—a level playing field, where everyone had access to the same information and could compete on the same terms as anyone else. As a software engineer, I worked for a couple of Silicon Valley companies, and I had even cofounded an early e-commerce site. This got me thinking that maybe the Internet was the place to create such an efficient market. Not just a site where big corporations sold stuff to consumers and bombarded them with ads, but rather one where people "traded" with *each other.* I thought, if you could bring enough people together and let them pay whatever they thought something was worth (in other words, have them bid in an auction format), real values could be realized and it could ultimately be a fairer system—a win-win for buyers and sellers.

Around the same time, Pam (who was then my fiancée) mentioned that she wished she could find other Pez collectors with whom she could buy and sell dispensers so she could complete her collection. It occurred to me that the Internet might again be the perfect medium for accomplishing this. After all, the Net was becoming pervasive—businesses and households were getting hooked up at an amazing rate. With such a critical mass, you'd be bound to have a few Pez purveyors—and who knows what else? Best of all, the Net was interactive: I

could imagine people not only communicating with each other one on one around a transaction, but also sharing information about their passion.

However, when eBay's AuctionWeb (the name was later shortened) launched on Labor Day, 1995, I never dreamed that the site would become the leading Internet destination for people buying and selling just about anything. It all seems more of a happy accident than a grand business design—like that old commercial where the guy with the chocolate bar runs into the guy with the peanut butter and—eureka!—the peanut butter cup is born. Indeed, eBay.com is the perfect convergence of technology and great people. Person-to-person online trading in an auction format is a fascinating concept, but it merely provides an infrastructure for an even more fascinating sociological experiment. There have been millions of positive transactions on eBay, proving time after time that people are basically honest and trustworthy and eager to do a good job. Without the passion and goodwill of collectors and small entrepreneurs, eBay would no doubt have been just a blip at the end of the twentieth century.

I have to admit that it wasn't until almost a year after the first auction that I really understood who our users were. My business partner Jeff Skoll, an analytical powerhouse, had finally talked me into having a focus group, which included people from all walks of life. One of them was a truck driver who said, "I don't use eBay that much—I'm on it only two or three times a day. But my son is on all the time. He has packages coming and going constantly." Then the truck driver and everyone else in the group asked to take a break so they could go check their auctions. Wow! Not only were these people dedicated, but I could see that eBay had become a part of their lives.

Of course, I'd been well aware that we were on to something for some time. I launched eBay on the space my personal Internet service provider allocated to me as a member. After a few months, I was getting so much traffic they kicked me off the personal site. In February of '96, *I* had to start charging people. My initial goal was just to cover my rising costs of Internet service; I wasn't even thinking profit. People seemed happy to pay for the service, except I was so busy keeping the site going, I couldn't even get to the mail and open the checks that were piling up. That's when I realized my little hobby/experiment had taken on a life of its own. A couple months later, I had to buy my own server and hire a part-time employee to open the mail. We were no longer working out of my house, but this was still very much a start-up company. The three of us worked out of one room and Jeff kept a suit at the office "just in case" he had to meet with some business bigwig. Neither of us quit our other jobs until August of that year.

By the time Meg Whitman joined the company in early '98 as our CEO, we realized that eBay was a collector phenomenon. But, of course, the collectors already knew that—and they guided us. Their fingerprints are all over the site, from policies and categories to chat rooms to the new interface introduced in 1999. We listen to all user suggestions and, as we add and improve our services, we will continue to do so. eBay is today what our members have built and will be tomorrow what they want it to be. I always tell our members "if you don't like something on eBay, change it." Whether you're a collector or dealer or both, the worst thing you can be is apathetic or disaffected.

One of the most unexpected and gratifying aspects of eBay is the impact it's had on people's lives. eBay has given many people a way to achieve success on their own terms, whether that means becoming a self-sufficient businessperson, finding all the lost toys from one's childhood, or simply finding a bunch of like-minded souls. eBay's strength depends on our members' ability to connect with other members of this new global trading community.

That's what this book is all about. *The Official eBay™ Guide* is the only book authorized by our company. In the following pages, you'll find clear explanations of the ins and outs of the site, tips for selling and bidding smartly, do's and don'ts of eBay etiquette, and strategies for building and maintaining a stellar collection. In short, our goal is to help you the user be as successful on eBay as possible.

I may not be a collector, but I have found a few treasures on eBay, and sweated snipers in the process. In fact, I bought Pam's wedding gift—a rare "Pez pal bride" Pez dispenser, of course—on the site. (The staff then chipped in and bought the matching groom for her in another eBay sale.) Winning that for her was much more of a kick than I expected. And that's really the point of eBay—to have fun. No matter how much the eBay universe expands, I hope we never lose that sense of wonder.

Welcome to *The Official eBay™ Guide to Buying, Selling, and Collecting Just About Anything.* This book's mission is to help you be a successful eBay user. On a point-and-click basis, eBay isn't hard to master. But there's much more to

HOW TO USE THIS BOOK

eBay than words and images on a screen. The world's largest person-to-person, auction-format online trading site has spawned, for many people, a new way of life. Getting the most out of eBay means—among other things—mastering new technical skills, searching for amazing stuff (both online and beyond), understanding the economics of the collectibles market, becoming a savvy buyer, perhaps running your own small business, and interacting with other traders (and friends) who make up the eBay community all over the world.

In this book, we attempt not only to demystify the technological intricacies and philosophical underpinnings of eBay, but also to help people get the most satisfaction out of building their collections, no matter what they collect. The book is organized into five sections:

● **Part I: The Thrill of the Hunt** gets you started on eBay with information on registering, finding great stuff, and bidding strategies.

● **Part II: Parting Is Such Sweet Sorrow** helps you sell your items on eBay, from writing good descriptions, posting images, and using HTML to thinking through the details of being in business on eBay.

● **Part III: Making Contact** covers what happens when the flush of bidding is over—getting items shipped and dealing with problems. And just in case, you can find the help and support you need from eBay staff and your peers.

● **Part IV: You Are What You Collect** delves into the heart of collecting, including becoming an expert, sources of antiques and collectibles, and making buys in the field.

● **Part V: Putting It All Together** is about the care and feeding of your collection, from keeping track of your eBay activities to documenting your "babies" for their own good.

The book follows a logical progression of its own, but each chapter is also designed to stand alone. This book contains the collected wisdom of many eBaysians, but if you can't find what you're looking for, let us know so that we may include it in a future edition. Success on eBay comes from sharing. Send your feedback and tips for eBay success to: ebayguide@ebay.com.

PART ONE

THE THRILL OF THE
hunt

If the idea of cyberauctions seemed far-fetched in the early 1990s, the results now tell a different story. In just a few years, eBay, the world's largest person-to-person online trading community, has **CHAPTER 1** become a high-powered magnet for traders, linking buyers and sellers from all around the world. eBay's mission, in a nutshell, is to help people buy and sell just about anything on earth. Every day the number of items for sale mushrooms, spawning new categories and subcategories. When eBay started there were only two categories: *Collectibles* and *Computers*. At this writing there are more than 1,600—including subcategories—with more to come.

In the process, a fascinating and diverse eBay community has grown up. It's made up of people who come back to eBay time after time—sometimes hour after hour (but far be it from us to say, "Hey, get a life!"). They like hanging out with other friendly users who support each other in the acquisition or sale of the next great thing. Never mind that some of those buddies are halfway around the world. The global marketplace is only a mouse click away.

For some, eBay has opened new avenues to earn a living. Alexandra L. Carter, for example, started selling electronic equipment with a computer (bought on credit) and little else in the depressed area of Yavapai County, Arizona. With her profits she was able to pay off her PC before the interest kicked in, buy a car, and start her own company, Carter Cybernetics. "The best thing about eBay is that it rewards intelligence and hard work, regardless of race or class, and largely regardless of resources," she says. "You need electricity, a phone line, and a computer, and that's about it."

The eBay Revolution: The Mouse That Roared

Taking advantage of all the Internet has to offer, eBay breaks down traditional barriers between bidders and sellers—people who might otherwise never meet because they live in different states, time zones, or continents. Unlike other Internet sites that simply make life more convenient by saving a trip to a bookstore or posting movie reviews, eBay has actually created a cybermarket where millions of people buy and sell twenty-four hours a day, prices are set through competition, and there are no middlemen. This enhanced ability of collectors to locate new acquisitions they can't find anywhere else and for sellers to tap into broad markets has forever altered the face of commerce. To hear some "eBaysians" (a term of endearment among community members) tell it, you'd think that time began on Labor Day 1995, when eBay came into existence. Looking at how the playing field has changed since then, we have to agree that, indeed, a new era has dawned.

Completed eBay Auction	Number of Bids	Selling Price
Star Wars R2D2 Cookie Jar	4	$158.00
Sammy Sosa rookie cards (5) No reserve	8	13.51
Rosie's signed golf set from her Orlando trip	40	1,600.00
Tiffany Lamp Tyler Original 18"	26	40,800.00
Luke Black Lab Puppy Ty Beanie Baby	3	7.50
California '64 Corvette Roadster "Awesome"	47	30,100.00
Roseville Blue Primrose Vase MINT LARGE	15	228.00

The Four Pillars of eBay

People may come to trade for different reasons, but if you ask them why they love eBay, they usually cite one—or all—of the following reasons:

● **Amazing stuff:** With its awesome volume, eBay attracts the finest items available in all categories of collecting. Where else can you type in *fire extinguisher* and, in a few seconds, have nearly 150

Meet eBay Ambassador Alexandra L. Carter

SPECIALTY:
Technical Equipment

eBay HANDLE: carter@goodnet.com   AGE: 36

I'VE BEEN COLLECTING SINCE: High school—my first project was an audio oscillator built in a cigar box. Now I have 2,600 pieces of neat phone stuff.

WHY THIS STUFF IS COOL: A good oscilloscope is always handy to have, and telephone test equipment is just plain fun to have. Top-quality test gear by Hewlett-Packard and Fluke is so well made, it's beautiful.

TO BE AN EXPERT IN THIS AREA: You should have a ham radio license and at least a two-year degree or the equivalent in electronics.

THE BIGGEST MISCONCEPTION: That old Heathkit catalogs aren't worth anything. Aargh!

I'M DYING TO ADD: The radio-controlled pterodactyl flown by Dr. Falken in the movie *WarGames*.

MY eBay CONVERSION: I listed a Sun Hemmi slide rule, figuring I'd double the $7 I paid for it at a swap meet. I got $60. Wow! I thought. There are other people who care about this stuff.

SINCE THEN: I started my own company and make more than I ever did in the electronics field—and it's a lot of fun. My buying and my selling puts me in contact with a lot of really neat people.

TO SUCCEED ON eBay: Be organized. Always include the item number and your address in emails.

MY BEST eBay FIND: A bumper sticker on my van that says "LINUX—for IQs Over 98." I get a lot of laughs over it at computer shows and ham radio fests.

QUESTION I'M ASKED THE MOST: Did you send it yet?

WHAT I TELL NEW COLLECTORS: eBay is the largest single database of its kind. Searching current and completed auctions is unparalleled for learning about things you're interested in.

BEST eBay TRANSACTION: I got a copy of *Computer Engineering: A DEC View* by Gordon Bell et al. for $7 and sold it for $185. That was certainly the best in monetary terms. In human terms, every time someone buys a good book for their kid or a tool they really need, or anything that helps them or someone, that's the best you can get.

Only on eBay

Theories abound about the origin of the name "eBay." Some people think it stands for "East Bay"—even though the company is located in the South Bay area of San Francisco. Others assume it's a mysterious acronym. Customer support manager Uncle Griff (meet him in chapter 9, "When You Need a Friend") prefers to think of it as pig Latin for "be." The real answer might seem mundane by comparison: founder Pierre Omidyar coined the name to convey two things close to his heart— e-commerce and the Bay Area. For him, "bay" also connotes other images: ships coming into trade, a port in a storm, a safe harbor . . . you see where this is going. And when it comes down to it, eBay is a heck of a lot catchier than the site's original name, eBay's AuctionWeb.

matches pop up, ranging from new fire extinguishers to glass fire extinguisher grenades from the 1880s?

The thrill of the hunt: eBay makes searching for the next wonderful addition to a collection easier—and more exciting—than ever. Collectors can see more items in an hour at home than they can in a year of scouting flea markets, garage sales, and shows. Once they've located their quarry, they have the heart-pounding experience of competing against equally passionate bidders at auction.

Connections with people: eBay is not only where collectibles and collectors intersect, it's also where people meet like-minded folks and share information about their passions and interests.

Success: Bidders and sellers alike get a rush from mastering the auction game. Success breeds success, and the more savvy eBay users become, the more satisfying the experience is for all involved. And the learning curve is fairly easy. In short order, sellers discover how to create listings that get results—which has spawned a cottage industry of collectibles entrepreneurs—and bidders find shortcuts to the items they desire, sending them to new levels of collecting.

Who Makes Up the eBay Community?

The people who use eBay are people like you: collectors, hobbyists, small dealers, unique item seekers, bargain hunters, opportunistic sellers, and browsers. The growth of the community comes from meeting and exceeding the expectations of these special people. You don't just pass through eBay on your way to the next antiques or collectibles show. eBay is a destination in

before ebay	after ebay
Collectors wade through thousands of objects at flea markets, garage sales, and shows—often going long stretches before finding a single item worthy of their collection.	One-stop shopping for collectors who can search a vast database tailored to their area of interest.
The hunt is restricted to your free time (whatever *that* is) and the hours of local vendors.	Bidders and sellers trade twenty-four hours a day, seven days week—when it's convenient for them.
Buyers and sellers constrained by geography and ability to travel.	Bidders can shop the world without leaving home.
Dealers buy merchandise in the hope that the right collector will (someday) cross their path.	Sellers have immediate exposure to thousands of new potential customers who are searching for that exact merchandise.
Assessing the state of the market and value of items is a guessing game based on a limited pool of buyers and sellers.	Anyone can instantly access sales information and prices of similar items based on transactions by a global network of traders.
Sellers are concerned that they're getting fair prices for their merchandise.	Sellers benefit from fair market value that results from an open and competitive auction.
Selling done mostly by dealers, who have overhead expenses that they pass on to buyers.	Individual sellers as well as dealers can take advantage of eBay's reasonable fee schedule to inexpensively post items for sale.
Individual sellers can't compete with dealers who have large inventories.	Anyone can turn a single find into instant cash or sell hundreds of items at a time.
Collectors isolated from each other, unable to share their passions and exchange hard-to-find information.	Like-minded people available online all the time to share war stories and provide support.
Buyers and sellers go about their business with no stake in the marketplace, taking out only what's good for them.	Everyone shares in eBay success by being the best buyers and sellers they can be.

Only on eBay

itself, where you can "click in" for a few minutes to see what's new for sale, whether your Partridge Family album collection has any new bids, or what's up in your favorite chat room.

Besides the chat rooms, which are developed around specific collectibles categories, there are also several support boards where you can ask a question or provide help to eBay brothers and sisters learning the ropes. Real friendships form on eBay and users have reported getting together offline for picnics, vacations, and other gatherings.

Meet Our Extended Family

eBay is not just a bunch of wigged-out collectors basking in the glow of their computer screens, clicking and typing away in anonymity. We're a family whose members are scattered around the country and the globe. From among the millions of users, eBay has identified some key players who've set the pace for eBay's phenomenal growth. These include:

- **Ambassadors:** eBay's Ambassadors play an important part in making the real-life connection between eBay the site and eBay the people. These experts come from all corners of the collecting globe, and their diplomatic mission is to spread goodwill throughout and beyond the eBay community. You can email them questions about their specialties or talk to them in the eBay chat rooms. Also look for them at major antiques and collectibles shows. You'll get to meet many of them throughout this book.

- **PowerSellers:** If you sell more than $2,000 worth of goods a month on eBay, you're in the big leagues. These are the folks who bring a significant amount of that great stuff online. PowerSellers receive varying levels of personalized customer support depending on their monthly volume.

Only on eBay

Don Millbranth, a retired cabinetmaker and engineer from Indiana, listed a book, *How to Make Shaker Furnishings for Doll Houses or Miniature Rooms,* on eBay in November 1998. Mary Ellen Gibb, an Alabama clinical systems analyst and dollhouse miniatures enthusiast, won the auction, and the two struck up an email correspondence. A friendship blossomed, but since they lived six hundred miles apart, neither Don nor Mary Ellen (both of whom were widowed) felt ready to move beyond a virtual relationship. But as their email exchanges accelerated—up to two hundred a day—their feelings deepened. In December Don proposed and Mary Ellen accepted, although it wasn't until February that they met in person. Having exchanged photos online, they spotted each other in the airport. "We both had been alone for many years, and our meeting was just so comfortable. We walked arm in arm to get the luggage, and it was just as if I were coming home," he says. They wed in May. Among their guests were thirty from the eBay community. In addition to the traditional wedding cake, a separate groom's table (a Southern tradition) featured a cake topped by two miniature computers. "I think we got to know more about each other by communicating through email," Mary Ellen says. "You get past all the physical awkwardness. I've heard it called 'falling in love from the inside out.' We had explored such issues as religion and politics—all those subjects that make a difference in building a life together—so that it was as if we had known each other forever." Now that they've combined households, Don has retrieved the book that started it all and begun making dollhouse furniture that he and his bride sell on eBay, continuing their partnership where it began.

Mastering the eBay Way in Five Easy Steps

Part auction, part classified ad listing, eBay is actually a sophisticated way of bringing order to the otherwise chaotic world of buying and selling stuff. Simply stated, eBay is an electronic bazaar with millions of cybervendors and cyberbuyers. Sellers take pictures and write descriptions of items for sale and bidders search by category for items of interest. There's a minimum of "paperwork"—registering, filling out an About Me profile (if you want)—and if you're a seller, it does help to have a scanner or digital camera. Sellers pay a small listing fee (between $0.25 and $2) and a commission of between 1.25 percent and 5 percent. (These fees are eBay's primary revenue source.) Buyers pay no fees.

Only on eBay

Chris Agarpao will forever be known as eBay employee number one. Back in the spring of 1996, Chris was thirty and looking to get into the computer field when he happened to attend a Jackie Chan movie with his sister, her fiancé, and the future best man at their wedding—Pierre Omidyar. Around this time Pierre had his hands full running the new site and needed help opening envelopes and processing bills. After an informal interview at the picnic table in Pierre's backyard, Chris started working part-time. The office comprised a laptop, an old school desk, and a filing cabinet in Pierre's small apartment. That was fine with Chris: "The hours were flexible, and I could wear shorts." After about a month they moved to a real office in Sunnyvale, California, where Chris graduated to a card table for a desk. "About eight months into it, I thought we were doing pretty well and (Vice President) Jeff Skoll said, 'You haven't seen *anything* yet!' It was then that I knew this was going to be big."

Overall, doing business on eBay couldn't be simpler. A typical transaction can be broken down into five steps:

1 Bidders, who must be registered users, find and bid on items they want—as many times as they want—or bid their maximum once and let eBay's *Proxy Bidding* function bid against all comers until their maximum price is reached.

2 After a prescribed time—three, five, seven, or ten days—the auction ends and the high bidder wins. In reserve price auctions, the high bidder wins only if the seller's reserve price is met or exceeded.

3 The seller and high bidder contact one another to finalize payment and shipping terms.

4 The winner sends the seller payment.

5 Upon payment, the seller ships the item.

It's that easy and even more fun!

Winning bidders arrange for payment with the seller. Some eBay sellers take credit cards, and most allow bidders to pay by check or money order. Your payment is sent directly to the seller, not shot into the great cyberspace void. Upon receipt of payment (or after the check clears), the seller ships the item directly to the buyer. How soon you get the goods depends on how quickly you send payment, what type of payment you use, and how quickly the seller can ship. If you were to mail a money order on the day the auction ended and the seller shipped the day the money order arrived, a transaction could be completed in seven to nine days. Typically, it's two to three weeks from auction end to receipt of goods. But if you need something in a hurry, most sellers are willing to work with you.

Why Buying on eBay Is Safe

Anyone familiar with the world of antiques and collectibles knows that, for the most part, people in this business are decent and fair. Maybe it's because they share an underlying respect for the objects being traded or because they know that treating people with dignity is easier and more profitable. In any case, the civility of the marketplace makes it a wonderful place to spend your time.

Building on this rich tradition, eBay was founded on the idea that people are basically honest. To make sure they stay that way, eBay allows users to establish a reputation for quality and square dealing just as they can in any other marketplace. And, through the *Feedback Forum*, one of eBay's many special services for registered users, that reputation is available to anyone in the eBay community. If you visit this part of the site and peruse the feedback that registered users have given and received, you'll quickly note that the vast majority of comments are positive. In fact, many users report that people go out of their way to make transactions as pleasant as possible. That is the eBay way and one of the reasons the site is so popular. Users like you make or break eBay's reputation.

Some people have shied away from buying or selling items on the Internet because they fear sending their credit card number into cyberspace. However, statistics show that the fear of credit card fraud in e-commerce is greater than its actual incidence warrants. When a seller uses a secure server to process credit card transactions, it's actually safer than paying with a credit card in person, when you consider how easy it is for an unscrupulous vendor to get your number from your "paper trail"—a receipt or carbon copy.

Perhaps the biggest concern people have about buying stuff over the Net is fraud. Is this stuff for real? Can I trust the seller? How can I tell the true condition from a grainy picture? All valid questions, to be sure. Interestingly, the number of complaints is relatively small—about two hundred per one million transactions. Most of those get resolved between users. The cases where someone files an official fraud complaint hovers around thirty per one million transactions, which is less than .001 percent. But bear in mind that just as eBay believes that most people in its community are on the up-and-up, your best protection as a bidder is to know your stuff. Do your homework, ask sellers questions, review their feedback no matter how high their rating, and keep tabs on the market for your area of collecting.

Okay, so we know that the world is not a perfect place. There are no civility, kindness, or intelligence tests for becoming a collector or a seller. Real disagreements can occur between perfectly reasonable and rational people. That's why eBay has created mechanisms for users to address these issues. For details on reporting and resolving such problems, read about the *Feedback Forum* and *SafeHarbor* program in chapter 2, "The Perfect Setup," and on formal eBay offenses in chapter 8, "*SafeHarbor* and Happy Trading."

A Nickel Tour of the Site

eBay is a big Web site to sort through, but once you get your bearings, you'll be able to find exactly what you're looking for in seconds. One of the most helpful places to start is the eBay site map, which lists topics or "areas" on the site. The site map can be accessed from the navigation bar at the top of every page. From there, you just scroll down until you find the link to the area you need. For example, if you want to change your password, look under *Services*, click on *Services Overview*, and locate *Change My Password.* We recommend bookmarking areas or pages you'll need often, such as *Feedback Forum*, or adding them to your favorite places folder.

The eBay site is built around the functions buyers and sellers perform. At the top of every page on the site is a menu bar, which when clicked on takes you to the associated content area. On the upper-right-hand side of a page you will see a link to the site map. Information on the site map is broken down into the following major areas:

- **Browse:** a list of main categories and all the item listings

- **Sell:** Sell your item form

- **Services:** Registration, Buying and Selling, Managing Items for Sale, Seller Accounts, Buyer Tools, My eBay, About Me, Feedback Forum, SafeHarbor

- **Search:** Search for items and members, Personal Shopper

- **Help:** Help Overview, Buyer Guide, Seller Guide, Community Standards, Support Boards

- **Community:** News, Announcements, Cool Happenings, Latest Buzz on New Features, Calendar, Letters to the Founder, Chat (including eBay Café and category-specific rooms), eBay Life, Library, Charity, Giving Board, eBay Store, Suggestion Box, About eBay

SPECIALTY:

Elvis

eBay HANDLE: kingthings@aol.com   AGE: 51 years young

IN THIRTY-FIVE YEARS I'VE COLLECTED: Some forty thousand pieces of Elvis memorabilia, from books and photos to his shirts and a lock of his hair.

QUESTION I GET ASKED MOST: Is Elvis really dead?

ROYAL TOUCH: My favorite memento is a photo of Elvis Presley giving me a scarf and a kiss on May 6, 1975, at the Sahara Tahoe Hotel in Lake Tahoe, Nevada. I also cherish a memory of a squirt gun fight we had there, which Ed Parker (an Elvis bodyguard) wrote about in his book, *Inside Elvis*.

I'D LOVE TO ADD: An Elvis jumpsuit with belt and cape. Elvis himself would also be great.

I SOLD eBay STOCK TO BUY: Elvis's dental chart, including X-rays and the patient card he filled out in 1967. The dentist who later bought the Palm Springs, California, practice found them in the back room.

ADVICE TO NEW COLLECTORS: Don't buy the first thing you see unless you're positive of its history. Look around—you might find it for less money elsewhere.

What Makes eBay Auctions Unique

If you've ever been to a live auction and found yourself waving a paddle in a white-knuckled, sweaty-brow bidding war, you're no stranger to the rules and customs by which traditional auctions are run. In many ways eBay auctions are similar. But there are also crucial differences to bear in mind, as the following chart indicates.

The heart of eBay is accessibility for everyone. While the site has become a great equalizer, its success hinges on the integrity of millions of users. They recognize the value of person-to-person online trading in an auction format and are making it work every day. In the process, they've built a vibrant community and helped shape a new economy. To further that process, this book is designed to help you get the most out of your eBay experience and become a great collector.

Traditional Auction	eBay Auction
Bidding is on a last-person-standing basis—that is, bidding continues until no one is willing to bid more.	Bidding ends at an established time—three, five, seven, or ten days—after the seller posts the listing.
Auction house actively engages in marketing items for sale and bringing potential buyers to the sale.	Sellers are free to write their own descriptions—eBay doesn't get involved in the marketing of any auction items.
Some auction houses will research items guaranteeing authenticity, authorship, provenance, date of manufacture, condition, and so on.	eBay leaves it up to sellers to provide such information and to bidders to do their homework and know the market. eBay neither authenticates nor guarantees any item.
Auction houses provide appraisals and presale estimates of potential selling price.	Sellers must assess value themselves.
Reserve auctions are those in which a confidential price is agreed upon between the seller and auction house below which the item will be passed and not sold.	Sellers can pick either a *reserve* auction, and specify a price below which they're not obligated to sell, or a *no-reserve* auction, where the high bidder automatically wins.
Some auction houses accept returns if bidders can disprove an item's authenticity.	Individual sellers decide on postsale policies such as returns and refunds.
Auction houses set terms of sale such as payment policies and pickup policies.	Seller sets policies about methods of payment and length of time for contact.
Some auction houses charge commissions to both bidders and sellers.	Sellers pay a nominal listing fee and small percentage commissions on each successful auction. Bidders pay nothing.
Sellers must wait for auction house to pay them after a sale.	Bidders pay sellers directly.
Sellers consign items for sale to auction houses and wait anywhere from a few weeks to several months until the auction actually takes place.	eBay sellers post items as fast as you can say "upload a picture."

I didn't know how to turn on a computer until my husband told me that people sold glass on an auction site called eBay. My son says that he created a monster because now they can't get on the computer until Mom "does the eBay thing." But I've gained computer skills I might never have if I hadn't looked at eBay that first time. It's opened up a whole new world for me. I've met great people and gained a lot of confidence.

—Dixie Hardesty, eBay Ambassador of Fire King and Kitchen Glass

CHAPTER 2

the

perfect

setup

You Gotta Be in It to Win It: Technical Stuff

There's only one route to eBay: the Internet. In other words, to get in on the fun you need a personal computer, a modem, access to the Internet, and your own email address. Most computers for the home market come Internet-ready with enough power, memory, and disk space to get you off and surfing. You just need to set up an account with one of the 4,500 Internet service providers (ISPs) in the United States. These companies give you phone numbers that your computer dials to access the Net and an email address, which should look something like this: youraccountname@yourISP.com.

The Need for Speed: Bits and Bandwidth

As you surf the Net, you are actually downloading, or bringing files onto your computer so you can view them. The speed of that process depends

SPECIALTY:

Fire King and Kitchen Glass

eBay HANDLE: randix@ascenture.net   AGE: 42

I STARTED COLLECTING: Fire King, 8½ years ago—before it was cool. My mother-in-law brought a sapphire blue casserole to a family dinner. She never did get it back.

WHAT'S SPECIAL ABOUT FIRE KING: Anchor Hocking Glass Company produced the Fire King line from the early 1940s to the late 1970s in Lancaster, Ohio—fifteen miles from my home. It brings back memories of eating at the local diner or Grandma's kitchen.

ON THE ONE HAND: People say, "You're paying *what* for that piece? I threw a bunch of that out when I cleaned out my grandmother's house!"

ON THE OTHER HAND: People assume that you can't find this stuff for a dime at garage sales anymore.

MY FAVORITE PIECE CAME FROM: A dump in the woods. It's a chipped Jade-ite Fire King mug that my son dug out when he was four.

I'M NOW DYING TO ADD: A Jade-ite Philbe table server with tab handles. (Philbe was one of the first oven-safe glass products. The dinnerware is as scarce as hen's teeth.)

I DREAM ABOUT FINDING: A Jade-ite Sheaths of Wheat demitasse and saucer. No one's ever heard of such a thing, but I dreamed I found it at a church bazaar.

BEFORE YOU BID: Watch other auctions in the category you're interested in to get a feel for the prices.

WHEN LISTING AN ITEM: Cut the fluff. Little hearts and flowers don't sell your item. A piece that's desirable will sell itself. Besides, people get impatient and don't like waiting all that extra time for pictures to load.

MY BEST eBay TRANSACTION: I sold an item to a gentleman in Denmark. My son happened to be doing a report on that country, and the customer was most generous in answering his questions.

a great deal on the size of the file and the speed of your modem and Internet connection. In general, graphics—photos, intricate artwork, fancy type— take longer than plain text to "load" onto your computer. Most personal computers (PCs) ship with modems rated at 56K (kilobits per second), the fastest available at this writing. If you have a slightly older PC or modem, you could be operating at slower rates of 28.8K or 14.4K. You might want to upgrade to a faster modem (which can be done without buying a new PC), so you can scan eBay pages as quickly as flipping through a book.

Internet service is changing rapidly, and new technologies will soon allow Internet access at blistering speeds, perhaps eliminating the need for dial-up service as people are hooked up twenty-four hours a day. The Net will be working for you all the time, grabbing files and alerting you to new items of interest. Four technologies are vying to provide the next wave of high-speed Internet access—and capture your heart, mind, and wallet. Many people are touting these "broadband" services as the next version of the Internet or Internet 2. One or two will come out winners, relegating the others to Betamax status of the information age. When that day comes, your current modem, no matter the speed, will be obsolete and you *will* need to buy new hardware. These are the technologies to watch:

ISDN (Integrated Services Digital Network):
A phone line with the capacity to handle Net access, phone, and fax simultaneously. Internet access can reach 128K (more than twice a 56K modem), depending on how much of the capacity you are using for phone or faxes at the same time as you're surfing. ISDN has actually been around for a while, but in some places phone companies are just now making it available for home use. Contact your local phone company for information about availability and fees.

DSL (Digital Subscriber Line):
Similar to ISDN in that it uses a standard phone line, DSL can achieve speeds five times faster than ISDN and eleven times faster than 56K. DSL creates a direct link between your computer and the Internet—it's like being hard-wired to the Internet. With DSL, when you turn on your PC you turn on the Internet. DSL is already available in some markets and may soon be available through your phone company or a third-party provider.

Cable modems:
The cable that brings five hundred television channels to your TV screen can also handle high-speed Internet

Only on eBay

If you've reached the point where you dread being away from your computer for fear you'll be outbid or because you can't wait to see how much your Russel Wright butter dish sold for, *eBay a-go-go* is a dream come true. With eBay a-go-go you receive auction alerts on any small wireless device—pager or cell phone—that accepts text messaging and has an Internet email address.

You receive automatic notification when: you've won an item, you're outbid, or your item sells. eBay a-go-go also sends messages to your pager and regular email address so when you get home from a long day on the road, you can follow up with buyers and sellers. And, you can activate and deactivate anytime by using your Web-based eBay a-go-go profile.

If you have your own hardware that meets the eBay a-go-go requirements, all you have to do is sign up for the service. However, if you don't have a pager or also want to receive free eBay news and access your messages via telephone with SkyTel Page Recall, you'll need an official eBay pager. Two models are available: one by Cirkisys, free when you activate the service and purchase 2,000 message units ($75 total) or Select Motorola's WORDline FLX, for $100. Looking ahead, the time is not far off when you'll even be able to place bids from your wireless device. For more information on eBay a-go-go and signing up, see www.skytel.com/ebay.

access. If your cable company doesn't already offer this service, it most likely will soon.

● **Satellite PC:** Just like satellite TV, you can get Internet access through a satellite dish in your yard or on your roof. Speed falls somewhere between that of ISDN and DSL.

Note: The speed with which you access the Internet also depends on whether the Web sites you visit have the capacity to handle the hordes of people logging on. That's why even with the fastest modem you occasionally hit "traffic jams," resulting in sluggish speeds.

Registering to Become Part of the eBay Community

To really get going on eBay, you have to become a registered user. Anyone who's over eighteen years old and has a valid email address is eligible. And rest assured that eBay adheres to strict privacy guidelines and will not disclose any registration information for marketing purposes or to any outside party. (See chapter 8, "*Safe-Harbor* and Happy Trading," for more on eBay's privacy policy.)

Setting Up an Account
You can access the registration menu in several ways: 1) from the home page (www.ebay.com); 2) through the *eBay site map*; or 3) by clicking

on *Services* on the navigation bar at the top of your screen found on most pages on the eBay site and going to *Register Now*. However you get there, the rest is simple:

1 **Complete the eBay initial registration form.** After providing basic information such as your email address, name, address, and phone number, double-check that it's accurate and submit.

2 **Receive your confirmation instructions.** eBay quickly emails a message to the address you've used on the form, confirming your registration. Write down or print out the confirmation code—you'll need it to complete the registration process.

3 **Confirm your registration.** Go to the eBay *user agreement* and read it. (Note: The URL address will be in the email with your confirmation code from eBay; URL stands for universal resource locater—the fancy name for an Internet address that begins *http://.*) Yes, it's long and legalistic and you may be tempted to just scroll quickly to the end. But these are the rules that govern eBay and your participation. Should you run afoul of them in the future, ignorance of the law is no excuse. Besides, you can learn a great deal from the fine print. At the end of the user agreement, either accept or decline. If you decline, then it's bye-bye, eBay. But if you accept, you can proceed to the next step.

4 **Enter your email address and your confirmation code from eBay.** (Aren't you glad you saved it earlier?) Now, create a password. Remember, your password is your protection from other people accessing your account or information. For safety, pick a password that's at least six characters and uses a combination of letters and numerals. Don't use anything obvious like your birthday or girlfriend's name. Try something a bit obscure—but not so obscure that you can't remember it! (You can get a new password if you forget yours by going to *I forgot my password* under *Services* on the site map.) To be supersafe, change your password every so often.

Only on eBay

As of July 1, 1999, the eBay community included more than 5.6 million registered users.

5 Choose a user ID or nickname (optional). This name will appear when you place bids or list items for sale. One's "handle" is a matter of personal taste. Some people choose names that reflect their areas of interest, such as *kingbeanie*, *dollnut*, or *toyfanatic*. You can pick any name you'd like or just use your email address. Anywhere on eBay where a user ID is required, you can use either your user ID or your email address. The one advantage to using your email address is that it can save people a step when they want to contact you. However, if you don't want your boss to see you out there on eBay, pick a nice alias.

6 **Click the *Complete Your Registration* button.** You're ready to go!

What's in a Name?

Your user ID, which must be at least two (2) characters long, is case insensitive. For example: *MadBidder* is the same as *madbidder*. While you may use letters (A through Z), numbers (0 through 9), and/or certain symbols, your user ID cannot contain the following:

- The "@" symbol unless your user ID is the same as your registered email address. This is to prevent anyone else from using your email address as his or her user ID.

- The "&" symbol.

- Spaces.

- Anything obscene, profane, or hateful.

As soon as you register, eBay extends you a $10 courtesy line of credit. This way you can start listing items for sale immediately until your credit limit is used up. At that point you'll be unable to add new items until you create an account and choose a method of payment. Despite the $10 line of credit, if you want to hit the ground running and put a lot of items up for sale, you'll probably want to set up an account for automatic billing right away.

Automatic Billing

eBay charges buyers no fees. Sellers, however, are subject to an insertion fee upon listing an item and a final value fee based on the item's final price. eBay's fees are based on a sliding scale depending upon opening bids and reserves and the final sales price of an auction. Insertion fees start at $0.25, and final value fees can be as low as 1.25 percent of the ending price. For an additional cost, you can take advantage of services such as *Featured Auctions*, *Boldface Titles*, and *Gallery* pictures. (For more on these options, please see chapter 5, "Putting It on the Block"). eBay's fees are modest—especially when you think about what it might cost to sell an item in other venues. Compared to paying a premium at a large auction house, taking a booth at a flea market or show, or taking out an ad—even a classified ad—listing your item on eBay, where millions of potential bidders might see it, is one of the world's last great bargains.

The easiest way to pay these fees is to have them billed to your credit card. eBay then debits your credit card account once a month and you can go happily on your way, selling, selling, selling. To set up an automatic billing plan, click on *Services*, go to *Buying and Selling Tools*, and fill out the credit card information form. Once you have submitted your credit card number, eBay attempts to authorize your card. The response from your credit card company appears on your *account status* page within twenty-four hours as either declined or approved. You can access your account status through *My eBay* (see chapter 15, *"My eBay* and Other Ways to Keep Track of It All") or under *Buying and Selling Tools*. Once approved, eBay bills your credit card each month for the previous month's activity. Remember that eBay knows the date your credit card expires and will suspend your account if you do not keep your card information up-to-date.

If you prefer not to set up an automated account by credit card, you can pay by check or money order. eBay invoices you by email on the first day of each month for the previous month's activity. You then go to *Make Payments Toward My Account* (under *Buying and Selling Tools*) and print out a coupon to mail in with your payment. (The snail-mail address is on the coupon.) Payment is due by the end of the month. Keeping your account up-to-date is important. eBay can and will block your ability to list items if your account is past due.

What eBay Charges Per Item

One of the first questions that new or potential traders frequently ask is, "How much does using eBay cost?" eBay makes money by providing the venue for bringing people together to trade. There are two kinds of sliding fees—insertion and final value—based on the value of the item listed and its final sale price. A fixed fee structure applies to certain types of listings.

Insertion Fees

When you list an item, you pay an insertion fee based on the amount of either the minimum bid or the reserve price that you've set. (For more on reserve-price auctions, please see chapter 5, "Putting It on the Block.") Insertion fees are nonrefundable. However, credits can apply if an item fails to sell and you relist it (see chapter 6, "Taking Care of Bidness"). eBay notifies you of the insertion fee amount when you post your listing and charges your account automatically. Here is the insertion fee schedule:

opening value or reserve price	insertion fee
$0.01–$9.99	$0.25
$10.00–$24.99	$0.50
$25.00–$49.99	$1.00
$50.00 and higher	$2.00

Reserve auctions are charged an additional fee of $0.50 when reserves are below $25 and $1 when reserves are greater than $25. if the auction meets the reserve, this fee is refunded.

Final Value Fees

If your item has sold when the auction ends, eBay automatically assesses your account a final value fee based on the selling price. For regular and reserve auctions, the final value fee is based on the winning bid. Final value fees are based on the closing auction price on an escalating scale as follows:

final value	fee
Up to and including $25	5%
$25.01 up to and including $1,000	5% on the first $25 and 2.5% on the high bid between $25.01 and the selling price
Greater than $1,000	5% on the first $25, 2.5% on the next $975, and 1.25% of the amount over $1,000

Example: Let's say your artist-signed Rookwood pottery vase sells for $1,200 (no reserve). The final value fee would be $28.13, calculated as follows:

1. $25 x 5%   = $ 1.25   *The fee on the first $25*
2. $975 x 2.5% = 24.38   *The fee on the next $975*
3. $200 x 1.25% =   2.50   *The fee on the portion of the sale greater than $1,000*

$28.13 Total

You will *not* be charged a final value fee if: there were no bids on your item, or the bids received failed to meet your reserve price (note: you will be charged $0.50 or $1.00, depending on your reserve price, if the reserve is not met).

You should note that final value fees are charged immediately after an auction ends. Should the bidder fail to complete the transaction, you can request a full or partial credit. (See chapter 6, "Taking Care of Bidness.")

Going Dutch

For *Dutch auctions*—where you offer more than one of the same item—insertion fees are based on the minimum bid multiplied by the number of items you're selling. For example, if you're offering six copies of the same Village People LP and the minimum bid is $10 for each, your insertion fee would be $3 (6 x $0.50). Final value fees are calculated by multiplying the lowest successful bid by the number of items sold. (For more information on Dutch auctions, please see chapter 4, "Let the Bidding Begin.")

Fixed Fees

eBay has created a fixed-pricing scheme to make it easier to list certain kinds of items. The following schedule delineates the pricing:

Category Type	eBay Category	Insertion Fee	Final Value Fee
Real Estate	Miscellaneous: Real Estate	$50	None
Vehicles	Miscellaneous: Vehicles: Cars	$25	$25
	Miscellaneous: Vehicles: Trucks	$25	$25
	Miscellaneous: Vehicles: RVs	$25	$25
	Miscellaneous: Transportation: Automobilia: Classic Cars	$25	$25

Only on eBay

Ersula Balbo and her husband, C. J. Balbo, have been selling antiques and collectibles since 1980, doing as many as twenty-eight shows a year. Last year C.J.'s sister Patty bought a computer after a friend of hers who worked at the post office told her about people selling on the Internet and the volume of boxes they were mailing. Using Patty's PC, the couple registered on eBay and listed a few items. In two weeks they'd sold as much as they normally did at two shows. They then bought their own PC as well as a scanner and digital camera. In two weeks, they recouped that investment, and in nine months, they became eBay PowerSellers, doing more volume than they would in a year of shows—and making more profit. "The beautiful thing about eBay," says Ersula, "is that there are no two A.M. setups, no unpacking, packing up, fighting the elements, or breakage. And, it costs less."

Note: These fees are based on selection of these categories at the time of listing, not the content of the listing. If you choose to list a book about cars in the "Miscellaneous: Vehicles: Cars" category, you will be charged the same $50 (insertion fee + final value fee) as someone selling a late-model Mercedes-Benz for $50,000.

Who You Are: Picking a Handle and Password

As mentioned earlier, when you register you pick a handle known as a user ID, and this becomes your persona in more ways than you might imagine. As you bid and sell your way across the eBay landscape, other buyers and sellers come to know you and, if they share a similar interest, may even track your activities. (See chapter 3, "The Quest for Amazing Stuff.") If you are what you eat, then you most definitely are what you collect. Fellow eBaysians know something about you by your name as well as by some kooky icons next to your name.

What That Pair of Shades Means

It's not uncommon to see a user ID with a pair of pink shades alongside it. Why would that be? To indicate a recent name change. Perhaps you wake up one morning and decide you are no longer a "doll-nut" but instead are "marblecrazy." On eBay you're allowed to change your user ID. However, each time you do, the pink shades appear for thirty days. These notify users that you've gone through an identity transformation and, more important, serve as an eBay safety feature to thwart fly-by-night scammers using multiple aliases or disguising themselves for illicit purposes. eBay keeps track of users' name changes, and when you see the pink shades you can click on them to see someone's name history.

Why There's a Zero by Your Name

When you first register, a zero in parentheses (0) also appears. Don't despair. The zero reflects neither your personality nor your IQ. It's your feedback rating, and since you have yet to engage in any bidding or selling, you have no feedback. Once you start participating in the action, your feedback quickly adds up. A feedback rating of 100 or even 1,000 is fairly common now. Your feedback rating follows you no matter how often you change your name. See the feedback section later in this chapter for the ins and outs of feedback.

About Me: Creating Your Personal Web Page

As a member of the community you may want to let other people know about you and your interests. eBay has created the option to let everyone create their own Web pages within the site. An icon with the word *Me* then shows up by your name. By clicking on the icon, other users can go directly to your page.

eBay has made setting up *About Me* pages simple. You can choose from three formats, and by completing a simple form, your page will be up in minutes.

You can use your page for the following purposes:

- Create links to your favorite sites on the World Wide Web.

- Let the world know about your collection.

- Explain why you collect what you do.

- Tell people about your greatest find.

- If you're brave, reveal your greatest mistake.

- Let it be known what stuff you seek.

- Create a link to your feedback, current auctions, or both.

- Share what you like about eBay.

- Let people know about your involvement in the eBay community.

- Create a link to pictures of your collection.

- Promote your favorite charity.

- Promote your auctions.

- Clarify your shipping and payment terms.

home | my eBay | site map

Browse | Sell | Services | Search | Help | Community

find items | find members | personal shopper

▸ Never be outbid again! Check out our new eBay a-go-go service. [ ] Search tips
▸ Review mockups of new item pages. Tell us what you think. ☐ Search titles and descriptions

This page is maintained by yellowsmileyface (243) ☆
08/19/99, 05:29:32 PDT

YellowSmileyFace's About Me Page

Welcome to my page!

Some call it a sickness. Some call it an obsession. I call it SmileyFace Fever. So what if the yellow smiley faces sometimes talk to me late at nite, there is nothing wrong with that!!

How the illness began.....

It started 5 years ago when I casually told my boyfriend Kerry (kerryz here on ebay) that I liked smiley faces. He bought me a McCoy Cookie Jar which became the first in my collection and it's been a circus freak show ever since - just can't stop! Who doesn't get happy looking at the lil' faces? Make sure you check out my auctions because I always have different items available!

Or click the smiley face if you just want to say hi!

Have a Happy Day! (I couldn't resist)
Thanks for stopping by!!

Visit anytime. I'm under constant construction :)

Designed by yellowsmileyface and kerryz. Programmed by kerryz

Creativity counts. Users nominate their favorite About Me pages for the monthly list published in eBay's online newsletter, *eBay Life*.

Becoming an Accredited User: A Badge of Honor

How you behave in the eBay community and what others think and say about you is important to your success. You should be proud to accumulate as many positive feedbacks as possible. On eBay, you have the freedom to establish yourself and your identity.

As a bidder, you can show people that you're conscientious by

- Responding quickly to emails after you win an auction.

- Sending payments promptly.

- Reading sellers' shipping and payment terms and respecting their wishes even though it may not be the way you'd do business.

- Asking questions before the sale ends so no surprises occur later.

- Reviewing a seller's feedback.

- Letting sellers know when they can expect payment.

- Informing sellers when merchandise arrives.

- Acting reasonably if problems arise and trying to reach mutually acceptable solutions.

- Rewarding sellers with positive feedback if you are so inclined.

As a seller, you should endeavor to make transactions go as smoothly as possible by

- Making descriptions as clear and complete as possible.

- Answering email questions quickly while a sale is under way.

- Setting reasonable shipping and payment terms.

- Charging reasonable shipping fees.

- Shipping merchandise promptly upon payment.

- Alerting buyers when items are shipped.

- Being reasonable if problems arise, and trying to reach mutually acceptable solutions.

● Rewarding buyers with positive feedback when the transaction is completed successfully.

How eBay Keeps You in the Loop

Although some eBay addicts sit riveted to their PCs monitoring their auctions by the nanosecond, others check in periodically to tally their sales. eBay helps all with automated emails to keep bidders and sellers posted.

The following chart shows when you can expect an automated email from the eBay genies:

Automated Email Schedule	Bidders	Sellers
Bid confirmation	◆	
Outbid notice	◆	
Auction ending notification (only winning bidders)	◆	◆
Daily update on bids and auctions under way	◆	◆
Listing confirmation		◆
Monthly invoice		◆

Don't want so many messages cluttering your inbox? Tell eBay what emails you want to get—or not get—by clicking on the link to email preferences from your My eBay page or on *Change My Notification Preferences* under *Services*. (For details on My eBay, see chapter 15: My eBay and Other Ways to Keep Track of It All.")

Community Customs

For any community to work, its members have to respect each other and take an active role in running things. That's especially true of the eBay community. If people just logged on to do a little buying and selling, that would be fine. But there's a lot more to eBay life than that. People get involved on the site because something amazing happens when they start talking about what they collect. For one thing, they connect on a level they never would have under different circumstances. Sharing their passion is an intimate exchange. They also become invested in the process and more than a little

protective of their eBay brethren. If someone gets out of
line, he hears about it. If he doesn't shape up, he risks
public humiliation and possible ostracism. It's not as if a
cyberposse runs him out of town, but, well, let's just say
that the key to success on eBay is to treat others as you
would have them treat you.

Only on eBay

eBay sends out an aver-
age of 2.5 million emails
to its users a day.

Ground Rules

Although you don't need to have memorized *Robert's
Rules of Order* to navigate eBay, community members
adhere to a code of honor:

- Don't leave feedback until a transaction is totally
complete (payment is made, item is received, and
buyer is happy).

- Don't leave negative feedback in a fit of pique or
before you have made reasonable efforts to resolve
disputes.

- Go out of your way to make transactions run
smoothly.

- Be respectful of other users and cultural differences that may exist in a global marketplace.

The Proof Is in the Feedback

In the world of commerce most of us are used to buying and selling by dealing face-to-face or over the phone.
As we conduct our various transactions, we make judgments about people's characters and our desire to do
business with them. When we need to purchase a new
product or service, we rely heavily on word-of-mouth
and turn to friends, neighbors, and family for referrals to
quality operations.

Feedback is eBay's electronic word-of-mouth. This
innovation allows buyers and sellers to establish a track
record in the community that can be viewed by potential
buyers and sellers. Viewing a user's feedback is an
important part of the shopping process. At first you may
feel intimidated to be cruising through eBay with a zero

among all these seasoned eBaysians with high feedback ratings. Don't be. We were all there once and have shared the excitement of completing our first deal and then giving and receiving our first feedback.

Feedback comes three ways: positive, negative, and neutral. Your feedback rating is calculated using a simple mathematical formula. For every positive feedback, your rating increases by 1. For every negative feedback, your rating decreases by 1. Neutral feedback does not change your rating either way.

Clicking on the number in parentheses next to a user's name takes you to that person's feedback page, where you can read the comments left by others.

Here are some basic rules of feedback:

- You can leave feedback for any user for any reason (you'll want to leave nice comments when community members help you outside of buying and selling things).

- Negative feedback can be left only in association with a transaction—a purchase or sale—that has taken place between users. You can't "flame" (gang up on someone and get others to leave negative feedback) someone just for the heck of it.

- No matter how many transactions you have with a user, you can move a user's rating only one point in either direction. For example, if you left someone a negative feedback but later made peace, you can leave two positives and that increases the user's positive rating by one. However, give feedback for every transaction—repeat customers are a significant sign of high-quality business dealings.

- You can't trade feedbacks just to boost your ratings.

- You can't leave feedback for yourself.

- You can't artificially have your feedback raised by getting a bunch of people to shill feedback for you.

- You can't threaten to leave negative feedback if another user won't do what you ask.

- There is no way for you to withdraw feedback—so get it right the first time!

Leaving feedback is easy and can be done in several ways. The fastest is to go to the listing screen of the auction (either through *My eBay* or a bid-

home | my eBay | site map

Browse | Sell | Services | Search | Help | Community

overview | registration | buying & selling | my eBay | about me | feedback forum | safe harbor

▸ Never be outbid again! Check out our new eBay a-go-go service.   [Search] tips
▸ Review mockups of new item pages. Tell us what you think.   ☐ Search titles and descriptions

Overall profile makeup

40 positives. 39 are from unique users and count toward the final rating.

2 neutrals. 2 are from users no longer registered.

0 negatives. 0 are from unique users and count toward the final rating.

ebY ID card	tommy-boy (39) ☆

Summary of Most Recent Comments

	Past 7 days	Past month	Past 6 mo.
Positive	0	0	6
Neutral	0	0	0
Negative	0	0	0
Total	**0**	**0**	**6**

Auctions by tommy-boy

Note: There are 2 comments that were converted to neutral because the commenting users are no longer registered.

You can leave feedback for this user. Visit the Feedback Forum for more info on feedback profiles.

If you are tommy-boy (39) ☆, you can respond to comments in this Feedback Profile.

Items 1-11 of 42 total

= 1 = [2] (next page)

User: (47) ☆ **Date:** 06/23/99, 07:57:20 PDT	**Item:** 116001661

Praise: Great to deal with!! Very fast payment!! Good communication!!AAA+++

User: (87) ☆ **Date:** 04/24/99, 10:37:35 PDT

Praise: Prompt payment and a smooth transaction. Recommended!

User: (380) ☆ **Date:** 03/18/99, 13:50:48 PST	**Item:** 71807215

Praise: Nice doing business with, quick response&payment. Thank you AAA+++ :o)

User: (54) ☆ **Date:** 03/14/99, 18:28:47 PST

Praise: Fast and Friendly!!! A true credit to eBay!! A+++++++

User: (102) ☆ **Date:** 03/07/99, 11:59:05 PST	**Item:** 66417088

Praise: EXCELLENT CUSTOMER!! FAST payment..good email contact..A+++++

User: (324) ☆ **Date:** 03/04/99, 08:12:46 PST	**Item:** 67044965

Praise: Fast pay, friendly mail, smooooooth as can be, A++ buyer, so deal with confidence

User: (194) ☆ **Date:** 02/18/99, 05:57:27 PST	**Item:** 63629971

Praise: Excellent communication, fast payment! RECOMMENDED buyer!! Thanks!

User: (241) ☆ **Date:** 02/04/99, 13:00:22 PST

Praise: Fast payment, good communication, would deal w/again. Highly recommended AA+++

User: (710) ☆ **Date:** 01/15/99, 20:56:16 PST

Praise: very prompt..would recommend...thank you very much

User: (248) ☆ **Date:** 12/31/98, 08:21:44 PST

Praise: Fast Payment, Great E-mail, Highly Recommended. A+A+A+

User: (917) ☆ **Date:** 10/20/98, 17:03:27 PDT

Praise: great transaction. would do business with again. A+++++

= 1 = [2] (next page)

Items 1-11 of 42 total

This feedback is ordered most-recent first. Each comment is attributed to its author who takes full responsibility for the comment. If you have any questions or concerns about a particular comment, please contact the author directly using the e-mail link provided with the author's User ID.

Only on eBay

eBay, like your favorite grade-school teacher, encourages, recognizes, and rewards good behavior. As your feedback grows, eBay posts stars next to your rating, each color signifying a feedback milestone.

The Star Chart

Feedback Rating	Star Color
10—99	Yellow
100—499	Turquoise
500—999	Purple
1,000—9,999	Red
10,000 and up	Gold—and shooting!

der's or seller's search that includes past auctions) you're commenting on. To the left of the seller and high bidder user names are links for leaving feedback. Going this route automatically posts the eBay item number in your feedback—identifying your feedback as transaction related—and your user name in the feedback input form. You need only enter your password, indicate the type of feedback you are leaving—positive, negative, neutral—and write your comments. You're limited to eighty characters, so be pithy.

The next easiest way to leave feedback is to click on a person's feedback rating, which is in parentheses next to their name. On their feedback page, a link that says *Leave Feedback for This User* takes you to the *Feedback Input* form with the user's name already posted. You can also go to *Leave Feedback on a Member* under *Services* on the navigation bar.

Thumbs up

Leaving positive feedback is straightforward. Let people know what was good about the transaction—speedy email responses, fast payment or shipment, quality merchandise, good packaging, or whatever you felt went smoothly. You might also say whether you'd buy or sell from that person again since that's the question foremost in other members' minds. Before you write your first feedback, check out the kinds of things people have said about others. As you can see, everyone develops their own reviewing style.

Thumbs Down

As you can tell by scanning feedback pages, negatives are rare. Most eBaysians view even one negative as a blight on their record. Who wants that glaring red complaint sticking out in a sea of green praise? Solid eBay community members do all they can to rectify and resolve problems. (If your best diplomatic overtures fall flat, head for *SafeHarbor;* see chapter 8.)

There may come a time when you feel you have no choice but to warn other community members about a user's behavior or business practices. Choose your words carefully. Remember: Under no circumstances can you retract feedback. Your words are cast in stone. Before damning someone for eternity, weigh your decision.

Keep negative feedback related to the transaction. Avoid libelous comments, threats, and personality attacks. Don't make accusations you can't substantiate. You want to warn people, not get yourself in trouble. If you feel you have been defrauded, take formal steps to complain by going to *SafeHarbor;* (see chapter 8). Be forewarned: If you leave negative feedback, that user will likely return the favor.

Every story has two sides, and users now have a chance to tell theirs in response. Go to your *My eBay* page, scroll down to *Feedback*, and click on *Respond to Feedback Others Have Left About Me.* This takes you to a page with all your feedback. On the right-hand side of each one is an envelope with a little arrow icon. Click on this and you're at the response form. You can also access the form by clicking on the Feedback Forum under *Services* on the navigation bar and then the link to *Review Feedback Others Have Left About You.*

Briefly and calmly explain your position. Avoid bashing the person who left the negative feedback. Casting aspersions doesn't reflect well on you. You can say you made efforts to resolve the dispute to no avail. Be honest. Maybe you really did kind of louse things up or you have a legitimate excuse. Take the high road and 'fess up to your own mistakes. Say you'll do better next time.

Don't give up trying to resolve the problem. Users sometimes reach an accord after they have gone the negative feedback route. Go back and leave a new positive feedback indicating that the situation is resolved.

Why Spam Ain't Kosher

The Internet has spawned a great deal of new lingo and rules of engagement. One such concept is *spam*. No, it's not that little blue can of gelatinous pork parts, but the Internet version is just as appetizing. Spam refers to unwanted, unsolicited email, and *spamming* is the process of sending out junk emails. For good reasons, eBay has banned spam from the menu.

What is unwanted or unsolicited email? By joining the eBay community as a buyer or seller, you are going to send and receive messages from new people with whom you've never communicated before. All those basic emails are fine. You can even reach out to people to ask questions. Maybe you see a Mickey Mouse doll for sale that's similar to the one you found at a flea market. It's okay to email the seller and ask questions. However, emailing any of the bidders for the Mickey Mouse doll and offering to sell them yours is not only spamming but bid siphoning as well—another serious infraction of eBay rules. Even if the bidder is glad to get your email, this still constitutes a spam. For a full explanation of such offenses, see chapter 8, "*SafeHarbor* and Happy Trading."

It's easy to think, Gee, all these people out there are interested in the same stuff I am. Why don't I create a list of email addresses and send an announcement of my new GI Joe Web site? This is a definite no-no and a classic example of spamming. It may also seem like a good idea to put together a list of all the winners of your auction to notify them when you put new GI Joes up for sale. No can do. Have faith that if they are interested and you list your item properly, they'll find it.

As you explore the vast eBay universe, your success is proportional to your ability to sort through the millions of items for sale and land on the perfect match with your desire. To become

CHAPTER 3

the quest for amazing stuff

an expert, put on your thinking beanie, grab your mouse, and click boldly where no collector has clicked before. Okay, so maybe you won't be the first eBaysian on the planet to explore all 4,282 listings of "Kiddie Car Classics," but rest assured that somewhere out there in cyberspace an item with your name on it awaits your bid.

Homing In, Category by Category

Some folks may think of eBay as a gigantic cyber–flea market, but it's a far cry from a bunch of virtual tables with tons of unrelated stuff dumped on them for you to dig through. For one thing, eBay is larger and more far-flung than any flea market or show you've ever attended. But eBay is also highly organized, making it easy to zero in on items of interest. The heart of eBay is the more than 1,600 categories in which items are listed. You can begin with a broad category such as *Books* and in moments have narrowed down your search to just *Nonfiction* books on *Paranormal* subjects.

If you collect in a specific area, you can work that category endlessly and get to know the other regulars who buy and sell there. But for many items, especially obscure or less popular collectibles, there is no established category (yet). Instead, similar items may be listed in very different categories, depending on how the seller sees them. For example, suppose you collect advertising rulers. You scroll down the list of subcategories under *Advertising*, expecting to find *Ruler* between *Restaurant* and *Seed Feed*, but it's not there. You then click

Only on eBay

Ever wonder what happens to the category suggestions you send to eBay? Meet Brian, the Category Guy. Every query ends up on his desk. His job is to then accommodate as many as he can into a spreadsheet that eventually becomes what you see on the site. "Due to the volume, it's impossible to respond to every email," he says. "But, rest assured, every one is read and considered. Our categories are a work in progress, and no idea is too small or mundane and nothing is ever discarded. If you don't see your suggestion in one implementation, it's still being considered for the next." Brian was among the first 5,000 users on eBay, back in the days when all items were just on one big list. As that compilation became harder to wade through, he volunteered to help Mary Lou Song (employee #3) break out a few categories. A year later there were more than 1,000, and collectors were petitioning him to give their specialty (no matter how obscure) a line on the list. Weighing everyone's opinions against the technical demands of the site can be daunting (even prompting him at times to consult the "real category guy"—his cat, Gizmo, who has proven to be amazingly unhelpful). "People think it's easy, like drawing lines on a parking lot," he says. "So did I, at first. But it isn't. So many items are cross-collectibles that it takes a bit of doing to present them in the proper structure in a way that promotes growth. But when it all comes together, it's a thrill to see a category go live from nothing and fill up with thousands of items."

on the search box, type in *ruler*, and click on *Search*. Voilà! All the rulers that are listed on the entire eBay site pop up. They were out there all along, just not in one place. To find them you would have had to go through dozens of other categories—*Tools, Advertising—Coca-Cola, Vintage Sewing*, and so on—looking for a ruler in a haystack.

The ad ruler example brings up another point: Sellers must also be familiar with the eBay categories. Putting an item in the right category can dramatically increase its final sale value. The more broadly you sell, the more you need to keep up-to-date with the categories. You do this by scanning the *Category Overview* under *Browse* and by checking in and seeing what's really for sale. (For more tips on listing items for sale, please see chapter 5, "Putting It on the Block.")

The Big List at a Glance

Whether you're looking for or selling a particular item, it helps to be familiar with the hundreds of categories—as well as subcategories and subsubcategories (or specialties)—on eBay. For example, under *Collectibles* there are over a dozen subcategories from *Airlines* to *Lunchboxes* to *Utilities*. As a further example, under the *Collectibles* subcategory of *Gasoline* there are close to twenty specialties, including *Humble*, *Pennzoil*, and *Sunoco*. At this writing, major categories include the following:

Antiques
Automotive
Books, Movies, Music
Coins & Stamps
Collectibles
Computers
Dolls, Figures
Great Collections
Jewelry, Gemstones
Photo & Electronics
Pottery & Glass
Sports Memorabilia
Toys & Bean Bag Plush
Miscellaneous

When in doubt, head for the *Miscellaneous* category, which covers an eclectic assortment including *Tobacciana*, *Railroadiana*, *Equestrian Equipment*, *Plants/Seeds*, *Pet Supplies—Reptile*, *Golf—Putters*, and just about anything else you can think of. When you're up for a surprise or you're listing something that truly resides in its own world, there's always the *Collectibles* subcategory of *Weird Stuff*, which ranges from *Slightly Unusual* to *Really Weird* to *Totally Bizarre*.

For a complete list, please see the appendix of this book or, for the very latest, click on *Category Overview* under *Browse* on the eBay site map.

What You Won't Find

Because eBay takes its responsibility to the larger community seriously, there are some items you can't sell on eBay. Besides illegal items such as controlled substances, the list of prohibited items includes, but is not limited to, the following:

● **Artifacts and historical items:** Native American human remains and gravesite-related items; Native American masks and "prayer sticks" from southwestern tribes; artifacts taken from any federal, state, public (Bureau of Land Management), or Native American land.

Firearms: eBay ended the sale of guns and ammunition on the site in early 1999. Included in the firearms restriction are BB guns, silencers, air guns, kits (to create firearms), converters (to make firearms automatic), high-capacity magazines, and ammunition with propellant.

Dead animals: Generally you can sell pelts, skins, hides, and rugs of nonendangered species. However, you cannot sell bear products of any kind, stuffed migratory birds or the eggs or nests of migratory birds, products that contain any part of a mountain lion, or any endangered species remains.

Live animals: Even though livestock auctions are a lively part of the local economy and social life in many places, eBay does not permit the sale of live animals. Pet stores and humane shelters are much more appropriate places to help animals find safe and loving homes.

Fireworks and pyrotechnic devices: Most states heavily regulate or ban these items, which include bottle rockets, firework kits, chasers, roman candles, firecrackers, skyrockets, party poppers, and smoke bombs.

Human parts and remains: Examples of prohibited items include bone, blood, waste, sperm, and eggs. However, items that contain human hair such as lockets or dolls are okay.

Police-related items: Because of the risk of individuals misrepresenting themselves as law enforcement officers to the public, eBay forbids the sale of law enforcement badges and other related items—unless the law enforcement organization states in writing that it doesn't object to the sale and you post that letter on the site with the badge. That list includes state or international badges, badges in Lucite, movie prop badges, identification cards, credential cases, and raid jackets. Exceptions include historical badges and souvenir items such as mugs and tie clips that do not contain badges.

Stock and certificates: Also prohibited is any other documentation that is accepted as proof of a current investment interest in any entity.

Switchblade knives and weapons:

Switchblade knives with blades over two inches are prohibited, as are brass or metal knuckles, nunchaku, zip guns, hand grenades or replica hand grenades, throwing stars, blackjacks, billys, sandclubs, saps, or sandbags. In addition, knives that are disguised to look like harmless items such as belt buckle knives, lipstick case knives, air gauge knives, and penknives are prohibited.

Rated R

eBay does believe in freedom of speech and so allows adult materials to be listed and sold on the site. However, out of respect for the wishes of members of the eBay community to restrict access to such materials, eBay requires users to provide a credit card number to verify that they're over eighteen years of age. (If you have registered as a seller with a credit card, you don't have to re-register again to view these listings.) Users must also agree to a *terms of use* agreement before registering to enter the *Adults Only* category. This is the only category that requires proof of age.

Alcohol and wine are allowed but you must adhere to the signature and shipping requirements for your state and the state where you're sending the goods. For a state-by-state analysis of wine-shipping laws, see http://www.wineinstitute.org/shipwine/analysis/state_analysis.htm

If you see something for sale on eBay that you don't think should be for sale, you can report it to eBay for investigation. See chapter 8, *"SafeHarbor and Happy Trading,"* to find out how to report illegal items and to learn more about infringing items such as software and games. For the most up-to-date list, go to *Help* on the navigation bar; under *Community Standards*, click on *Prohibited and Infringing Items.*

Finding What You're Looking For

Sellers have many options for listing items, and you'll sometimes find that their process of selecting one category over another is rather subjective and idiosyncratic. And, occasionally, sellers stick items in completely inappropriate categories, perhaps because they don't know what they have and don't understand the market. Such foibles can work in favor of the bidder who's aggressive and creative in searching. Many collections (and sellers' profits) are built on other people's mistakes.

In effect, searching allows you to create your own customized eBay cat-

▸ Never be outbid again! Check out our new eBay a-go-go service.　　[Search] tips
▸ Review mockups of new item pages. Tell us what you think.　　☐ Search titles and descriptions

Find Items

Search menu:　Listings Title Search - Item Number Lookup - Seller Search - Bidder Search - Completed Auctions

New regional search feature!
Search eBay LA for items listed in the Los Angeles area.

Listings Title Search eBay's most popular search feature	[Search] Enter what you're looking for (e.g. "brown bear" -teddy) Easy tips
Price Range	Between $ [ ]　And $ [ ]
Country where item is	⦿ located ○ available [Any Country ⧩]
Order by	[Ending Date ⧩] ⦿ ascending ○ descending
	☐ Text-only results　☐ Search title AND item description
	Search completed auctions

Item Number Lookup Use only if you have the item number (#)	Item Number (#) [ ]　[Search]

Seller Search Find all items currently listed by a specific seller	[Search] User ID or email address of seller. See your favorite seller's listings.
Include bidder emails	⦿ No ○ Yes
Completed items too?	⦿ No ○ All ○ Last Day ○ Last 2 Days ○ Last Week ○ Last 2 Weeks
Order by	○ Newest first ⦿ Oldest first ○ Auction end ○ Current price
# of items per page	[25　⧩]

Bidder Search Find all items currently bid upon by a bidder	[Search] User ID or email address of bidder. Use if you want to see what you bid on.
Completed items too?	⦿ No ○ Yes
Even if not high bidder?	⦿ Yes, even if not the high bidder ○ No, only if high bidder
# of items per page	[25　⧩]

Completed Auctions Find auctions that have completed	[Search] Words to search for in title (e.g. "brown bear" -teddy) Easy tips
Order by	[Ending Date ⧩] ⦿ ascending ○ descending
	☐ Text-only results

egories. If you collect in diverse areas, set up a search that encompasses those interests under one set of results. Say you collect items related to John Deere tractors. You notice that a seller has a mint owner's manual for a two-cylinder Deere. However, out of ignorance (he doesn't realize there's a *John Deere* subcategory under *Farm* listings) or cunning (he's betting on a higher price), he lists the item under the *Vehicles* section of the *Nonfiction Books* category. Unless you're on top of these and all other areas where John Deere items might be found (advertising, signs, and so on), you could miss out. Another happy bidder, oblivious to your pain, walks away with the booklet for $10 less than you might've been willing to bid.

eBay's search engines are powerful yet simple to use. You can search in five ways: by title, item number, seller, bidder, and completed auctions (searching by title in a database of past auctions). All you have to do is give your computer the right command; ask and you shall retrieve.

These options can be found by clicking on the *Search* option on the navigation bar or by using the search box that appears on pages throughout the site. You have the option of searching the category or the entire site by title and description (see following) or just by title. Limiting your search to the category takes you directly to items and saves you from paging through thousands of listings.

Reminder: Once you've created searches that work, bookmark or add them to your favorite places.

Searching by Title

The fastest way to get started is to type in the word or words describing the items you're seeking. Click on the search button and the little computer wizard scans every listing in every category, looking for titles—the "headlines" sellers write to describe their wares—that contain your keywords. Up pops a list of "hits" (items for sale that meet your criteria). Click on any listing that catches your eye. Then use your browser's back function to return to the search results.

This method is the most flexible but also a little unforgiving, which puts the onus on you to be precise. Keep these rules in mind:

- Spelling counts, but grammar doesn't necessarily.

- eBay's search engine doesn't recognize such words as *and, or, an,* or *the* except as part of a title.

- Punctuation—commas, parentheses, plusses, minuses—takes on new meaning, as explained later in this chapter.

● eBay's search engines are not case sensitive. Whether you type in all lowercase or all capital letters or a mix, it doesn't matter—it's all the same to the computer.

Experiment with different words and word combinations. The more words you add to the criteria, the fewer results will be returned. For example, if you collect American art pottery, try casting a wide net with makers' names such as Fulper, Ohr, Rookwood, or Roseville. Typing in the words *green Fulper vase* will likely yield few if any results unless a seller happens to have used those very words in a listing heading. (Then again, you might type in that phrase on a day when you have great eBay karma and find a dozen green Fulper vases for sale.)

On the search results page, you can further modify your criteria or re-sort the data. Options include the following:

● Finding keywords beyond headings:
Check the *Search Text* box and search item descriptions as well as titles.

● Seeing the latest listings first: Check the
descending box and reorder the search so new items are listed first. By default, eBay lists items in *ascending* order, which means that the sooner the auction ends, the higher it is on the list.

● Refining or starting over: Type in a more pre-
cise—or entirely new—keyword or phrase and search again.

Getting Good: Advanced Title Searches
As you become more savvy, why not refine your technique? Here are some timesaving tricks:

● Search for hidden keywords: In the box for title
searches, you can request that the search encompass not only titles but also item descriptions by clicking a box that reads, naturally, *Search Title AND Description*. This box also appears with the search results, so you can augment your title search later to make sure nothing has escaped your dragnet. Note that you're likely to get many unwanted results in these kinds of searches because a keyword need crop up only once in a description for the listing to qualify. So if you're searching for Tiffany glass and do a text search for *Tiffany*, you get every listing

where the word *Tiffany* happens to be mentioned: cufflinks, watch fobs, or anything else sold by Tiffany & Co.; albums by 1980s one-hit-wonder pop singer Tiffany; Tiffany baseball cards; Tiffany studio lampshades; and a fantasy Pez set of celluloid terror Chucky and his bride Tiffany.

Put phrases in quotes: Using quotation marks around phrases takes you only to listings or text with that exact phrase. For example, results from a search for *"green fulper vase"* would not include any listings such as *Fulper vase green.* Use quotes only if you're dead sure the item is listed that way.

Use parentheses and commas (no spaces after the commas): By placing two or more keywords in parentheses and separating the words by commas, you'll turn up all listings with any of those words. For example, if you type in *(designer,jewelry)*, you'll get all listings that contain either word. You can also use several words such as *(costume jewelry,chanel,balenci-aga,gucci,tiffany,cartier)* and you will get a rich return. Note: The phrase *costume jewelry* without commas limits returns to costume jewelry, not all jewelry.

Add a minus sign: Using a minus sign to separate words bars from your search all listings containing the word(s) following the sign. For example, if you put in *dolls −bisque* you get all listings for dolls—except bisque ones. Note: Include a space only *before* the minus sign.

Plug in a plus sign: Employing a plus sign after a word specifies that the word must appear to get a match. For example, if you put in *yellow bakelite +radio*, your returns will include only those listings that have yellow Bakelite *and* radio in them. Without the *+radio* you'd get tons of yellow Bakelite earrings, bracelets, pins—and perhaps the occasional radio.

Pick a wildcard: Using an asterisk (*) enables a search when you know only part of a word. For example; typing *camp** would return items such as Camp Fire Girl, camper, camporee, Campobello, campaign, Campbell, and so on. Wildcards also work well with dates. If you are searching for a Mercury dime from the 1940s, enter *mercury dime 194*.*

● **Find an exact number or date:** To home in on an exact number or date, just type it in (for example, *1945* or *Compaq Armada 1573dm*).

● **Pick two out of three:** If you're looking for a green vase and you'd like it to be Fulper but want to know all your options, you can use the @ symbol. By typing in *@1 green Fulper vase*, the search engine will hunt down the intersection of any two words and return text with the occurrence of: *green and vase, green and Fulper*, or *Fulper and vase*.

● **Order a combo platter:** You can combine search functions to create more complex searches. For example, the search *jewelry 195* −(Gucci, Cartier)* will provide hits of 1950s jewelry but exclude those that have Gucci and Cartier.

The search field is limited to one hundred characters. Got a lot to look for? Make two or more searches.

Avoiding Parameter Pitfalls

Like your dear aunt Loretta, who has to have every joke explained to her, search engines are very literal minded. The engine will dutifully search for your criteria exactly as you type it in—errors and all. For the best results, make sure your searches are free of these common bloopers:

● **Misspellings:** You may be comforted to know that many people spell as badly as you do, but if you misspell a word, you get returns only on those items that sellers have listed with the same misspelling.

● **Plurals:** If you collect beer coasters, you might be tempted to type in a search for *beer coasters* because

The No-Frills Search

By specifying *Text-only results* in a title search, you get a listing that's free of all the icons eBay uses to denote new items or other special features so the listing pages load faster and you can whiz through them. This is really helpful for those using modems of less than 33.3 bps. (If that's you, your first search should be for *modem fast.)* The text-only is for search results. Once you click on an item, though, the page opens just as the seller listed it, complete with photos and, yes, the other eBay icons.

that's how you think of your collection. After all, you'd sound pretty goofy saying, "I collect coaster." However, you usually buy one coaster at a time because that's how most sellers list them. Try typing in *coaster* (singular) and see how many more results (plural) you get. Note: Using *coaster** returns both coaster and coasters.

● Shorthand: Skip nicknames and abbreviations unless they're the common parlance for advertising or discussing an object.

Putting Item Numbers to Work

eBay assigns a reference number to every item listed. The number appears at the top of each listing and shows up in some searches. Typing or pasting the item number into the *Item Lookup* field takes you directly to the listing faster than you can say, "I gotta have it!" This function comes in handy when friends email you the numbers of listings they think will captivate you, or a trader inquires about a listing and provides only the number. The latter instance brings up a point of etiquette. To make things easier all around, get in the habit of including both the item number *and* the description in all correspondence.

Checking Completed Auctions

Results of auctions that have already ended are a valuable resource for buyers and sellers. You can determine the going rate for identical items you're selling or bidding on. And you can gauge the supply and demand by seeing how many similar items have shown up recently on eBay. To look at auctions that have ended in the past thirty days, go to *Search* and do either a title or completed auction search. However, be forewarned: Searching auctions that have already taken place can be depressing. What would you do if you discovered that just last week you missed a rare signed photo of the Beatles during their Hamburg days with Pete Best on drums?

Only on eBay

In the future, eBay plans to implement the ability to list items and conduct searches regionally in the top fifty-four metropolitan areas in the United States. If you live in Los Angeles, this regional search feature is already up and running.

Close to Home

Even as eBay facilitates global trading, it's also developing ways for people to shop locally. Trading can take on many dimensions, and in some instances sellers have items that just aren't conducive to or worth the effort of shipping. In the spring of 1999 eBay launched the eBay L.A. home page, enabling people to search for items listed in the Los Angeles area.

What's the advantage of all this? Some people feel more comfortable buying from folks in their neck of the woods. This way, buyers can inspect big-ticket—or just plain big—items in person. People buying cars, for example, can make an appointment, drive across town, and kick the tires. Pickup and delivery are easier and less costly, too. The same goes for furniture, houses, boats, and planes—anything that's not accepted by the local post office.

Follow the Leader:
Tracking Like-minded Bidders and Sellers

We hate to break it to you, but your collection is probably not unique. However, you can turn this ego-deflating realization into a way to hunt down great items by checking in on and tracking the brilliant aficionados who share your fancy for Victorian doorknobs. This may strike some folks as underhanded or sneaky, but since who's bidding on what is a matter of public record on eBay, just think of it as accessing information you're entitled to.

But first, some background: eBay instituted the bidder and seller search options to prevent fraud by detecting "shill bidding" and other devious practices. Suppose you notice that a user bids on every auction hosted by a particular seller. By doing a bidder search, you can see whether it's a coincidence or a ringer. If the bidder never bids on other sellers' auctions or wins any auctions and has no feedback, chances are that person is a shill and should be reported to eBay for investigation (as described in chapter 8, "*SafeHarbor* and Happy Trading").

Another way to use the seller search is to check in with your favorite dealers and see what they've got for sale. You'll notice that they do get repeat bidders, but that doesn't mean they're shills. More likely they're just interested in the same stuff you are—they're your competition. You can see what other great items they've sniffed out by doing a bidder search.

From the *Search* menu, put the bidder's or seller's user ID or email address in the appropriate field. The search engine returns a list of all the auctions the user is involved in. Modified searches are also possible. With a seller search, for example, you can view completed as well as current auctions. On the bidder search you can specify all auctions that buyers have bid on or just those where they're currently the high bidder.

Tracking bidders is great sport, and it allows you to satisfy that voyeuristic urge in a safe, legal manner. Don't get cocky, though. Watchers can also be watched.

Personal Shopper

If you've ever wished for a genie who intuited your collecting desires and tirelessly traveled the world for items that fit the bill, eBay's *Personal Shopper* is for you. You type in what you're looking for, and eBay emails you (up to once a day for ninety days) a list of auctions that sound promising.

To use this automated search function, look for the *Personal Shopper* on the site map or under *Search* on the navigation bar. Enter your favorite search phrase(s). Once you've defined a search, eBay gives you back a sample page of results. If they include what you're looking for, great. If not, tinker with the parameters until the shopper gets it right. Save the search and indicate the frequency with which you'd like your Personal Shopper to notify you of new items and how long it should do your legwork (thirty, sixty, or ninety days). The service then emails you a listing of all the new items that meet the criteria. You can cut and paste the URLs of those auctions into your browser address bar and—*zoom!*—you're there. Or you can access them through your Personal Shopper page.

You can store up to three Personal Shopper searches at a time. But you can maximize their effectiveness using these techniques:

● **Combine searches:** Put a couple of your favorite searches together so you can be alerted to what's new in your favorite areas.

● **Broaden the scope:** Write searches that cover the fringes of your collecting area. Normally, such strings produce an overwhelming number of results. But *Personal Shopper* alerts you only to the fresh ones, making the results manageable.

● **Bookmark searches:** Can't wait for *Personal Shopper* to email you? Bookmark your *Personal Shopper* searches or save them in your Favorite Places folder so you can check on them with a mouse click.

SPECIALTY:

Old Las Vegas/Casino Collectibles

eBay HANDLE: Babydino@pacbell.net   AGE: 32

WHY THIS SPECIALTY'S COOL: Most of the old Las Vegas is gone, and this stuff reminds me of the swingin' days—when the Rat Pack ruled the Strip!

I GOT HOOKED: After witnessing the Dunes implosion in 1993, I bought an ice bucket from the hotel.

QUESTIONS I GET ASKED THE MOST: "Do you gamble a lot?" and "Are you crazy?"

MY ALL-TIME FAVE: A photo of Liza Minnelli, Sammy Davis Jr., and Frank Sinatra, autographed by all three of them "To Dino" (probably for Dean Martin, after whom I named my son).

THE PIECE I'M DYING TO ADD: *Anything* from "Dino's Lodge."

WHAT MY COLLECTION SAYS ABOUT ME: I'm a hip, swingin' guy! Cocktails, anyone?

Gallery Hopping and Shopping

Most folks are used to shopping in stores or by catalog—where you see stuff before reading a description or label about it. That's why eBay created the *Gallery*, a place where you can digest a few dozen items for sale at a glance. The current bid price and the auction end date appear under each image. Clicking on the image takes you to the full listing page.

For every category that has its own listings page there is a Gallery where sellers can post pictures from their ads in thumbnail (as in thumbnail sketch) format. Sellers pay a small fee for this service. Therefore not all listings with photos show up in the Gallery, and those without photos certainly don't. The Gallery is like a category sampler, so don't give up searching and looking in categories, but add the Gallery as a regular stop on your eBay grand tour.

Beyond Collectibles: Everyday Wonders

Two or three million items for sale at a time is a lot of merchandise, which makes eBay a great place to undertake all kinds of shopping expeditions. Need a faster modem (who doesn't)? Perhaps Junior could use a new (or new to you) computer since you're on eBay every night. Maybe the time has come to spice up your listings with pictures. Thousands of digital cameras and scanners are offered for sale every day. Many vendors have set up virtual storefronts to sell the latest technology, complete with the manufacturers' warranty. Others specialize in used or refurbished equipment.

Before bidding on new products, price them at retailers—both in person and online. Be sure that models have the features you require. Sellers sometimes don't know or understand all the features or capabilities of the gizmos they're selling. Check manufacturers' Web sites for full descriptions. Keep in mind that although interstate commerce over the Internet is not subject to sales tax, you do have to pay shipping. Even so, it may still be possible to get it cheaper through eBay.

You can customize searches to zero in on other types of purchases as well:

● **Gifts:** For a birthday or anniversary, type in the age or year. You're likely to turn up hundreds of items dating from that year, such as books, sheet music, signed art, cigarette cards, or memorabilia. You might also find lots of odd objects with the significant number—sports jerseys, Magic 8 balls, Union '76 advertising memorabilia, toy race cars, real race cars, and so on. Also try searching by the recipient's inter-ests—bird-watching, fishing, quilting, pulp fiction mysteries—just as you do for your own hobbies and collections. Baby, wedding, and grad-uation gifts can also be found by searching for such traditional things as silver, china, leather, books, and writing accessories. Fifteen min-utes on eBay will yield more possibilities than hours slogging around the mall will. Tip: Search by text, as people don't always list dates in titles. Also keep your eyes peeled for those items featuring gift icons in their listings. These icons are a seller's way of letting you know they think their item might be that something special you are looking for.

Home furnishings: Need a new bedspread? Looking for a work of art to go over the mantel? The rug in the foyer looking thread-bare? Need a new set of chairs for the dining room table? Let eBay become your personal design store to spruce up the old homestead.

Personal library: Looking for a good book? How about that one Stephen King novel you still haven't read? eBay has more than highly collectible first editions—it's a virtual used-book store with lots of bargains.

Heritage: Want to hang some meaningful objects on the family tree? Type in your family name. You may be surprised to find books written by or about people with the same surname as you—perhaps they're relatives or ancestors. Or you may discover advertising memo-rabilia and novelties emblazoned with your name.

Clothing: Besides vintage or designer garments, you can find everyday clothes on eBay. Military families, who've had difficulty finding things they need while stationed abroad, have turned to eBay for back-to-school shopping. Others have merely typed in their size to mentally "try on" what's available. Note to sellers: Your "gently worn" duds can find a happy buyer on eBay—and often for more money than you'd get at a consignment shop. Just make sure your merchandise is clean and in good condition.

Computer games: As long as they're original, you can legally buy them on eBay. However, beware of pirated versions or hard-ware add-ons such as mod chips that allow you to play illegal copies of games. Not only is selling bootleg games illegal, but *playing* them is ille-gal, too. If you believe you've purchased an unauthorized copy, contact the Interactive Digital Software Association at www.idsa.com, or fill out a *Community Watch* report by going to: *Help*, then *Community Standards;* once there, locate *If Something Goes Wrong* and click on *email.*

● **Car parts:** Actually, it's accessories and entire cars, too. The automotive categories are among the most popular on eBay, especially with the acquisition of the Kruse International classic car auction company.

● **House hunting:** Real estate listings include Montana ranches, Florida condos, and even cemetery plots. The advent of regional pages is changing the way many buyers shop for property on eBay. (See "Real Estate Reality Check," below.)

● **Business supplies:** Whether you're looking for bulldozers, heavy-duty Swedish speed juicers, stainless-steel surgical instruments, hydraulic hose crimpers, or high-speed copiers, you can find them in *Business*, *Office*, *Equipment*, and *Show Supplies* categories. You can also stumble across career-related items such as leather attachés (sold, no doubt, by Dilberts-turned-full-time-eBaysians). And, of course, you'll never run out of people selling bubble wrap and resealable plastic bags— the mainstays of every eBay seller.

● **Pet paraphernalia:** From custom-made dog cots to pet chinchilla guides, you can find the products, books, and toys to make your animal's life complete.

● **Sports closet:** If you're wondering where old gravity boots and *Buns of Steel* videos go to die, look

Real Estate Reality Check

Due to the wide variety of laws governing the sale of real estate, eBay auctions of real property are not legally binding offers to buy and sell property. Instead, they are a way for sellers to advertise their real estate and meet potential buyers. At the close of the auction, the seller should contact the high bidder to discuss entering into a contract for the real property. However, neither party is obligated to complete the real estate transaction.

The purchase and sale of real estate is a complicated matter frequently governed by local laws, and laws in the country where the property is located. You are strongly advised to seek the help of a licensed real estate professional and/or a real estate attorney for assistance in finalizing a real estate transaction.

no further. They actually get reincarnated under eBay's *Sporting Goods* category, along with archery equipment, wet suits, rock-climbing pitons, and the like.

● **Foods:** Maine lobsters, Kona coffee, beef jerky—everything you need for a nutritious breakfast. Note: When selling food, you are subject to certain laws and regulations. Please see eBay's *Community Standards* in the *Help* section regarding such issues.

● **Garden goodies:** Better than a greenhouse, the *Garden Items* category covers small (heirloom tomato seeds), medium (gargoyle wind chimes), and large (edible Japanese plum trees) items for your patch of green.

● **Vacations:** Plane tickets, hotel rooms, tours, and so on go to the high bidder. Luggage and other accoutrements abound as well.

● **Services:** The idea of auctioning skills is catching on. Math tutors, songwriters (who'll compose a ditty for your loved one), and high-tech consultants have all put themselves on the block. Occasionally you can even buy an entire staff or company.

The "Great Collections" Connection

Although eBay did not start out trying to beat traditional auction houses at their own game, online trading in an auction format has revolutionized the industry. eBay now hosts thousands of sales a month for items over $1,000 and even over $10,000. With this influx of high-end merchandise have come requests for eBay to offer special services—vetting, or authenticating, and so on—to encourage buyer confidence. So in the fall of 1999, eBay launched the *Great Collections* category for authenticated, premium items.

The genesis of Great Collections was eBay's purchase of a bricks-and-mortar auction house: Butterfield & Butterfield. Founded in 1865 in San Francisco, Butterfield & Butterfield is one of the world's oldest and largest houses, specializing in the appraisal and sale of fine art, antiques, and objects in all collecting categories. By teaming up with them, eBay gains not only a staff of experts who can authenticate and appraise items, but also a global trading partner—Butterfield has galleries in San Francisco, Los Angeles, and Chicago, and representatives throughout the U.S. and Europe. So if you've ever felt too intimidated to preview a sale at a big auction house, let alone bid at one, you can now rub virtual elbows with the bigwigs at auction houses around the world.

You can browse items in Great Collections just as you would in any other category. Items from G.C. will also turn up in regular searches and be designated by a special icon. If you win a G.C. item, you send payment directly to the seller or firm listing the item (just like on any other eBay auction). It's also possible to keep a credit card on file with Butterfield and authorize the charge for a winning bid. All items sold in G.C. are guaranteed to be authentic based on the terms and conditions as specified by these sellers. At a live auction, you would normally pay a buyer's commission, but these are eBay rules, and there's no fee to buyers.

Great Collections isn't only about what you can buy. It's also about getting help from the experts. Auction houses participating in G.C. will vet items, although only by an in-person inspection. If you prefer, these firms will list your item for you. As an eBay user, you qualify for a reduced rate on the normal commission.

Kruse Control

Cars have done well on eBay since the beginning, partly because collectible cars are unique and the people who buy them are passionate. By early 1999, more than 1,000 cars a week were selling in the automotive category—and eBay sought an alliance to make trading cars an even better experience. All roads led to Kruse International of Auburn (like the car), Indiana, the world's largest auctioneer of unique and collectible cars.

Kruse has some interesting parallels with eBay. Both companies held their first auction on Labor Day (thirty-five years apart). Both were started by men who saw a way to create an efficient marketplace using an auction format. And both were pioneers in their fields. In the fifties, the concept of a collectible car was pretty new. Buying a classic car meant buying a used car that was really old. The market was fragmented, and sellers had difficulty realizing good values for their vehicles. Dean Kruse changed all that by consolidating the market and making the process less of a hassle by, among other things, arranging financing and shipping. Kruse travels the country and holds auctions throughout the United States. Kruse's flagship auction (held every Labor Day, of course) attracts 150,000 people bidding for a slice of automotive history.

Cars are not just big-ticket items—they're big physically. There are only so many cars that even Kruse can bring to one place for people to view.

What's more, the overall $370 billion used-car industry is still highly ineffi-cient. That means buying a used car isn't fun—it can be downright painful. By combining Kruse's automotive expertise with eBay's ability to reach mil-lions of people, eBay hopes to further revolutionize this process. Kruse is continuing its successful live auctions with some enhancements:

- Ability to sell collectible cars at Kruse's live auctions. If the car doesn't sell, it can automatically be listed on eBay.

- Access to Kruse's expertise in title management, financing collectible cars, insurance, and shipping.

This partnership unites two of the largest non-dealer car marketplaces in the world. Whether you're looking for a second family car or a perfectly detailed 1929 Duesenberg, eBay is a great place to kick the virtual tires.

You've got your user ID and mastered the eBay search machine. You are now ready to engage in the competitive pastime of kicking the butts of fellow buyers—other-wise known as bidding. Some eBaysians con-sider bidding part art, part blood sport. They invest countless hours strategizing as if they were Gary Kasparov training for a rematch with IBM's *Deep Blue* chess computer. Certainly bidding is serious business, and everyone has a pet theory on what works. In this chapter we cover several ways to attack the situation, all geared to help you bid to win.

CHAPTER 4

let the

bidding

begin

Demystifying the Bidding Process

eBay doesn't charge a fee to place a bid, but you must be a registered user. (Registration is also free.) After that, bidding is as simple as counting the fingers on one hand:

1 Identify an item on which you want to bid and click on its listing page.

2 Either click on the bid paddle icon to the left of the description or scroll down to the bid form.

3 Enter your bid amount and submit it (press *Enter*).

4 Review and confirm your bid.

5 Type in your user ID and password on the next form and submit it. Through proxy bidding eBay does the rest.

eBay immediately confirms your bid by email. eBay also emails you when someone outbids you and when the auction is over, reminding you (if yours is the winning bid) to get in touch with the

home | my eBay | site map

| Browse | Sell | Services | Search | Help | Community |

item view

Classic Hubley cast iron racer w/ driver
Item #152757882

Toys, Bean Bag Plush:Vintage:Cast Iron

Description

Bid!

Currently	**$10.00**	First bid **$10.00**
Quantity	**1**	# of bids **1** (bid history) (with emails)
Time left	**6 days, 23 hours +**	Location **New York, NY**
Started	08/25/99, 14:14:51 PDT	(mail this auction to a friend)
Ends	09/01/99, 14:14:51 PDT	(request a gift alert)

Seller   **rock1230 (23)**
(view comments in seller's Feedback Profile)   (view seller's other auctions)
(ask seller a question)

High bid   **icen(2)**

Payment   See item description for payment methods accepted
Shipping   See item description for shipping charges

Seller assumes all responsibility for listing this item. You should contact the seller to resolve any questions before bidding. Currency is dollar ($) unless otherwise noted.

Description

This is a classic cast-iron racer with the driver behind the wheel, ready to roar into your collection. Manufactured by Hubley, circa 1920s, this car is in very good/excellent condition. There is some loss of orange paint on the nose, sidefins, and tailfin as detailed in the photo. The black paint on the driver steering wheel is perfect. The white rubber wheels have seen better days (but can easily be replaced). The red "hubcaps" on the right are faded, but the ones on the left are bright. The car is 7" long and 3" wide. It is marked HUBLEY underneath. It is easy to see how a child could have gotten hours of pleasure from this toy—it rolls beautifully. Terms and conditions: Buyer to pay shipping costs of $5.40 USPS Priority Mail. If you prefer another method click here to use iShip.com to view your shipping charges. I will happily accommodate any shipping method you prefer. I don't think paying should be a hassle, so personal checks are encouraged, but I also accept money orders or other certified payments. I do wait five days for personal checks to clear and ship within 48 hours upon receipt of certified funds, so if time is of the essence you make the call. Every item I sell is satisfaction guaranteed and you can return it for any reason. Just notify me within 3 days of receipt. You pay return shipping and insurance (let's not tempt fate).

Bidding

Classic Hubley cast iron racer w/ driver (Item #152757882)

Current bid	**$10.00**
Bid increment	**$0.50**
Minimum bid	**$10.50**

Registration required. eBay requires registration in order to bid. Find out how to become a registered user. It's fast and it's **free**!

To finalize your bid, you will need to submit your User ID and Password in the next step — once you click on Review Bid.

[_____] *Current minimum bid is 10.50* [**review bid**]

Enter your maximum bid

- Remember to type in **numbers only** and use a decimal point (.) when necessary. **Don't include a currency symbol ($) or thousand separator**. For example: 1000000.00

Bid efficiently with Proxy Bidding — here's how it works:

- Your maximum bid is kept **secret**, and it's **not necessarily what you'll pay**. eBay will bid on your behalf (which is called proxy bidding) by steadily increasing your bid by **small increments until your maximum is reached**.
- **Why?** Because it means **you don't have to monitor the auction** as it unfolds. You also **don't have to worry about being outbid at the very last minute** unless someone bids over your maximum dollar amount. Want more details? Check out an example of proxy bidding.
- **Choose your maximum carefully**, though, as you won't be able to reduce it later.

Your bid is a contract

- Only place a bid if you're serious about buying the item; if you're the winning bidder, you **will** enter into a legally binding contract to purchase the item from the seller.

What It Means to Bid

eBay is not a game. By placing a bid, you're committing to purchase the object if you are the high bidder. Failure to follow through and complete the transaction is a serious breach of eBay rules and can result in punishment. Some sellers make their livelihoods on eBay and count on you to stand behind your bid. Although sellers have the option of relisting an item if the buyer defaults, this can hurt their business and tarnish their image. People may remember the object and wonder why it's for sale again. Potential bidders might assume the item is defective or the seller is a flake. So please bid only on items you want to own. You expect to get paid for your work—why should eBay sellers expect any less? For more information on bad bidders, please see chapter 8, "SafeHarbor and Happy Trading."

seller within three days and complete the transaction. In cases where two users bid the same amount, the first one takes precedence.

eBay auctions are time limited, which means they last three, five, seven, or ten days, depending on the seller's wishes. The ending date and time are prominently displayed in military format (24-hour clock) on every listing. A typical entry might read:

Starts: 09/11/00, 14:33:49 PDT
Ends: 09/18/00, 14:33:49 PDT

That means the auction begins September 11, 2000, at 2:33 (and 49 seconds) P.M., Pacific daylight time and ends seven days later at the same time. Some diehard eBaysians—as well as those who, for the life of them, can't get the time zones straight—set their computer clocks to eBay time (which is Pacific daylight time). On top of each category listing page is a link to the time at eBay.

Until the auction ends, you can bid

● At any time.

● As many times as you want.

● Again, even if you're already the high bidder, you can raise your maximum to keep others from outbidding you.

● As much money as you want (although your spouse, credit card company, or bank might disagree).

● On as many items as you desire at any one time.

As uncomplicated as placing a bid is, you can increase your chances of winning by understanding the process and finding a strategy that works for you.

Retracting a Bid

eBay bids are binding, but you can retract a bid if you have good reason. The bid retraction form is under *Services* on the navigation bar. Your retraction is publicized under the item's bid history, and you may be asked to explain your reasons. If your reasons aren't legitimate, you expose yourself to negative feedback. Here are a couple of circumstances under which it's okay to retract:

- Seller changes the description of an item after you bid.

- You made a clear and substantial error in the amount you bid. For example, you meant to bid $19.95, but bid $1995 (a little excited, were you?) by mistake. Having second thoughts is not the same as a typo, so think before you bid.

Note: When you retract a single bid, you retract all of your preceding bids for that item. You must rebid to stay in the game.

You Absolutely, Positively Have to Have It: Bidding to Win

The only way to come out on top when the dust settles is to bid more than the next guy. Although eBay is full of bargains, to ensure you snare that set of Pokemon trading cards you've been lusting after, you should bid the maximum you're willing to pay. The operative word here is *willing*, which indicates an amount you think is fair and within your budget, and what the item is worth to *you*. You have to think, "If I got this cool piece for that price, I'd be psyched." That way you won't feel you've overpaid. If you get outbid, you'll know you did your best but it wasn't your day. You won't be kicking yourself for cheaping out—especially if the item sells for significantly less than what your high bid would've been.

If you consistently bid your top amount—an amount that's not delusional for your market—you'll win many auctions and steadily grow your collection. eBay's proxy bidding works well with this philosophy.

Proxy Bidding

On eBay, you need not be present to win. In other words, you tell eBay the maximum amount you're willing to pay and the computer acts as your proxy,

Capitalism for the Rest of Us

An auction is one of the purest forms of economic competition—a true test of supply and demand. Bidders express their desire, or demand, by bidding their hard-earned dollars. They decide the price based on what they can afford, what they perceive the supply to be, and what they think the item is worth to them personally. The rarer or shorter in supply an object, the higher people bid.

Unlike a commodity such as oil, which everyone continually needs to survive and which is traded in vast quantities on world markets, antiques and collectibles are "needed" by a relatively small group of people whose passing flights of fancy can send the market up or down. In some cases it takes only two people bidding on an object to drive up the price no matter what the actual supply. Then again, if those two don't happen to be in a buying mood that day, the price might never rise above the opening bid—and other buyers might conclude that the "supply" has exceeded the "demand." Likewise, nothing moves stuff onto the market faster than rising prices.

Why this little economics lesson? To remind you that to fetch the highest and fairest price at auction, an object needs to be exposed to the greatest number of potential bidders who recognize its value. By expanding the community of sellers and buyers globally, eBay creates a more efficient marketplace. Even so, part of what make auctions fun is their unpredictability—and the chance to either make a huge profit or find great pieces for amazing prices by being in the right place at the right time.

placing bids for you against other bidders until your maximum is hit. Here's how it works:

1 Your relentless search has turned up a terrific item—a must have. The *opening bid* is $10, but you're willing to pay $45. You scroll down to the bid form or click on the *bid paddle icon*. Enter $45 as your bid and confirm with your user ID and password.

2 Your bid of $45 is the first, so the *current bid* goes to the minimum: $10. The listing now indicates that the *minimum bid* someone can make is $10.50. ($0.50 is the next standard bidding increment at this price; for a list of bidding increments, see page 67).

3 Another bidder, "Archrival," comes along and bids $18. eBay knows that you're willing to pay up to $45, so Archrival is informed that he's been outbid. Now the minimum is up to $18.50 (again, the standard increment over your competitor's bid). Archrival, of course, has no idea how much you're actually willing to bid, and your $45 secret is safe with eBay.

4 Several days go by and you're still sitting in the catbird seat at $18.50. Not to be out-

done, Archrival bids with only two minutes left in the auction. Assuming—wrongly—that the maximum you'd pay is $25, Archrival smugly bids $27.

5 eBay exercises your wishes, and once again Archrival is frustrated to see the bid zoom to $28 (the next bid increment—but you know this by now, right?).

6 With forty seconds to go, Archrival desperately bids $30. Archrival doesn't really want to pay that much, but now his aim is not merely to get the item, but to beat you (always a bad reason to bid).

7 eBay exercises your wishes, and the bid ups to $31, foiling Archrival again. With pride on the line, Archrival punches in $35.

8 Too late! Bidding has closed for that auction.

9 Later that day you arrive home from the beach and log on to eBay to find you've won the day—and the item for $31.

Proxy bidding isn't foolproof. You still need to check in on your auctions periodically. eBay does email outbid notices, but they don't always come in time if Archrival outbids you in the closing minutes.

Two-Minute Warning—Sniper's Paradise

Archrival's attempt to finesse a bid at the closing bell is known as "sniping." eBaysians love to complain about snipers, who swoop in at the last possible second to pick off items. However, despite its bad rap, sniping is a perfectly legitimate tactic.

At live auctions the bidding continues until everyone but the current high bidder drops out. The only way to snipe at a live auction is to wait until the auctioneer starts saying, "Going . . . going . . ." and you jump up like a jack-in-the-box and bid. But that just keeps the bidding open, of course, and unless you're the last person standing, someone could pull the same maneuver on you.

As eBay auctions end at specific times, snipers play beat the clock, squeezing in a higher bid in the last nanoseconds. They're often successful, especially when the current bid amount is low. Snipers can succeed only if bidders allow them a window of opportunity by bidding less than they're really willing to pay.

Here's how snipers operate: Suppose your search turns up a lovely vintage Japanese lacquer sushi set with an opening of bid of $35, no reserve.

Meet eBay Ambassador Rebecca Chen

SPECIALTY:

Popples

eBay HANDLE: popples@ucla.edu   AGE: 20

TO BE A POPPLEOLOGIST: You need to know a lot about the cartoons these toys were based on, the characters' names, who was produced, who wasn't, who's rare, their accessories, and so on.

MY PREMIER POPPLE: My dad bought me Prize Popple when I was five in 1985. She was the only one I owned until I was "grown up."

WHAT MY COLLECTION SAYS ABOUT ME: I'm in touch with my childhood, and I love stuffed animals. I long for the old days (the 1980s) when cartoons were happy and cheery. Cartoons today are so dark and violent. Popples didn't even have villains.

THE GREAT POPPLES CHALLENGE: None of the '80s toys I like are produced anymore, and most of the manufacturers don't even remember producing them. A lot of people think they're just junk.

IF IT WEREN'T FOR eBay: I wouldn't be able to collect Popples at all. eBay has connected me with owners who are willing to sell. For instance, I didn't realize that Net Set, the Tennis Popple, was made into a stuffed animal until I found him on eBay. Unfortunately, I was outbid at the last minute.

SOMEDAY THAT SNIPER WILL BE SORRY: Sniping is a risk because you never know when your Internet connection will decide to be slow.

MY BEST eBay TRANSACTION: I was the highest bidder for two Popples glasses sold at Pizza Hut in 1986. One arrived shattered, but the seller gave me a full refund and let me keep the intact glass. eBay users are some of the nicest people around. Some have given me free Popples with items I won just because I love them.

Although you'd gladly pay $90, you decide upon a maximum bid of $50, thinking that'll cushion you against bumps from other bidders. On the last day, sitting pretty with a bid of $39, you go to bed confident you've won, since the auction ends at 2 A.M. The next morning you log on and discover the set went for $51—you've been sniped in the middle of the night! Adding insult, the winner has beaten you by an insignificant amount (one bidding increment above your proxy bid), although you'll never know how much a sniper has really bid.

How do snipers achieve these magical wins? Some stay up to all hours and place their bids in the final seconds of an auction. Others use software programs that handle their bidding for them. eBay's success has spawned a host of third-party software packages that facilitate the use of eBay. Several applications feature automated bidding programs that log you on to eBay and execute bids at specified times. Although eBay neither endorses nor prohibits these products, you can read more about them in chapter 15, "My eBay and Other Ways to Keep Track of It All."

Is There a Right Time to Bid?

At a live auction, the only one time to bid is during the few minutes when the object is on the block. At some auction houses you can leave bids and the house will exercise them (in a similar fashion to eBay's proxy bidding) or bid by phone when the item's in play. But you can't place a bid and then think about it for twenty-four hours before bidding again.

Since eBay auctions take place over several days, you have more options to decide when to make your move. Proxy bidding and sniping are two approaches, but when you bid depends on the style that works for you.

Know Your Style

Most eBaysians develop their own bidding styles, which can be summed up as follows:

Only on eBay

On a seven-day average, eBay hosts more than two million auctions, with more than 300,000 new items joining the "for sale" list every twenty-four hours.

● **"I know what I like":** You bookmark your favorite searches and check them every day (or hour), monitoring the action or plunging in whenever you see something that piques your interest. Sometimes you buy stuff just because it's a good deal, not because you really need or want it. You are learning to exercise self-control.

● **"Bid early and often and low":** You deal in volume, surfing your favorite categories and placing numerous small bids early on. You lose more than you win, but given the law of averages, you do win enough by default to keep you happy. And those victories don't make much of a dent in your wallet. This is not a smart strategy for folks prone to depression when they don't get what they want.

● **"Late bidder take all":** You specialize in the misunderstood and the mislabeled—anything that appears undervalued by the bidding public as the auction draws to a close. You hang out in the *Ending Today* and *Going, Going, Gone* sections of your favorite categories and place bids on items that seem to be overlooked. You hope you're alone in this strategy (unlikely), but you score often enough to convince yourself that you know something others don't.

● **"That's my final offer":** Also known as the "Take it or leave it" bidder. Smart and confident, you know exactly which pieces have to be yours and you've calculated the maximum you're willing to pay for them. You bid at various times, and your proxy bid says it all. You will not under any circumstances raise it. You feel that people who get caught up in feeding frenzies deserve to pay more.

● **"A little bid at a time":** Like the proverbial inchworm, you slowly make your way up the reserve tree—without going out on a limb—bidding in small increments until you land exactly on the reserve. You tend to tucker out the higher you go.

● **"Mind your own beeswax":** You're an active bidder in several areas, and it's likely your competitors have come to recognize you and follow you. So you wait until the last minute to throw them off your trail. Sometimes you bid on an item several times in the last few hours or seconds, working your way up to the winning bid or making the reserve.

● **"Keep 'em guessing":** You bid early, you bid late—inconsistency is your trademark. You might bid low on several items at once and monitor them on *My eBay*, and then up your bids later. Sometimes you keep yourself guessing because you forget when auctions end and forget to bid, losing out. Not to worry; there's always another auction out there.

Up and Up: Bidding Increments

On eBay bids are placed in fixed increments based on the current price. As you can see by the following chart, these bumps follow a sliding scale:

Current Price	Bid Increment
$0.01—$0.99	$0.05
$1.00—$4.99	$0.25
$5.00—$24.99	$0.50
$25.00—$99.99	$1.00
$100.00—$249.99	$2.50
$250.00—$499.99	$5.00
$500.00—$999.99	$10.00
$1,000.00—$2,499.99	$25.00
$2,500.00—$4,999.99	$50.00
$5,000.00 and up	$100.00

eBay automatically calculates the next bid and lets you know the minimum bid that will be accepted. For example, if you bid on a vintage Pucci bag and the current price is $104, you couldn't get away with bidding $105; you'd have to increase your bid by at least $2.50—the increment at that price level—to $106.50. To find a chart of bid increments, go to *Help* on the navigation bar; click on the *Basics* box, go to *Glossary Terms*, and click on *Bid Increment*.

Cracking the Bid Code

eBay continually compares all bids and then grants high bidder status to the person who offered the most or, in the case of equal bids, got there first. The top amount you bid is confidential until you are outbid. You can, however, unintentionally signal your high bid like a flashing neon sign. Of course, this means you can sometimes figure out what the other guy bid as well. Here's how:

Some users think that bidding an oddball amount—such as $126.77—somehow cushions them against an even bid like $125 and makes it impossible for someone to figure out their number. Nothing could be further from the truth. Although the odd-amount bidder will indeed beat any bid between $124.28 and $126.76, it doesn't take much for sharp eBaysians to deduce that they've been outbid by less than a full bid increment (in this case $2.50). By upping their bid one increment, they beat out the oddball.

Others take the tactic that they can win by a penny. They bid, for example, $50.01 on the assumption that they'd beat out a last minute bid of $50 by a good old Lincoln copper piece. Technically they're correct. But, like the oddball bidder, they're tipping their hand. Because the eBay genies are programmed to raise the bid by the next full increment, a proxy bid that falls short of the next increment ends up raising the bid by a lesser amount, which again is obvious to your competitor. The next increment over $50 would be $51. Only in a case where the bids come in at the last second might the bid of $50.01 take the day. You don't get much in this world for a penny, and you'll rarely win an auction by that amount on eBay.

The winning strategy is to bid an amount that's an established increment. Your high bid is better disguised, and you get a psychological edge as well. Suppose our penny-pincher had sprung for another $0.99 and bid $51. A $50 bargain hunter's bid would be outbid by a full increment. The bargain bidder might figure, "Wow, this guy really wants this piece; who knows how much he bid," and move on to something else. You win by a buck instead of losing by one.

Checking Up on Your Competition

To the right of the portion of the listing that shows the number of bids an item has received is a link to *Bid History*, where you can view the date and time of all bidders on the item. The bidders are listed from the current high bidder to the lowest. Viewing the bid history is fun and informative. Here's the place to find out if Archrival has hunted down the item as well. One of the most valuable pieces of intelligence to be gleaned is who is bidding.

When the same names keep cropping up, think about doing a bidder search (see chapter 3, "The Quest for Amazing Stuff") and checking into what other treasures they've found.

When the auction is over it's possible to view bid amounts as well. You won't be able to see the winning bidder's top bid—just the amount they needed to win—so you'll never know how high they would've gone. That's always a secret.

Understanding Reserves

Sellers have the right to hold a *reserve price auction*, where they set a price below which they are not obligated to sell. Don't confuse minimum bids with reserves. Every auction has a minimum bid set by the seller. You can tell an item has a reserve price by looking at the current or starting price. Next to it is a parenthetical notation that says *(reserve not yet met)*, *(reserve met)*. In a *no reserve auction*, there isn't any notation and the high bidder wins. However, if the reserve hasn't been met when the auction ends, the seller isn't obligated to offer the item again or sell it to the highest bidder. (The seller is subject to a fee if the auction fails to achieve the reserve.) Likewise, the high bidder isn't obligated to buy the item.

The only way to find out the reserve price is to bid high enough to reach it. Here's how bidding works in such an auction:

1 You find a smashing Mont Blanc roller ball pen—mint in the box—that would make a great high school graduation gift for your nephew.

2 There have been no previous bidders, and the opening bid is $19.99. You see that in parentheses, next to the opening bid price, is the phrase *reserve not yet met.*

3 You bid $35, and the confirmation screen informs you that your bid has been placed and the current price is $19.99 (reserve not yet met). You think, What the heck—I don't get it. That's because if your bid is less than the reserve, eBay raises the bid only to the next bidding amount (either opening or next bid increment). eBay's proxy bidding then kicks in and bids for you until the bidding exceeds your $35.

4 You type in $75. The bid zooms to $50—and now, next to the listing, is the phrase *reserve met.* This tells you that the reserve was $50 and your proxy bid is still the high bid.

5 You eventually win the pen for $62.50, and the story ends happily for you—and for your nephew.

Dutch Auctions

When sellers have multiple identical items to sell, they hold a Dutch auction. This format can be confusing and results can take many forms, depending on the number of people and bids, the quantity bid for, and the amount bid.

To start, the seller specifies the minimum price (the starting bid) and the number of items available. There are no reserves allowed in Dutch auctions, so the minimum bid is actually the minimum purchase price. Over the course of the auction, bidders bid at or above that minimum and on whatever quantity they are interested in purchasing.

At the close of the auction, the highest bidders purchase the items at the lowest successful bid. Sound convoluted? It's not so bad once you get the hang of it. Consider the scenarios that could result in an auction of ten digital cameras, each with a minimum bid of $100:

- Twenty-five people bid $100 for one camera each. The first ten win, since the bid amounts are the same and earlier bids take precedence (as in all auctions).

- Eleven people bid for the cameras. Ten bid $100 and the eleventh bids $150. The latter and the nine earliest bidders win a camera for $100.

- Ten people bid $100 and ten more bid $125. The ten who bid $125 each win a camera for $102.50—the next bid increment over $100.

- Eight people bid any amount over $100, and all eight win a camera at $100.

If the lowest buyer bid for three cameras, she might be entitled to only one, since nine others could be allocated to higher bidders. The only way around this problem is to ensure that you are not the lowest bidder. Occasionally a bidder may reserve the right to refuse purchase of a partial quantity. In that case the seller may skip that bidder and move on to the next one, if any.

Special note: You can sell in the Dutch auction format only if you have a feedback rating greater than 10 *and* have been a member of eBay for more than sixty days. These rules took effect in early 1999 based on feedback from community members to help keep eBay a safe trading environment.

Do Your Due Diligence

Because you can't inspect items in person prior to sale, you have to rely on the seller's description and photo. The quality and resolution of photos vary greatly, so you need other ways of evaluating what you're looking at. Do your homework before placing a bid. Here are some assignments to tackle:

- Always check sellers' feedback to figure out whether you want to do business with them. eBay is growing a community with new registered users joining every day. Undoubtedly it won't be long before you'll want to bid on an item from a user with a feedback of 0. Most users are honest, but a good option with new users is to shoot off an email and make personal contact to see if the person can actually get it together to respond. Seeing a slew of positive feedbacks can give you an added level of confidence when placing a bid or having others bid on your items.

- Ask for input in one of the chat rooms if you're not sure what an item is.

- Hit the books—the special reference library that, ideally, you've been compiling. (See chapter 12, "Becoming an Expert.")

- If you're interested in an expensive item or dealing with a new user, consider using an escrow service. (See chapter 8, "*SafeHarbor* and Happy Trading.")

- Take advantage of the power of email to quiz the seller. Under the seller's name, there's an option called *Ask the Seller a Question.* Just click and query.

Good Questions to Ask

The vast majority of sellers are honest, forthright people who more often than not go out of their way to provide significant detail about an item's condition. Just like you, they don't want any surprises after the auction. However, just because they sell something doesn't make them an expert. Sellers often leave out important information such as dimensions or identifying marks. (We've seen sellers list pieces of art glass as signed but then not mention the name of the artist or studio.) This is rarely intentional. Many sellers are just getting into the business of selling online, and in the rush to list items they may forget critical information. Then again, they might not know what they're really selling, be familiar with the market, or otherwise have a clue what a collector looks for.

So it's up to you to gently investigate. Be clear and polite. Avoid using overly technical language that might not be understood by sellers who aren't up to speed with the lingo of your area of collecting. Who knows—you both might end up learning something. Typical lines of inquiry to email a seller include the following:

- Is that a blemish on the piece or an optical illusion in the photo?

- Is the color more blue green or yellow green, and so on?

- Does the piece have a date or copyright?

- Where did you find this piece? (Warning: Not all sellers will reveal their secret sources.)

- Is anything printed on the back of the piece?

- Does the piece come with original paperwork or packaging?

- What is the size or what are its dimensions?

- What material is it made of?

- Would you please be more specific about the condition with regard to such and such? (The more specific *you* are, the better information you'll get.)

- Ask about a return policy if there is no mention of one in the listing. Then you have it in writing should something go wrong.

Sellers Set Their Own Rules—So Read the Fine Print

eBay sets only broad rules for conducting trades. Sellers set their own terms for many aspects of the transaction, including (but not limited to) the following:

- **Methods of payment:** Most sellers state in their listings whether they accept credit cards, personal checks, or money orders. Because most sellers wait seven to fourteen days for checks to clear, you're better off sending a money order if you want your purchase in a hurry. These terms are at the seller's discretion, and if you want to pay in some other way, contact the seller *before the auction ends* to prevent any miscommunication. Most transactions are in U.S. dollars, so international buyers should make arrangements with sellers in advance. Merchandise gets shipped after the seller has received payment.

Shipping costs and methods:

Unless you live close enough to a seller to pick up an item in person, you need to arrange and pay for shipping. Sellers usually give the cost in the listing and preferred method, so read the terms closely and be sure to include the cost with your payment. If the seller fails to mention shipping in the listing or you want to deviate from the stated terms, clarify the arrangements *before the auction ends.* You don't want to be saddled with excessive shipping costs that weren't specified. International buyers, even in Canada, should note that costs for international shipping are significantly higher than those for shipping within the United States and that some dealers will not ship outside the United States.

Contact terms: Many sellers specify

contact terms and time frames for completing a sale. eBay stipulates that traders should contact each other within three days or the item can be relisted or offered to the next highest bidder. It's not uncommon for sellers to set a "drop dead date" for payment as well. Expediting matters is in everyone's interest. Some sellers are more flexible than others, but it helps to be proactive. For example, if you know you're unreachable for a while after the auction, or you can't get to the bank until the weekend for a money order, email the seller even before the auction ends and give an estimated time of arrival for your payment.

Common sense rules, and if you make the effort to be conscientious, community members respond in kind. Just check out the feedback of buyers and sellers—"thanks for your patience," "went out of her way to accommodate my needs," "great communication and email responses"—to see that little touches such as prompt emails, expeditious shipping, and courteous communication are a major part of making eBay work smoothly.

PART TWO

PARTING IS SUCH

sweet
sorrow

You've done it now. What started as a quaint assemblage of 1939 New York World's Fair memorabilia has burgeoned into a voracious beast, sweeping into its maw goodies ranging from state fair ribbons and 4H

CHAPTER 5 putting it on the block

patches to carnival glass and circus posters—and even a herd of life-size carousel horses. Your family, if they're still talking to you, has pleaded with you to get rid of this "junk"—their word, not yours—that clutters every square foot of your home. Your car hasn't seen the inside of the garage in years. It occurs to you that you might be suffering from MCD, or multiple collections disorder.

Far from a fatal disease, MCD has a simple cure: Sell some stuff! eBay's just the place to do it. Where else will you find a whole community of collectors waiting to jump on a brochure from the General Motors Futurama exhibit?

The first step is to sort through your collections and decide what gets the ax. Despite an initial urge to become a minimalist, resist the temptation to sell *everything*. You just want to get down to fighting weight. To do this you need to refocus. (For tips on building and upgrading your collection, see chapter 10, "Collecting Your Thoughts.") You're sure to come across scores of old finds that someone might want. Pump them into the eBay pipeline. Get some boxes together and mark them BFE— bound for eBay.

In this chapter we tackle the nitty-gritty secrets of selling successfully on eBay, from writing an irresistible description to posting pictures that get results. This material might seem highly technical at first, but it's easier than you might think. Once you get the hang of it, you'll have to stop yourself from selling every last possession.

Details, Please: Listing Your Item for Sale

When a big-time company really wants to move a product, it launches a slick advertising campaign and pays people like Michael Jordan to say how wonderful their product is. Obviously you aren't going to those lengths to sell your Howdy Doody doll. But you can steal a few tricks from the copywriters, art directors, graphic designers, photographers, spokespeople, and marketing geniuses who create those memorable ads. On eBay you get to wear all those hats (or high-tops)—a challenge that can be broken down into a few simple steps.

By completing a simple form, you can have your item up for sale in minutes. Success comes from being creative and strategic. Here's what you'll need to do:

- Describe your item in a few to-the-point words (for the title).

- Figure out under which category your item is most appropriately listed.

- Write an accurate, winning description.

- Think through the entire transaction, including payment, shipping, terms, and conditions.

- Take a photograph or several and get them into your "ad." (This is optional, but photos do boost sales.)

- Respond to questions from potential buyers.

- Wait for the bids to rack up.

Perfect Form

All you need to start selling is to access the *Sell Your Item* form (see pages 80–81) from the *Sell* button on the navigation bar. Mastering this document is the art of eBay. Fortunately it's as simple as following a recipe.

What's in a Name?

Your first task comes right at the top of the form: creating an eye-catching title. With a few well-chosen words you telegraph the essence of your goods. This crucial one-liner then appears in category listings and in listings of all search results.

Brevity is imperative. You're allowed only forty-five characters (including spaces), so it's a little like stuffing everything you need for a month-long cruise into a fanny pack. Titles are plain text—no HTML (HyperText Markup Language, discussed on page 89) allowed—so you need to use the power of words to your advantage. The more precise and descriptive your language, the better.

Take some time to peruse eBay listings and do some searches. What titles draw you in? Which ones turn you off? Can you identify any phrases or words that seem to work? Don't hesitate to copy good ideas.

Prioritize what must be included in the title, and use the argot of the category where your item is going to be listed. For example, if you're trying to reel in people who collect fishing gear, you'd be better off saying, *Creek Chub Wiggler No. 100 fishing lure*, as opposed to *GREAT FISH HOOK—WOW!!* You want to hit the high points, so decide which of the following pieces of information will both be search friendly (see chapter 3, "The Quest for Amazing Stuff") and entice category cruisers:

Brand name, maker, or manufacturer:
Go with what's recognizable. Many people search by these names, whether there's a category for them or not. For example, you might list your set of Speedy Gonzales Pepsi glasses under *Comics*, where a Pepsi collector would never find them. Because you can list your item in only one category (see page 84), you might miss many potential buyers if you don't use the Pepsi name. Also, names of brands and manufacturers signal the level of quality no matter what the item.

Artist or designer: The creative hand behind an object
is of prime importance in art, decorative arts, clothing, and furniture. If you have an Armani jacket, you would say so, not call it just "nice woman's jacket." If your object is signed, it's almost a given that you'd include the name or mark in the title.

Country of origin: Many collectors focus on items from a
particular country or region, so consider whether your object might be of interest to them.

Medium or material: Mentioning that an object is fab-
ric, ceramic, paper, wood, and so on might be redundant, depending on the category you choose. However, in certain cases this information could make the difference for a buyer. For example, a rattan window

▶ Subscribe now! Get your charter subscription to eBay magazine.   [   ] [**Search**] tips
▶ Review mockups of new item pages. Tell us what you think.   ☐ Search titles **and** descriptions

Sell Your Item

Related Links: • New to Selling? • Seller Tips • Fees •
Registration
• Free Shipping Estimates from iShip.com

Registration required. You must be a registered eBay user to sell your item.

Title required	(45 characters max; no HTML tags, asterisks, or quotes, as they interfere with Search) see tips

If you prefer to use the old-style method of choosing a category, click here.

Category required   You have chosen category # [   ]
Just click in the boxes below from left to right until you have found the appropriate category for your item. The chosen category number will appear in the small box to indicate that you have made a valid selection.

Antiques ->
Books, Movies, Music ->
Coins & Stamps ->
Collectibles ->
Computers ->
Dolls, Figures ->
Jewelry, Gemstones ->
Photo & Electronics ->
Pottery & Glass ->
Sports Memorabilia ->
Toys, Bean Bag Plush ->
Miscellaneous ->

---------------------------   ---------------------------   ---------------------------

Description required	▲ ▼
	You can use basic HTML tags to spruce up your listing. see tips
	You can add links to additional photos, but enter your primary photo in the Picture URL below. If you want more than one photo for your item, insert its URL in the Description section in the following format: <img src=http://www.anywhere.com/mypicture.jpg>
Picture URL optional	http:// [ ] 📷 It's easy! Learn the basics in the tutorial, and enter your URL here.
The Gallery Don't get left out! Items in the Gallery get more bids! learn more	◉ Do not include my item in the Gallery ◯ Add my item to the Gallery (only **$0.25!**) ◯ Feature my item in the Gallery (Featured fee of $19.95) 🖼️
	http:// [ ] If you leave the Gallery URL empty, your Pic URL will be used as your Gallery URL. (Only jpg, bmp, or tif files can be used in the Gallery. Please note that **gif** files will **not** appear in the Gallery!)

Make your item stand out and get more bids! Try these winning options.	
Boldface Title?	☐ $2.00 charge
Featured?	☐ $99.95 charge learn more
Featured in Category?	☐ $14.95 charge learn more
Great Gift icon?	[Not Selected ⬍] $1.00 charge learn more

Item location required	City, Region (e.g., San Jose, CA) Zip or postal code (e.g., 95125) [United States ⬍] Country

Payment Methods Choose all that you will accept	☐ Money Order/Cashiers Check ☐ Personal Check ☐ Visa/MasterCard ☐ COD (collect on delivery) ☐ On-line Escrow ☐ American Express ☑ See Item Description ☐ Other ☐ Discover
Where will you ship?	⦿ Ship to Seller's Country Only ◯ Will Ship Internationally see tips
Who pays for shipping?	☐ Seller Pays Shipping ☐ Buyer Pays Fixed Amount ☐ Buyer Pays Actual Shipping Cost ☑ See Item Description

Quantity required	1 If quantity is more than one, then you will have a Dutch auction. see tips
Minimum bid required	_____ per item see tips (e.g., 2.00 -- Please do not include commas or currency symbols, such as $.)
Duration required	[7 ⬍] days

Reserve Price optional	_____ see tips (e.g., 15.00 -- Please do not include commas or currency symbols, such as $.)
Private Auction? optional	☐ Please don't use this unless you have a specific reason. learn more

UserID / Password required	_____ _____ User ID or E-mail address Password (forgotten it?)

Press the "review" button below to see what fees are due immediately and what fees may be due if your item sells. You will not incur any fees until you accept the terms disclosed in the next screen.

Press [review] to review and place your listing.

Press [clear form] to clear the form and start over.

Note: If the Back button on your browser erases your information on this form, find out how to fix this.

shade might be of no interest whatsoever to someone who loves bamboo.

● **Technique:** In some mediums, such as ceramics, glass, metalwork, and textiles, the technique is as important as the maker or design. For example, a hand-tied quilt versus a machine-stitched one might appeal to very different people.

● **Date of manufacture or creation:** This might refer to a patent, an exact date as on a painting or letter, a publishing year, or an era such as *Victorian* or *17th century*.

● **Marks:** Is the piece signed or stamped by the manufacturer? If you're selling sterling, for example, you might want to consult a manufacturer's catalog or reference book to decipher the mysterious symbol(s) (also known as *hallmarks*) stamped on the bottom or handle.

● **Size:** Include only if it's an important selling point, as in the case of miniatures, clothing, rugs, bedspreads, engines (horsepower), and boats.

● **Color:** Think like a collector or searcher. Are people out there looking for only red items, or is red a rare color for this object?

● **Model number:** Include when model numbers are common parlance of the category, as in technical equipment, computers, and cars.

● **Reserve status:** People love a no-reserve auction, where they can jump into the action. If you have room and aren't setting a reserve, indicate so with *NR*, *No Res*, or *No Reserve*.

Take these two examples of titles for the same item. Which is more likely to be a match with item searches? Which one conveys useful information to the busy collector sorting through tons of items in the *Pottery and Glass: Pottery: Scandinavian Art* category?

1 *Really Pretty Vase L@@K!!!!*

2 *Finnish Arabia Vase Signed 1950s 12" NR*

If you picked number two, bingo—you win. (For the record, this title is forty-four characters.)

Here are some things *not* to include in your title listing:

- Exclamation points or other characters such as @, as in *L@@K!!!* Remember, searches are word specific.

- Misspelled words, which will severely limit the number of bidders for your item.

- Offensive language.

- Vague descriptions.

- Gratuitous mentions of brand names. People sometimes include other brand names to attract bidders to similar or lesser-quality goods. A typical example: *"Croc" handbag, NOT Prada, Gucci, Kleinberg-Sherrill.* Don't expect buyers to get a warm and fuzzy feeling about you or your merchandise using this technique. In fact, abuse of keywords can be a violation of eBay's keyword spamming policy and may cause eBay to end the auction early and issue an automatic credit to the seller for the insertion fee.

As you enter your title in the form's title field, you'll know when you've reached forty-five characters because you won't be able to add any more and your computer will let out a little *ding*. Instead of playing count the characters on a scratch pad, use the field to help you edit. The idea

The Key to Winning Titles

A well-written title undoubtedly already contains many words that collectors are likely to employ when looking for a specific type of item. Space permitting, use keywords strategically, but don't sacrifice vital information in favor of keywords. For example, you write a title, *Signed Bradley Hubbard Brass Inkwell,* for an item you are listing in *Collectibles: Writing Instruments: Inkwells.* Collectors of either Bradley & Hubbard or inkwells should find your item without a problem. Best of all, it's only thirty-three characters long, leaving room for an additional nugget of information. This inkwell has an organic, curvilinear form, so you update your title to read, *Bradley Hubbard Brass Inkwell Art Nouveau* (forty-three characters). You drop the word *signed* since you are identifying the maker, which is enough to get people to click on the description. By adding *Art Nouveau,* you reach a new audience interested in this important design movement from the turn of the twentieth century but unlikely to be hanging out in the *Inkwells* category.

Keywords are also essential when you write your description. When people opt to search by text and title, the eBay search engine scans your entire description for matches. Therefore, list or include in your description as many keywords as possible (without resorting to the keyword spamming technique discussed in this chapter).

is to keep refining and cutting words until you've covered the important points.

Pick a Category—But Not Just Any Category

eBay has more than 1,600 categories, and an item can fall into several of them. Sounds good at first, except you can list your item in only one. This restriction helps keep eBay an orderly place. If items were listed in multiple categories, it would be nearly impossible to keep all the bids up-to-date and accurate. Choosing the best category is a common dilemma. For example, you want to list a hard-to-find book on American toys of the twentieth century. It has excellent pictures, lots of pages devoted to pressed steel planes, cars, and trucks, and a strong section on dolls. The book could be listed appropriately in any of the following categories:

● *Books: Nonfiction: Collectibles*

● *Dolls: General*

● *Dolls: Antique: General*

● *Toys & Bean Bag Plush: Vintage Vehicles: Pressed Steel*

● *Toys & Bean Bag Plush: Vintage Vehicles: Trucks*

All these choices are enough to cause a rash. Don't book an appointment with the dermatologist. Instead be thankful that your book is probably appealing to a whole host of collectors; more collector interest equals more bids. To figure out the perfect category, start by researching where other people are selling similar books:

● Search *completed auctions* for *book toys*. If you get too many results, narrow the parameters to *book toy planes* or *book dolls*.

● From the results, identify the categories where similar books have been listed.

● Note final sale prices and compare prices in one category with those in another.

● Search current auctions by title and analyze categories and prices.

● You can also check into various categories and search within them (using *Search* at the top of every listing page).

● Note titles and descriptions carefully and model yours on successful ones.

This doesn't take long, and your final decision might surprise you. Initially you leaned toward listing in *Toys & Bean Bag Plush: Vintage Vehicles: Pressed Steel*, only to find through sales results that doll collectors are voracious purchasers of anything doll related. You wind up listing the book in *Dolls: Antique: General.* Other collectors are going to find your book because your title and description have good keywords that their search radar will pick up.

The mechanics of category selection are simple. Start on the left, clicking first on the major categories, and then on each subsection until you reach the category you want. Note: If your browser does not support JavaScript (WebTV, for example) or if you've turned JavaScript off, you select categories based on pull-down menus.

eBay policies stipulate that you must list your item in the appropriate category. Items listed improperly will be moved to the correct category. eBay moves approximately one thousand items per week to their correct categories.

Writing a Successful Item Description

On the Internet, content is king. Getting potential bidders to find your item is one thing; getting them to leave a nice hefty bid is another. Your item description is an opportunity to make your case to the jury.

Make your listing comprehensive, and anticipate what goes through a potential buyer's mind when evaluating your item. You have unlimited space for your listing, but that's not a license to write an epic. A good salesman conveys an item's strengths with-

Some Like Plain Vanilla

As you survey the eBay landscape, you'll see lots of listings with fancy additions such as elaborate backgrounds, colored fonts, animation, and even music. Before trotting off to the land of bells and whistles, ask yourself, What sells? A talking seagull cartoon or a few bars of your favorite song might amuse some customers, but chances are that most don't want to spend a few extra seconds waiting for their computers to download all that extraneous digital information. In addition, complex graphics often make text hard to read. eBaysians want to check in and check out as quickly as possible—there's a lot of virtual ground to cover before they have to hit the sack. Pithy, fact-filled listings are all they need to make an informed decision. Sometimes vanilla is the most powerful flavor.

out hyperbole. You can't make something what it isn't. If your item is not the top of the heap, no amount of salesmanship is going to improve it. Remember, you're in a marketplace where people aren't able to inspect your merchandise. Overselling results in disappointed buyers and hassles you just don't need. Honesty, and even modesty, results in more satisfied customers. If you're not well versed in the item, no problem. Use good pictures (you're not limited as to the number of pictures you can use, but quality is better than quantity), provide the basic information, and let the object speak for itself. The expert collectors will sort it out, ask you the critical questions, and bid to its value. Or stop into one of the category-specific chat rooms and ask your fellow eBaysians if they can help you identify your object and assess its value.

Here are some pointers for good listings:

- **Be accurate:** If your photo shows an unrealistic color or weird shadow that looks like a blemish, let potential bidders know that the image isn't a true representation and try to explain how the object differs in person.

- **Stick with the facts:** Give all the pertinent factoids that would be important for the bidder. It's amazing, but many sellers often omit critical information through ignorance or oversight: signatures, makers' marks, technique of manufacture, labels, and so on. If you don't know the significance of a mark, provide as much information as possible. Better yet, take a picture of the mark and add it to your listing. Collectors are good detectives. Given the clues, they can deduce the rest. When selling equipment, check the manufacturer's Web site for specifications and features.

- **Tell what you know:** If you are an expert in the field of what you are selling, let it all hang out. However, that doesn't mean you should act like a pretentious know-it-all. You are probably not the only expert out there, and you don't want to send a message that people are going to have to pay dearly for your knowledge.

- **Be honest about condition:** Condition is one of the most important variables in establishing value and also the hardest to evaluate from a photo over the Internet. Be straightforward. It's all right to err on the side of too much information. Any damage should be fully explained and your price set accordingly. If you're selling something in a new area and don't know how condition affects the value, encourage people to ask questions.

● **Point to documentation:** If your item or a similar item can be found in a popular book on the subject, reference the book and the page number. Skip esoteric books, however. Just because an item is in a book doesn't necessarily make it more valuable.

● **Let the provenance be known:** If the item has real provenance—you can document its ownership history—share that information. Just because a piece came out of a home with other similar or high-quality items doesn't confer a provenance or necessarily increase its value. On the other hand, if the four hand-painted porcelain Beatle figurines from the 1968 animated movie *Yellow Submarine* were given to you by your uncle Al, who produced the movie, don't hold back. That really means something.

Calling the Cliché Cops

One of the most common mistakes sellers make is loading their listings with hackneyed phrases and clichés. Avoid these at all costs. Although eBay is a chatty kind of venue, this kind of verbiage detracts from your credibility. Should you find the following verbal crutches creeping into your copy, delete them immediately:

● **"A great addition to any collection of . . .":** Collectors disdain this phrase for its presumptuousness. They will be the judge of whether your item is a great addition to *any* collection, particularly their own.

● **"Unique, one of a kind, rare":** The frequency with which these words appear in listings is enough to make rare items seem pretty darn common. Just because you've never seen it, don't assume that hardly any of the five million people using eBay haven't. Unless you're certain beyond a reasonable doubt that no (or few) others exist, come up with a better set of adjectives.

● **"I've never seen another one like it":** Most collectors would conclude that you need to get out more. Of course, if you've handled a significant number of similar items and none have shared these attributes, you should share your years of research with potential bidders by being specific.

● **"Reserve set to protect my investment":** Most bidders don't care about your investment, and they certainly don't want to hear you whine about it. They assume your reserve is your investment plus a profit. If your item fails to hit the reserve, you'll know you overpaid or were too greedy.

● **"Reasonable reserve":** Set a reserve you believe is reasonable, but don't advertise the fact. You wouldn't let the world know you've set an unreasonable reserve, would you? Bidders ultimately tell you if the reserve is reasonable by meeting or surpassing it.

Some Rules You Ought to Know

eBay has several policies that govern listings that you should keep in mind. Among them are the following:

● You are not allowed to use listings as advertisements (for items not for sale on eBay), as want ads (seeking items), or for trades (seeking merchandise in lieu of payment).

● You may not have a listing that doesn't sell anything but instead directs bidders to another auction on eBay. On a bona fide item listing, however, you may encourage bidders to check out your other auctions.

● Offering bonuses, raffles, giveaways, prizes, random drawings, or prizes as an enticement to bid is forbidden. Many states consider these promotions illegal lotteries.

● Listing techniques that avoid eBay's fee structure are prohibited. These include auctions with low bid prices and high shipping costs, selling items that require an additional purchase, offering items for direct sale, and offering bidders a "choice" of items.

● Auctions for catalogs from which buyers may order other merchandise are not allowed.

● When setting a reserve price auction, you may not 1) state there is a reserve when item is not listed as reserve auction; or 2) state that a bidder is obligated to purchase when reserve is not met.

● Although users may place simple links to other Web sites in their listing, these links may not be to other auction sites, sites offering the same merchandise for an equal or lower price, or sites offering merchandise that is prohibited on eBay.

When eBay determines a listing has violated these policies, it ends the auction early and issues a credit for the insertion fee. For a complete discussion of listing policies, see *Community Standards* under *Help* on the navigation bar.

Files with Style: Using HTML

You've mastered the basics of getting things listed in the proper category and writing stunning titles and item listings. Now consider jazzing up the visual appeal using some of the special effects that professional Web page designers employ. What's the magic behind Web pages? It's HTML, short for HyperText Markup Language, the programming language people use to create Web pages. You can add different-colored and different-size fonts to your item description by using HTML, an easy-to-learn tool for formatting text in interesting ways inside a Web browser. The good news is you don't have to be a computer wiz or have any special software to use HTML in your eBay listings and in chat rooms. (Think of HTML as a "built-in" feature on eBay.) If you can type, you can use HTML.

HTML uses symbols called *tag indicators* to determine the type of formatting and to alert the browser to display text or graphics in a special way. These tag indicators are the symbols < > and appear at the start and end of every HTML command. (They're above the comma and period on your keyboard.) Inside these tags you type the function that you want HTML to perform.

Suppose you're selling a 1970s Seiko watch that's never been used and is still in the original box, a condition known as *new old stock*. This adds considerably to its desirability and value. To focus bidders on this important asset, you want to highlight this text in color. In the description box, input your item as you always would:

Nice stainless-steel Seiko watch c. 1975. This disco-generation Seiko has an automatic (winds by the movement of your wrist), 17-jewel movement with a sweep second hand and quick-set date with number and day of week (just

---

The Great Listing Checklist

Have you covered all the bases for a terrific listing?

1. Easily searchable title.
2. Item listed in "right" category.
3. Accurate description.
4. Vital dimensions listed.
5. Reference books and/or provenance cited.
6. Photos clear, cropped, and of reasonable size.
7. Return policy stated.
8. Payment terms articulated.
9. Shipping costs and terms provided.
10. Realistic reserve or minimum bid set.

push in the stem to advance a full day). This watch has a great look with its deep blue dial and Roman numeral hour markers. Note the rectangular shape of the case and the cool stainless-steel bracelet. Best of all, it's <font color=red> new old stock /mint in box!! </font>. I have never had it worked on or looked at by a watchmaker. However, it keeps excellent time.

When your listing appears on eBay, the words *new old stock* and *mint in box* will be red. When performing some HTML functions, such as modifying text, it's critical to begin and end the command. The tag *<font color=red>* starts the command, while *</font>* ends it, returning the text to its normal appearance. You can choose from the following default colors: aqua, black, blue, fuchsia, gray, green, lime, maroon, navy, olive, purple, red, silver, teal, yellow, and white. Pick wisely; colors such as yellow are hard to read.

Not all HTML uses a tag at the beginning and end. Some commands are completely contained within one set of tags. Below is a list of common HTML commands eBaysians employ:

● Increase the point size:

<big> makes words bigger<big> makes them bigger still</big> reverts down one size</big> takes words back to the point size you were originally working in.

● Create paragraphs:

place this tag wherever you want to end a paragraph <p>
  And start a new one.

● End a line:

When you want lines to break, type
but note that doing so doesn't create a new paragraph.

● Boldface text:

makes words bold

● Italicize text:

makes words appear in italics

Underline text:

<u>underline words</u>

Center text:

puts words in the middle of the page

Create a bulleted list:

To have bullets, start by using this symbol<ul>

<li>followed by these tags</li>

<li>at the beginning and end</li>

<li>of each piece of bulleted text, and then end the command</li>

</ul>

Do a numbered list:

Creating fancy numerals use this tag:<ol>

<li>and then these tags before and after each block of text</li>

<li>as shown—the numbers will appear in ascending order</li>

<li>as easy as 1, 2, 3</li>

<ol>

Combine HTML codes:

<u><font color=green>*__Makes a plain statement bold, italicized, underlined, and green__** </font></u> Note: Tags are canceled in reverse order.

Create a link:

<a href="http:cgi3.ebay.com/aw-cgi/eBayISAPI.dll?ViewListedItems& userid=(your user ID goes here)">see my other auctions</a> puts the text *see my other auctions* in your listing as a colored, clickable link to

everything you have on sale at eBay. You can replace the URL and name of the link to create other links to your feedback, About Me page, another image or another Web site (as long as you conform to eBay's rules per the links policy discussed in this chapter). Note: The simplest way to get the correct URL is to copy it from the address bar on your browser from the page that you want to link to.

Of course, all this code requires a great deal of typing. You can make life easier by creating a template in your word-processing system that has the basics of your listing: payment terms, shipping information, and so on, as well as the HTML tags with no text in between. When you create a new listing, make a duplicate of your template, add the new information to the tags, and then, when logged on to eBay, copy (highlight text and hit CTRL-C) your new document and paste (hit CTRL-V) it into the description box. This way you can also use spell check (before you cut and paste onto eBay) to keep your listings clean.

Say It with Pictures

Photos make a huge difference in sales results. They build bidder confidence. Think of adding photos as the difference between buying through the classifieds and buying through a catalog. Photos make it possible to show things that words can't do justice, such as fine detail, technique, or signature.

Posting your photos in your listings can be accomplished in five steps:

1 Find a place to store your images on the Internet.

2 Photograph your goods.

3 Get your images into a usable form on your computer.

4 Upload the images to a server.

5 Add your photos to your listing.

Getting Your Photos onto the Internet

Talking about what to do with your photo before you've taken it might seem like putting the cart before the horse, but scoping out this part of the process ahead of time can greatly reduce your frustration later. Because you're shooting pictures with the purpose of inserting them into your eBay listing, you'll need to modify your technique, invest in some specialized equipment, and become adept at turning your photos into a format that your computer can read.

You see, when you add a photo to your listing, you're pointing eBay to a Web site that is "hosting" your image. If that sounds intimidating, think of this hosting service as an electronic filing cabinet where you temporarily store images so they can be easily retrieved. When the bidder clicks into your listing, eBay goes to the Web site where your picture resides and retrieves it—or uploads it, in techno parlance—into the listing. For this reason you must not remove your image from where it is hosted until your auction has ended.

This is also why you should look to your Internet service provider (ISP) and not eBay if your images aren't being displayed.

Your filing cabinet is actually a space on a server hooked up to the Internet. A server is a computer that connects other computers and "serves" information. The first place to look for this storage area is your ISP. Many ISPs allocate server space where you can

A Host of Options

Many image hosting services have cropped up in the last few years. Some are free, while others charge fees starting at around $0.50 to host an image for thirty days. Here are a few popular ones:

- www.photopoint.com: Provides the ability to email your photos and post them to the server as well as FTP.

- www.auctionwatch.com: Offers free hosting and lots of information about the online auction community.

- www.pongo.com: Posts images for $0.50 and has links to other image hosting services.

- www.pixhost.com: Fees start at $0.50 per image.

Film-processing companies such as Kodak (www.kodak.photonet.com) and Seattle Film Works (www.filmworks.com) offer a service whereby they not only send you prints of your photos, but also place digital copies on the Web. You can use this trick for your eBay listings as well as to create an electronic photo album that your friends and family can view.

create your own Web site that stores images for eBay. AOL, for example, allocates 2 megabytes of Web space/storage per each registered screen name (you're allowed up to five screen names per account, which is more than enough space to list many, many items at once). Contact your ISP to find out if it'll provide space for you. To load your pictures, some ISPs use standardized software known as FTP (file transfer protocol) or, like AOL, they may have built their own interface for loading images. If your ISP doesn't have space for you, other sites on the Web offer free Web space or free and low-cost image hosting services. After you've selected a site, check its terms of service to make sure it allows links from other sites. In any case, your ulti-mate goal is to load your pictures onto a server where it's assigned a URL.

Photographing Your Goods

Once you figure out where your photos are going to end up, you can turn your attention to perfecting your images for viewing on eBay. After all, even the most agile text falls flat without a powerful visual image attached to it. Although you might be tempted to do a slapdash job on your photos because you're not taking them for posterity, bear in mind that one well-composed shot is worth ten sloppy ones. Good photos equal sales, so take the time to develop your picture-taking proficiency and avoid these common quality issues:

● Low light that makes it hard to see details.

● Too much light resulting in overexposure.

● Reflective glare or "hot" spots on items from a flash or other lighting source.

● Fuzzy focus.

● Dinky image.

● Poor or nonexistent cropping.

● Distracting background.

Ninety-nine times out of a hundred, a poor photo is the result of operator error (that means you). You can improve your technique immensely by having the right tool for the job. For example, if you sell jewelry, and your camera does not have a macro function (the ability to focus items from a short distance), you may never be able to get good close-ups of earrings, rings, or brooches.

The best way to learn what works is to take photos in different environ-ments. Some people find it easiest to shoot items under natural light either in a sunny room or outdoors. The conventional rule is to have the light source behind and above you lighting up the surface of what you're shooting. This works fine when taking a photo of your mother, Aunt Helen, and Aunt Joan; it's likely to be a nightmare when shooting a silver-plate tea service pol-ished to perfection. Items with shiny surfaces—glass, metal, ceramics, glossy paper—are susceptible to glare, especially when you're using a flash. Photos often end up with hot (overlit) spots that you might not notice until after the photo is developed or you view it on a PC. To remedy this, try shooting outside on a cloudy day or in the shade; this can flatten colors and reduce contrast but could still give the best representation of your object.

If you have the space and the inclination, you can construct a small photography set consisting of a table and a few yards of background paper or fabric. Attach one end of the background material to a wall and drape it gently so it covers and then hangs over the table. When you shoot, you'll now have a "seamless" background as in professional photographs. Poster board, colored paper, bedsheets, and fabric all make good, inexpensive backgrounds. Avoid materials that are glossy or have a sheen, as they are likely to reflect light. Black velvet happens to be an excellent light-absorbing material. Stick with solid colors so the background doesn't detract from your object.

You can also try the "sky cam" method. Lay your background on the floor and place the item on it. Then stand directly above it and shoot. If the item is designed to stand upright, lay it on its side and shoot as straight down as possible. Your photo should look fine. You might need a stepladder (be careful) to put more distance between you and the item so it fits in the frame.

Note: Unless you have explicit permission to use photos from another source, the photos you post must be images that you've photographed yourself, have hired someone to photograph for you, or otherwise own the rights to use on eBay.

Making Your Photos Computer Friendly

Before you can move your images onto your hosting service, you have to put them on your hard drive. There are three ways to do this: 1) take a regular photo, develop it, and use a scanner to "copy" the picture to your hard drive; 2) skip the camera and put the object right on a scanner; or 3) use a digital camera that loads the image directly onto the computer (no rolls of film to develop).

Scanning Images and Objects

Scanners are like desktop photocopiers, except the resulting image becomes a computer file as opposed to a piece of paper. You lay the picture on the glass (hence the name *flatbed scanner*), press a few keys and buttons, and all those dots (called *pixels*) that compose a picture get turned into digitized bits of computer data. You can also scan flat items such as books, brochures, paper advertising, coins, stamps, and watches without ever taking a photograph.

Scanner images are measured in dots per inch (dpi). The higher the dpi,

Meet eBay Ambassador Jess Anderson

SPECIALTY:
Fiestaware
(and Assorted Junk)

eBay HANDLE: Buyzalott   AGE: 30

MY MOTHER WAS AN ANTIQUES DEALER: So I've been collecting Fiesta pottery and vintage books and clothes since I was 5.

HOW I GOT STARTED ON eBay: I used to drag the hubby around to endless garage sales, spending money on stuff that was "valuable" but did nothing but clutter my house. I turned to him as we were driving to yet another one and said, "Wouldn't it be great if I could just do this all the time for a living?" Someone up there must have been listening because the *next* day at my son's swim class I met a woman who told me about eBay. She showed me the ropes and I took off from there. Now I can stay home with my children, satisfy my compulsive garage sale/thrift store habit, and make money.

MY EXPERIENCE PROVES: You can sell anything on eBay. I've sold discarded library books no one would have thought had value for hundreds, Care Bears for tons, and other assorted junk. These folks will BUY, BUY, BUY!

TO SELL, SELL, SELL: Read all the books you can—research the stuff on eBay to see what it went for. Get an automatic advertising program such as Sam Cool—nicer ads with clear, detailed photos seem to do better.

MY BEST eBay TRANSACTION: Bought a vase for $10 not knowing what it was and found out it was worth thousands.

MY MISSION: To keep selling—I have eBay stuff all over my house.

the larger the image. The good news is that you don't need a high-end scanner for eBay because Internet images are composed of about 75 dpi, which fits the screen well. A 300 dpi image is four times as large, making it too big to fit on the screen and snail-like when loading. So set your scans to 75 dpi. Scans can be cropped like photos, and this helps reduce their size as well. A scanner suitable for eBay purposes costs less than $150.

Digital Cameras

If your budget allows, digital cameras are the way to go. Even though they cost from $200 to more than $1,000, the advantages are tremendous. For one, digital cameras use no film, so the savings in film and processing alone allows you to recoup your investment quickly. Going digital means that practicing costs nothing—if you take a lousy picture, press a button and it's gone. There's also no waiting around for pictures to be developed, which means you can have an object up on eBay in less than half an hour.

If you go digital, you'll probably want a camera with at least a 2–3x zoom lens and macro capabilities. Manufacturers use different methods to transfer pictures to your computer's hard drive, such as using a floppy disk that pops out of the camera and into your PC, or hooking the camera directly to the PC via a cable or port. Whatever you buy has to be compatible with your hardware. Talk to professionals at computer stores and camera shops. When you find the model you want, shop for price (including on eBay, of course).

Cameras take pictures in pixel sizes, such as 960×720 and 640×480 (the standard-size screen on a PC). The ideal pixel size for your eBay listings is 320×240, which translates into physical size of about 3×4 inches. At this size, your pictures load quickly and are more than sufficient for bidders to comprehend.

Actual image size is one consideration, but the amount of disk space or the file size is another. File size refers to the number of bytes your image takes up. The ideal size for eBay is between 20,000 and 35,000 bytes, which can also be expressed as between 20K and 35K. (By the way, a megabyte is 1 million bytes.) Two factors determine the byte size of your image: pixels and the quality at which you save your image. A 320×240-pixel size image saved at a medium quality (some applications use numbers, with 100 being the highest quality) should be around 30K.

Tweaking and Editing Images

Your scanner or camera should come with software allowing you to manipulate the images on your computer. These images must first be saved in a file format that your Internet browser can read. The two industry standard formats are *gif* and *jpeg* (also *jpg*). Photos are best saved in jpeg (imperative if you want to use the Gallery). You should be able to specify this as the default for your images or save them in this format with any provided software.

Most digital cameras and scanners include software to manipulate your images. Using these applications, you can adjust

● **brightness:** to bring up or lower light levels.

● **contrast:** to change the differential between the light and the dark areas of your image.

● **sharpness:** to bring images into focus.

Perhaps the software feature that's destined to become your favorite is the ability to crop your pictures. Cropping enables you to create a more professional look by cutting out any excess image that surrounds your item. If the best light you can find is outside on the hood of your car (draped in non-reflective material), cropping allows you to get rid of those pesky garage doors in the background.

Working with images on your computer is easy and risk free. On most programs you can undo whatever changes you've made to an image or just start over by opening a new copy of the picture on your hard drive.

When you are done saving an image, it should have a name like *myitem.jpg*. It won't be long before you have a slew of photos on your hard drive, so giving each one a unique name (butterdish, Venicepstcrd, etc.) as opposed to generic ones (item1, item2, etc.) will help you keep track. One tip: Sometimes it's good to create three folders: *eBay to be listed, eBay for sale*, and *eBay archives*. Good organization can reduce a lot of technostress when an image seems to go missing in action.

Uploading Your Image to a Server

The process for getting your pictures onto your ISP or image hosting services Web server is called *uploading*, and the specifics vary based on your hosting service. It may take a few tries to get the hang of it, but have patience. Becoming a pro is only a matter of sticking with it.

The result you seek is the same no matter where you upload your images. When you're done, your image should have its own URL or Internet address, which you need to put in your listing on eBay. As long as your images are sitting on a page on the World Wide Web, if you want your best friends to see the cool new thing you're putting up for sale, send an email with the URL and they can check it out. Want some help identifying an object? Load a picture of the mystery item, go to the relevant chat room, post a message with a link (HTML) or the address of the picture, and request the expert input of your fellow eBaysians.

Of course, you are going to have to keep track of all these URLs so you can have them handy to put in your listing. Either write them down or load your photos as you write your listings, copying and pasting in the URL onto the *Sell Your Item* form.

Adding Photos to Your Listing

There are two places to insert photos into your listing: on the *Picture URL* field and within HTML tags in your description.

eBay provides a *Picture URL* on the *Sell Your Item* form so your listing points toward your image. On this line you add the full URL, such as http://www.mypicture host.com/mypicture.jpg. (Of course, you add your real information here.) This makes your photo appear at the end of your written text, and eBay posts the little camera icon next to your listing to alert other users that you've included an image. Note: In this case, you use just the URL and no HTML tags.

Frequently it requires two or more photos to show your item in the best possible light. They can be merged with your item description by using HTML to pick up your images from your image hosting server. The basic code for adding a photo is as follows:

```
<img src=http://www.mypicturehost.com/mypicture.jpg >
```

AOL members use this:

```
<img src=http://members.aol.com/yourscreenname/
               mypicture.jpg >
```

Note: For AOL, there's no need for "www."

You can put this code at any point in the item description where you want your photo to appear. Images

Only on eBay

eBay receives an average of fifty million page views every day, which is about 1.5 billion page views per month.

embedded in your listing appear before those in the picture URL field, so think about the order you want. Consider putting the most general shot—the overall piece—as the opener in your description. As you progress through the text, add images that highlight what you're explaining, such as close-ups of technique or marks. You can use the picture URL field for one of these close-ups as well.

To specify the alignment of your image—such as centered, flush left, and flush right—use these HTML codes:

<img align=left src=http://www.mypicturehost.com/mypicture.jpg >

<img align=right src=http://www.mypicturehost.com/mypicture.jpg >

<img align=center src=http://www.mypicturehost.com/mypicture.jpg >

Using Photos in the Gallery

Every category on eBay has a *Gallery* where buyers can shop by picture (with the exception of the adult categories)—and your item can get some additional exposure (no pun intended). The cost is minimal: $0.25 added to your insertion fee. Your picture appears as a thumbnail photo of 96 × 96 pixels. To use this feature, click on the *Add Your Image to the Gallery* box, and the photo in the *Picture URL* field appears in the Gallery. If you prefer, you can specify another image by typing the URL in the space provided.

Special Options from eBay

eBay offers several ways to increase attention to your listing. You select these options from the *Sell Your Item* form when you create your listing. eBay adds the nonrefundable charges to your insertion fee. You can choose from among the following extras:

● **Boldface text in title:** Makes your title appear in the category listings in bold type. Cost: $2.

● **Category featured auction:** These auctions appear at the top of the category listings pages for the chosen category. At no additional charge, some are selected randomly for display in the *Featured Items* section of the related category page. Your item, along with those of other sellers who use this option, is among the first people will see in a category. Cost: $14.95.

Off-the-Shelf Software

Several companies and software designers are jumping on the eBay bandwagon, creating new applications to automate some of eBay's functions. eBay has no financial or other interest in any of these companies, nor does it endorse any of these products. However, eBay does endeavor to inform the public when changes are anticipated. When purchasing software, confirm that it's up-to-date and compatible with eBay.

Here are some popular applications:

● **Auction Poster 98**—http://www.auctionposter.com/: Helps create your ads and listings and automatically generates the HTML code. Create your listings offline then log on and load them onto eBay—up to one hundred at a time. This software will even upload your images automatically to your hosting service. If you don't have a site to host your pictures, use theirs. What's best about this site is that you can get an unlimited pass or pay per use, so you can try it out first and see if it works for you.

● **AdGen**—http://adgen.hypermart.net/: This free service will generate all the HTML for the item description part of your listings in a variety of different styles and post it directly to eBay's *Sell Your Item* form. You complete the form—user ID, auction duration, and so on—and post. A great way to give automated listing software a test drive.

● **Auction Assistant**—http://www.blackthornesw.com/bthome: A complete suite of eBay automation tools, including a tracking system, listing creation system, automated FTP, and data retrieval from eBay to store in your system (winning bidders and their email addresses, for example, to generate automated after-the-sale messages to buyers).

● **Featured auction:** Your item appears in the *Featured Auction* section accessible from *Browse* on the navigation bar. For no additional charge—and if you're one of the lucky sellers—eBay randomly selects featured auctions to appear on the eBay home page and in the featured section of related category home pages. Cost: $99.95.

● **Gift icon:** You can choose to add a special icon to your listing beside your title. This lets bidders know that your item would make a great gift. Your item also appears in the special gift section. Cost: $1.

● **Gallery listing:** Your item appears in miniature on a Gallery page. (For details, see "Using Photos in the Gallery" in this chapter.) Cost: $0.25.

● **Featured Gallery listing:** The featured Gallery listing places your item in the Gallery category in which you list your item. Larger versions of these listings also appear randomly at the top of the Gallery listing pages. Featured Gallery image size is 140 × 140 pixels. Cost: $19.95.

Once you make the move to become a seller, you have to start thinking like a businessperson. Uncle Griff, an early eBaysian whose life was changed so much by eBay that he now trains eBay **CHAPTER 6** customer support staff, puts it simply: "Even if you're selling only one thing, you've got to have a business plan."

Griff is right on the money. Every transaction on eBay is the most important one. Customers don't care if you are selling one thing or a million. They want the transaction to be completed as quickly and hassle free as possible. That means you need to make clear from the start your policies on shipping, payment, and return. And you have to adhere to the eBay honor code. In this chapter we go over strategies for managing your trades, from pricing and etiquette to after-the-sale details—all geared to make everyone come out a winner.

taking care of bidness

Name Your Price

Establishing a price is one of the most confusing issues for sellers. Before you even consider whether or not to hold a reserve auction, you must determine the lowest possible sale price that is acceptable to you. Note the use of the word *lowest*. A reserve or minimum bid is not what you hope the final sale price will be—it is the *lowest* price at which you are *willing* to sell. (Note: On an item listing page, the minimum price is called the *first bid*.)

From a seller's perspective, an ideal sale is one where you realize a profit of at least 100 percent of your investment. The market, however, doesn't always cooperate. Therefore it's best to keep your expectations low and your hopes high. To determine your minimum price for an item, first consider whether you would've been happy to pay double for it under different circumstances. If you

Is It Really What You Think It Is?

While it's best to become an expert in the stuff you trade, nobody knows everything. For a fee, the services below can help clear up any mysteries and assign a value to certain items.

● **Cataloging by Columbus— www.columbuscat.com:** The experts (from museums, auction houses, and specialist dealers) review items based on photographs and write your eBay item title and description for you. They have experts available in most areas, but Oriental art and antiques, silver, ceramics, and European works of art are their strong suit. Your listing reads like it's straight out of a catalog from one of the world's leading auction houses.

● **Professional Coin Grading Service** (access through *SafeHarbor):* Experts evaluate coins on a 70-point grading scale, and then encapsulate each coin in a tamper-evident holder with a label describing the coin and grade.

● **Professional Sports Authenticator** (access through *SafeHarbor):* Grading and authentication services for sports and non-sports trading cards. Experts evaluate on a grading scale and place your card in a tamper-evident protective holder with a certification tag that lists description and grade.

could conceive of doing so, then perhaps other collectors would, too. If not, what would be a more reasonable amount? You might have to concede that any profit is a good profit—especially if the alternatives are breaking even or taking a loss. Then again, no one is forcing you to sell (unless you've promised the fire marshal you'll empty the garage).

Do some quick research on eBay to see if your price is appropriate. Check both completed auctions and nearly over auctions for up-to-date results. (Refer to chapter 3, "The Quest for Amazing Stuff," for a search refresher course.)

As you review sales results, pay attention to condition and other factors that have an impact on an item's final sale price. Don't get starry-eyed if you find a pristine example of your item selling for twenty-five times what you paid; anything less than perfection is going to reduce value dramatically. Also look at similar items that *didn't* sell. Did they have high reserves that weren't met? Is your piece nicer and more likely to sell? The added benefit to nosing around in completed auctions is learning about other types of merchandise that sell well. Remember them when you're in the field hunting down new stuff for sale.

Resist being greedy. Even if you can double the amount you paid

SPECIALTY:
Breweriana

eBay HANDLE: atfab (AnyThing For A Buck)   AGE: 64

COLLECTING BREWERIANA SINCE: I was old enough to drink.

THE PIECE THAT GOT ME HOOKED: A regimental I bought at a small antiques store in Heidelberg, Germany, about 1960.

WHY THIS SPECIALTY'S COOL: Pre-Prohibition beer advertising glasses and such are getting harder to find, and many of the old German beer steins are truly works of art.

BIGGEST MISCONCEPTION ABOUT THIS SPECIALTY: That all steins are alike. I constantly see on eBay "German stein, made in Japan." Huh?

WHAT MY COLLECTION SAYS ABOUT ME: I spend too much money.

ADVICE TO NEW COLLECTORS: Don't buy junk.

BEST BIDDING TIP: Sniping is a waste of time, unless you absolutely have nothing else to do (in which case, get a life!).

BEST SELLING TIPS: After scanning the picture, use a good photo editor to crop, sharpen, and reduce the image. Keep your boilerplate verbiage in an MS Word document that you can paste onto the submission form.

MY BEST eBay TRANSACTION: The Japanese sword (circa 1700) that I bought for $300 and sold for $600? Or the RCA Nipper pin that I bought for $30 and sold for $120?

THE BEST THING ABOUT eBay: Worldwide access—I sold a Hummel to a man in Germany.

and still sell for a reasonable price, consider setting your reserve or minimum bid at 75 percent of that amount. This increases the likelihood that your item will sell. When you're really lucky—you paid $10 for something that could sell for $100—try a $50 reserve or minimum. No one should complain about a 500% return—it's better than what you get on Wall Street and the reasonable price gets collectors' blood flowing. Pure capitalism as a goal is nothing to be ashamed of. However, buyers are smart. Unrealistic pricing isn't going to make you rich. Getting a reputation of being "too expensive" can be disastrous. Buyers won't waste their time bidding if they've tried to win an item or two from you and could never hit the reserve.

To Reserve or Not to Reserve?

Having determined a reasonable price for your item, you now engage in the existential soul-searching inherent in being a seller: Should you have a reserve or not? The relationship of a reserve to a minimum bid brings to mind that old saying from geometry: A square is a rectangle, but a rectangle is not a square. On eBay, every reserve auction has a minimum bid but every auction doesn't necessarily have a reserve. When an auction has a minimum bid and no reserve, the high bidder wins. When an auction has a reserve, the high bidder wins only if the bid equals or surpasses the reserve. (For more on bidding, refer to chapter 4, "Let the Bidding Begin.")

To gauge the market for reserves, you have to get inside the heads of bidders and understand the sometimes contradictory logic that goes through their fevered brains. You also have to be aware of the market conditions that can affect their perception. Some variables worthy of consideration:

● **You don't want to telegraph a price:** If your minimum sale price is below $25, think twice before using a reserve auction. Bidders frequently equate reserve with expensive. Start your auction at the lowest possible minimum bid you can live with.

● **The market is hot, hot, hot for items like yours:** Forget a reserve, which can slow down the action as bidders flock to similar items without one. List your item with a reasonable opening bid and then let the market work its magic. This creates excitement for buyers. The top bid is a winner, and that's where everyone wants to be.

The market is unknown for your item: If your investment is low, set a reasonable minimum bid and see what happens. But if you're risk averse, set a reserve based on a realistic profit margin, and have a low opening bid to get the wheels of commerce moving.

You're selling a highly valuable item: A high minimum bid is a turnoff even to bidders willing to pay full market value. Humor them. Set your reserve and start the bidding low. Bidders are likely to bid early or track your item. Such auctions generate a lot of curiosity, which can translate into bids. If your reserve is reasonable, it'll be met soon enough—and then the bidding will get fast, furious, and fun.

You have a nice item and low investment: Put your piece on the block and have confidence that others will see what you see. If you got a remarkable deal, your minimum bid can include a profit margin.

Once you've made your choice, complete the appropriate fields on the *Sell Your Item* form. The minimum bid is a required field, reserve or not. Enter the amount of the opening that you have determined to be acceptable. If your auction is a reserve, enter your lowest selling price in the reserve price field. A caveat about fees: eBay charges you an insertion fee based on your minimum bid (no reserve auction) or reserve price, which is one of the reasons you can set a low minimum bid in a reserve auction. On reserve auctions, you are also charged an addi-

Only on eBay

To generate more bidding on Saturdays, which can be the slowest day for sales, a bunch of eBay community members got together and formed Club99. This independent group of sellers holds themed auctions—such as "Christmas in July"—the second Saturday of every month. Most of the auctions start at $0.99, and all have no reserve. You can access the group's auctions through its About Me page at:

http://www.isplaza.net/club99/ eBay/aboutme_frames.html

The Online Traders Web Alliance hosts Club99's message forums and FAQ pages at:

http://www.isplaza.net/club99.

You can reach OTWA's home page—which contains among other things a time-zone conversion chart to help you coordinate your auctions—through a link on the Club99 About Me page, or at:

http://www.otwa.com/index.shtml

tional fee of $0.50 (reserve less than $25) or $1 (reserve greater than $25). If the reserve is surpassed the fee is automatically refunded.

Establishing Payment Methods and Terms

What—you expect to get paid for all this fun? Of course you do, which means you have to decide what form of payment you'll accept.

Doing business on the Internet can seem a little scary at first, and some new sellers prefer to restrict payment methods to those using certifiable funds, such as a money order. However, when you limit the methods of payment you are probably limiting potential bidders as well. How long would you continue to shop at a local grocery store if they accepted only certified checks? So give some thought to being flexible when considering the options:

● **Personal checks:** For most buyers this is the easiest form of payment. Most eBaysians feel no obligation to ship goods until checks clear, so it's fine to state a waiting period. Be reasonable, though. Many sellers wait ten business days for checks to clear before they'll ship purchases, but unless your bank really takes that long to clear a check, it might be in your interest not to keep customers waiting. Like most people, collectors love instant gratification and appreciate anything you can do to expedite the process.

● **Money orders and other certifiable funds:** Vendors of money orders must be delighted by the emergence of person-to-person online trading. It has created a new market for money orders that no one could have imagined five years ago. Virtually every eBay seller accepts money orders, certified checks, or cashier's checks. Many places—the post office, Western Union, and banks—issue money orders. Don't specify postal money orders only: you are forcing customers to go to the post office and wait on long lines when they could likely get a money order at their local bank, possibly for free. Cashier's checks and certified checks also come with fees. If bidders choose to pay this way, fine. Forcing them to do so will probably lower the amount they are willing to bid to offset fees, and some people can't be bothered by the hassle of getting a specific kind of payment—they might skip your auction altogether.

● **Cash:** Accepting cash payments is highly inadvisable. There are no safeguards against loss in the mail. And requesting cash can raise questions about possible fraud. Some people might fear you'll take their cash and never send the goods. Cash can't be canceled or replaced like checks and money orders. Some international buyers prefer to pay in cash because they can't easily access money orders in U.S. funds. Work this out on a case-by-case basis, and warn these customers of the risks of lost mail. Conversely, some international sellers encourage cash payments to avoid high check-processing fees.

● **Credit cards:** Credit cards make it convenient for buyers and expedite payment and shipping. If you become a serious seller, you should consider accepting credit cards. Merchants pay a fee, usually a percentage of the sale price, to the credit card company. (See "Payments Made Easy," p. 110.)

● **Escrow:** When selling big-ticket items, a way to safeguard against fraud and build consumer confidence is to use an escrow service that holds funds while a buyer accepts or rejects merchandise. The escrow agent releases funds to the seller upon approval or returns funds to the buyer when the seller confirms the merchandise has been received. (See chapter 8, *"SafeHarbor* and Happy Trading," for information about escrow and eBay's relationship with i-escrow.com.)

You have two ways to indicate the kinds of payments you'll accept: by explaining the terms in your item description or by checking off a series of boxes on the *Sell Your Item* form. We recommend using both methods. The default for all eBay transactions in the United States is good old U.S. dollars. (As eBay goes global, the default payment will be local currencies; for example, at eBay UK, it's pounds sterling.) If for some reason you want your transaction in another currency, you must state so in your description.

Perfect Timing

eBay auctions end three, five, seven, or ten days from the moment you place your listing. There is no scientific formula for determining how long to have your auction last. Generally, though, the longer your auction runs, the more people potentially see it and thus bid.

The default time period on the *Sell Your Item* form is seven days, and that's the duration of most auctions. Yes, many bidders seem to be on eBay twenty-four hours a day and bidding on items the moment they come up for sale. Not all are that devout, however. Many people live under serious time

Payments Made Easy

In the spring of 1999 eBay purchased Billpoint, an online service for facilitating the use of credit cards between buyers and sellers on the Internet. eBay is planning to incorporate Billpoint's services into the site during the first part of 2000, bringing new services and convenience for buyers and sellers. Below are some of the benefits of the Billpoint program when it is fully deployed.

Sellers using Billpoint will:

- Be able to accept credit cards without obtaining a merchant account (which can be expensive) or acquiring hardware and software required to communicate with a financial institution handling that account.

- Have funds directly deposited into their account, eliminating waiting time for checks to be mailed and payments to clear.

- Have easy account management.

Buyers using Billpoint will:

- Have an extra level of security because their credit card number is given to Billpoint rather than a seller.

- Have the standard credit card convenience and protections (as provided by the card issuer and law).

- Have a quick and easy payment method that avoids the hassles of mailing checks or money orders and speeds merchandise on its way toward your collection.

Billpoint is yet another way for sellers to offer payment terms that are attractive to buyers and make it easier for bidders to get in on the action.

constraints or travel a great deal and can be away from a computer for several days at a stretch. The long sales period enables stragglers to get in their bids.

There is no consensus about the best time to end your auction. Some argue that auctions should end between nine and twelve P.M. eastern standard time to allow people on the West Coast time to get home from work and bid. Others say that auctions should start and end on Sunday evening because that's when most people are home. These theories are based on the assumptions that people always bid at the end of an auction and from home. Serious bidders find a way to get in on the action before it's over, whether it's through bidding by proxy (see chapter 4, "Let the Bidding Begin"), sniping from the office when the boss isn't looking, or using third-party software to execute a bid automatically.

That doesn't mean you shouldn't play it safe. Have your auctions end during hours that the majority of people (in the United States, at least) are likely to be awake. Avoid having your auctions end during a holiday. How many people are going to be bidding at nine P.M. PDT on December 31?

Note: In the rare instance that eBay experiences a hard outage (an unscheduled downtime that lasts more than two hours) and users can view items but not bid on them, eBay might automatically push back the ending time. Auctions scheduled to end during the hard outage as well as those scheduled to end within an hour after the outage will be extended for twenty-four hours. The extension policy is a courtesy. If your auction was scheduled to end during the downtime and you are happy with the results, you may end your auction. (See "Knocking Off Early," page 116.)

Sorry, You Can't Bid on Your Own Auction

You are not allowed, under any circumstances, to bid on your own item. In the early days of eBay, sellers were allowed to bid once on no-reserve auctions to increase the prices or if they decided they wanted to keep an item. However, this policy caused too much confusion and made other bidders feel uncomfortable, so it was changed.

Getting the Shipping Straight

Figuring out how to handle shipping is part of your planning process. It is customary for the buyer to pay shipping (as she would with almost any purchases through a catalog or from other online sites). As with payment methods, you can indicate your shipping terms via a check-off box in the *Sell Your Item* form and in the body of your description. Clearly delineate the costs, methods, and services you use (U.S. Postal Service, UPS, FedEx, and so on).

It's in your interest to set fair terms and limit shipping charges to the actual cost. People read the fine print. Excessive shipping charges are a turnoff—and make you look guilty of price gouging. If you feel compelled to charge for shipping materials, explain why. Packing some items, especially fragile ones, requires extra materials, and costs can add up quickly. Do not charge for the time you put into packing items; that's the cost of doing business.

Even though it costs more, it is strongly recommended that you insure items for shipping. Things do get broken in transit. When they do, it's a relief to know that the shipper will foot the bill and buyers and sellers are made whole.

Happy Returns

You're in business now with real customers who have hopes and expectations about the items you are selling. What are you going to do if they receive the item and are unhappy? Don't wait until you have a dissatisfied customer to formulate a return policy. In fact, a fair and generous return policy can be helpful in marketing your items.

No rules exist to force you to have a return policy. However, having one—and a liberal one at that—sends a message to prospective bidders that you stand behind your merchandise, you care about customer satisfaction, and nothing should inhibit them from bidding freely. State your policy clearly and succinctly, and include it in every listing. There are two kinds of return policies:

Unconditional returns: You accept returns for any reason, no questions asked. No harm, no foul. Your goal is a 100 percent happy customer each and every time. Note: Unconditional doesn't have to mean open-ended. Feel free to specify a time frame by which a buyer needs to contact you about a return.

Conditional returns: You accept returns only under certain conditions. These might include that the item was not authentic, not as described, or damaged (frequently an honest oversight by an unknowing seller). Buyer's remorse, where a buyer changed his mind or made a mistake, usually doesn't qualify. Neither does the excuse that a bidder found it cheaper somewhere else after the auction ended. Even with such restrictions, an up-front policy instills confidence.

Even if you don't specify a return policy you can expect to get emails from unhappy buyers. Of course, you're not obligated to accept returns. Take the time to hear people out and try to come to a mutually acceptable accommodation. This can lead to a great community experience and positive feedback all around. (See chapter 8, *"SafeHarbor* and Happy Trading,"* for other ways to resolve problems after the sale.)

Final Touches

You've made it. You've wended your way to the bottom of the *Sell Your Item* form and your listing is complete. (A drumroll, please.) Now you can click on the *review listing* button at the bottom of the page. eBay takes you to a new page with your listing's details: how your description will look, including HTML coding results; photos; and other parameters such as minimum bid, reserve, category, and so on. eBay also notifies you at this time of the total insertion fee, including extra charges for bold-face, featured auction, and the like. (Obviously, the final value fee is assessed after the auction.)

If your HTML or pictures don't appear correctly, or your text contains typos, it's not too late to fix them. Just hit your browser's back button to be returned to the *Sell Your Item* form with all your information ready to be edited.

The most common problem is that your images don't appear. In this case eBay shows a little box with a red x. Don't panic. More than likely you have a typo in the URL for the image. Go back and check your work. Even an extra space within the address could be the cause. When an error is not immediately apparent, go back and try finding the image on the Web either by copying and pasting the URL out of the *Picture URL* field into the address field at the top of your browser, or typing it in. If your browser doesn't take you to your picture on the World Wide Web, you probably have the wrong URL and must go back to your hosting

Only on eBay

When your sales volume starts growing, it's probably time to start using Mister Lister, eBay's bulk listing tool. Mister Lister allows sellers to prepare listings offline on your computer and then email them to eBay up to 100 at a time. Using Mister Lister to list 50 or more items at a time can shave hours off using the *Sell Your Item* form. After emailing your listings, you then go to eBay, where you can preview your listing and make changes if needed (as you would with any listing) and start the auction.

Sellers find that Mister Lister is a helpful tool for managing eBay activity. Listings can be created and stored and auctions can be started (and thus end) at times that work best for the seller.

Additional information on Mister Lister can be found on eBay at:

http://pages.ebay.com/services/ buyandsell/mr-lister.html

Customer support for Mister Lister users is handled through a dedicated email address, misterlister@ebay.com.

service to double-check the exact address. You know when you can't find your glasses because they're on top of your head? Well, sometimes people try to post images to their listings when they've yet to upload the pictures to a server.

Most HTML mistakes can be traced to typos as well. Common errors are plain old misspellings or forgetting the <> and </> tags to begin and end a code.

When everything works like a charm, you submit your listing by clicking on the button at the bottom of the review page. eBay will verify, "Your auction has begun!" by returning a screen with a link to your listing. Note: Don't expect bids right away. eBay updates listings periodically and it may be an hour or two before eBay updates the category listing you've selected and your item is available in the title search.

Forget Something?

With the auction up and running, you sit back and wait for the bids to roll in. After a day or so, say you get an email from a prospective bidder who wants to know the height of your cat-shaped cast-iron doorstop. Huh? But you were so diligent in following the little checklist. . . . You go to your *My eBay* page and click the listing. Sure enough, somehow amid your poetic prose you forgot the dimensions. It happens to the best of us. Measure the kitty and email the dimensions to the user. (You want to maintain your hard-earned reputation for speedy email responses to bidders.) Your next step is to update your listing, which can be done in two ways:

1 Use the *Add to My Item Description* form.

2 Revise your listing—but only if you don't have any bids yet.

And Another Thing: Adding to Your Item Description

At any time during your auction you can add information to your item's description. Jot down or copy (highlight and CTRL-C) the item's eBay number. You need this number to complete the process. You can access the *Add to My Item Description* in *Buying and Selling Tools* under *Services* on the navigation bar. When you click on this option a form appears. Complete the basics (user ID, password, item number). Below this will be a box where you can append your description, complete with HTML, photos, or other information. When you complete the form, you have a chance to review the new information before submitting it. Use your browser's back button to go back and make any additional changes.

When you finally submit your new information, it will appear at the bottom of the listing with a stamp indicating the time and date when "the seller added the following information."

New and Improved: Revising Your Listing

Until anyone bids on your item, you can edit some parts of your actual listing, including the title, description, payment options, and shipping terms; you can also change or add photos. (After the first bid, however, you can change only the category, unless you use the *Add to My Item Description* form.) Look at the *Update Item* line. You'll see a message that reads, "**Seller:** If this item has received no bids, you may revise it." Click on the underlined word revise. A screen will pop up containing the entire *Sell Your Item* form with your original information. The longer your auction has been under way, the fewer changes you should make. Just because there aren't any bids doesn't mean no one's interested. Some people wait till the last moment to jump in; others may be researching your item and contemplating its value before making a move. By all means, correct typos, but be careful about removing possible keywords.

The Big Category Switcharoo

If you put your item in the wrong category, you can change it any time through the *Change My Item's Category* page accessed through the *Services* menu.

If you get an email inquiring whether your Malibu Barbie is Mesopotamian or Babylonian—a perplexing question indeed—you may discover that your doll has inadvertently time-traveled to the category of *Antiques: Ancient World*. You'll want to correct that boo-boo as soon as possible and move the tanned goddess to the *Dolls:Barbie:General* category. However, don't change categories impulsively because your item hasn't gotten any bids after a day or two. Some folks out there are likely tracking it. If it disappears from their favorite category, then it's out of sight, out of mind and, in your case, out of bids.

Sellers, Please Stand By

You're not just listing your item for sale in cyberspace and returning several days later to collect your booty. Customers need attention. When a potential bidder has a question you need to be available and responsive.

Check your emails at least once daily—more frequently in the last thirty-six hours of the auction—and respond posthaste. If you're a new seller, understand that some bidders are not only seeking information, but also testing your business manner. Don't deny them the information they seek—use this opportunity to encourage bidding and let them know you're a responsible seller.

Knocking Off Early

In rare instances you may want to end your auction early. This is fine under the following circumstances:

- You damage the item or discover a problem with it.
- You realize the item is not authentic.
- You change the mind and decide you want to keep the item.

Note: Even under some of these circumstances you may want just to update your listing by adding to your item's description. If your item has received no bids or not reached its reserve, you can end your auction early without a hassle. Just click on the *Services* option on the navigation bar at the top of each page and use the link to the *End My Auction Early* form in *Buying and Selling Tools*.

If you've received bids and the reserve (if there is one) has been met, you are still obligated to sell to the high bidder even if you end early. If you must go through with ending the auction, all bids on the item need to be canceled.

Reach out to current bidders and let them know what's going on. For example, if you discover damage that you hadn't noticed earlier, email bidders and inform them of the problem and that you're ending the auction. Let the high bidder know you are open to still selling the item and try to negotiate a price. Act fast, because you could get bids at any moment. In fact, before doing anything, add a message to your item's description (see "New and Improved: Revising Your Listing," page 115) to wave off any potential bids: "Bidders, take note that I am ending this auction early because of recently discovered damage to this item. I emailed all bidders on [date] to let them know the bad news before I canceled their bids. Please, do not bid. Thanks for looking anyway."

You will be charged the normal insertion fee for your auction when you end your auction early. If you end your auction prior to canceling bids, you could be subject to a final value fee as well. In this case you can request a final value fee credit (see "Requesting a Fee Credit," page 118).

Canceling Bids

Sellers can cancel bids that have been placed on their auctions for various reasons, such as the following:

● A bidder contacts you to renege.

● You cannot, for various reasons, verify the identity of the bidder.

● You want to end your auction early (you must eliminate all bids).

Using the *Cancel Bids on My Item* form in *Buying and Selling Tools*, under *Services* on the navigation bar, cancel each bid individually (you actually can't cancel them all at once). Although eBay automatically notifies bidders when a seller cancels, it sounds better coming from you personally, so reach out before you take action.

Your bid cancellations are publicized in the bidding history for the auction. A notation will appear by each canceled bid, explaining that it was a seller cancellation. On the form you have the opportunity to provide a short explanation. Take the time to convey that your reasons are legitimate. Canceled bids can be frustrating for a bidder, and a wishy-washy explanation could lead to bidder dissatisfaction and possibly negative feedback.

Your Item Didn't Sell

Despite your best efforts, for some reason your item didn't sell. Do not feel bad. Items don't sell for many reasons. It could be a matter of timing. Maybe all the potential bidders for your Shriners memorabilia were at the annual convention the week you posted.

Rethinking Your Selling Strategy

When relisting and rethinking, eBay is on your side. You can relist your item within thirty days of the end of your auction. To start the process, go to the actual listing of your completed auction and click on the *Relist This Item* link.

No substitutions and no plate sharing! You are allowed to relist only the item that didn't sell. Changes to your listing are allowed and should be made. Take the time to review, and give some thought to the following:

● Title: Was it accurate and easily searchable?

● **Item description:** Did you really say all there was to say? Or have you since found some appealing aspects that should be highlighted?

● **Category:** Was the item in the right category? Is there another category worth trying where the item might get some more action?

● **Photos:** Do they do your item justice, or do you need to put your paparazzi skills to work?

● **Minimum price:** No bids? Do you think your minimum was too high? Are you ready to let it go for less money?

● **Reserve price auctions:** Did your reserve scare away bidders? Should you eliminate it or lower it substantially? (You are not allowed to relist the item with a higher reserve price.)

You have to relist in thirty days to get an insertion fee credit (if the item sells the second time around), because that's how long eBay keeps ended auctions in the database. When you restart your auction within that period is up to you. Items that received some action but didn't meet the reserve can be relisted right away if you intend to lower or eliminate the reserve. Use your lower price to encourage people to jump back in the bidding. If your item received no bids, wait two or three weeks. By that time perhaps a new crop of users will be interested.

Requesting a Fee Credit

If your item doesn't sell or the deal falls through, you can get credits for the final value fees you've paid.

Insertion fees are not refundable per se. However, if your item doesn't sell (no bids on a regular auction or fails to meet the reserve), eBay allows you to relist the item. If your item sells the second time around, the insertion fee for the relisted item is refunded when the auction ends. In other words, you will be billed one insertion fee if your item sells. (See "Rethinking Your Selling Strategy" in this chapter.)

eBay gives credits for final value fees if you cannot complete the sale in the following circumstances:

● No response from a bidder.

● Bidder no longer wanted item.

● Bidder did not send payment.

● Bidder bounced check or stopped payment.

● Bidder returned item.

● Bidder could not complete auction due to family or financial emergency.

● Bidder claimed terms were unacceptable and backed out.

If you complete a sale for lower than the final bid price, you can request a partial credit on your final value fee when the following occurs:

● High bidder backed out and lower bidder purchased item.

● Item is damaged and bidder ended up paying a lower price.

● Confusion about actual bid price (leads to selling at a price lower than the final bid).

● High bidder had an emergency and lower bidder purchased item.

To receive a credit, you have to make your request within sixty days from the end of the auction. eBay uses information from credit requests to identify deadbeat bidders who win auctions and fail to follow through. (See chapter 8, *"SafeHarbor* and Happy Trading," for more information.) To request a credit or partial credit, use the *Request Final Credit Fee* link from the *Services* menu or the site map.

Building a Business on eBay

Some sellers start by using eBay to weed out their collections or sell stuff that's cluttering the house. A few decent sales usually motivate folks to think about using eBay to expand their income. There are even sellers who have quit their day jobs to enjoy the eBay lifestyle. Before you tell the boss to take this job and you-know-what it, be sure you can make a living. Even if you're just moonlighting on eBay for extra spending money, you need a plan.

First of all, to be successful, you need funds to make purchases and a steady flow of quality merchandise. (For sources of antiques and collectibles for resale, see chapter 13, "Where the Action Is" and chapter 14, "Out in the Field.") One way to "capitalize" your new endeavor is to build a merchandise fund by setting aside some of the proceeds from your first eBay sales.

Proceed with caution. It takes time and energy to get even a small side

Only on eBay

eBay Power Seller Dave Dahl got his start selling about three years ago when he sold his construction business and his wife encouraged him to "lighten up" around the house. One of his first eBay trades was an R.S. Prussia bowl that commanded $225—four times what he could have sold it for in his hometown. "That got me going, and 4,000 items later I'm still selling," says Dave. "I've met some fantastic people, here and abroad—and I have never received a bad check." Other people commission Dave to sell for them on eBay, and he enjoys astounding them with the prices he gets for their items. "I've personally gotten several people to join the eBay community," Dave says. "They're now fully addicted."

business going. Start your resale efforts by sticking to what you know. More than likely this is your current area of collecting. Seek out familiar pieces that are desirable at prices that leave some room for profit. Avoid the end-of-the-rainbow mentality—looking for the pot of gold that's going to convert your $25 investment into tens of thousands of dollars. The odds of making the big score, or even reasonable purchases that can lead to a profit, are greatly increased by becoming an expert in several areas of collector interest, using your knowledge to buy wisely, and spending lots of time shopping.

Even if you start small, you're in business and need to think like a businessperson. The point of your effort is to make a profit. Selling things for more than you paid for them sounds simple enough. But how much are you looking to make? Start conservatively. While it might be nice to sell every item for a 100 percent markup (and this is how you should review every potential purchase for resale), high expectations don't always garner results. In fact, the law of averages means that some items will sell high, others low, and some in between. Setting lower margins can actually build your momentum faster than you might imagine. You want to be kind of a mini Wal-Mart and make money by lower profit margins on larger volumes.

Let's compare two approaches to profit margins. There are two sellers who have both put aside $300 from their spring cleaning sale on eBay and want to build a little sideline. Over a nine-week period they run auctions every two weeks. At each of these auctions they invest the entire proceeds from their previous auction. Seller number one marks up every item 40 percent because she wants to price her items somewhere between wholesale and retail. Most important, she wants them to sell. Number two feels that it's worth his while only to eke out every penny and make a 100 percent markup. Their strategies yield interesting results. On average, seller number one unloads all her merchandise every two weeks, while seller number two sells only about 50 percent. In each cycle both invest all available cash into new merchandise. Here's how their businesses would grow:

Week	Cash on Hand Seller #1 @ 40% markup selling 100% of merchandise	Cash on Hand Seller #2 @ 100% markup selling 50% of merchandise
1	$300	$300
3	$420	$300
5	$588	$300
7	$823	$300
9	$1,152	$300

This is hypothetical and oversimplified, and doesn't account for any of the costs of doing business. Technically, while dealer number two would have less cash, he still would have his unsold inventory as assets. Dealer number one is building her capital. At week nine, if she wanted to pull out a couple of hundred dollars to buy some additions to her collection or take the family away for a weekend, it wouldn't jeopardize her business. The lesson is similar to that of "The Tortoise and the Hare." Set a pace you can keep and, like the tortoise who beat the hare, you'll win in the end.

PART THREE

MAKING

contact

The bell has rung, the auction is over. Your magnificently tooled Western stock saddle captured the fancy of many bidders, and in a flurry of activity that would make the floor of the New York Stock Exchange look sedate, ten bids in the last ninety seconds sent the final sale price skyrocketing to $435. But before you can start spending your windfall, you must attend to a few details.

CHAPTER 7

the bidding is closed— now what?

Buyer Meet Seller, Seller Meet Buyer

After the auction ends, sellers usually reach out to the high bidder. This is a custom, not a rule. However, buyers who can't wait an extra second longer to get the goods should feel free to initiate contact. Within twenty-four hours of the end of the auction, eBay emails buyer and seller with the results. That missive contains particulars such as the final bid price, the parties' email addresses, and a line about the three-day rule, which states that you both have three days to make contact or the sale can be considered void. In short, seal the deal!

Many sellers contact high bidders within minutes or hours after the auction ends, before the flush of victory wears off. Compared with the high-tech transaction that just transpired, these next few steps can seem positively glacial in speed. But until the day arrives when Furbies and jet skis can travel via phone lines to your living room (a disturbing image to contemplate), payments must be mailed, checks cleared, items packed by hand, and packages shipped by train, plane, and automobile.

Some deals require only the exchange of mailing addresses to wrap up. Frequently it's a little more complicated. If you're shipping United Parcel Service (UPS) or internationally and/or insuring the item, you can't calculate the final cost until you

have the buyer's address and the final value. Getting it all straightened out can take several emails back and forth. Keep the process on track by responding promptly.

"A sale isn't a sale until you get paid," says eBay Ambassador Alexandra Carter. "A lot of people have busy lives and simply forget to send payment even though they want the item. By emailing winners an order 'ticket' to include with their payment, you can make it easier for them to remember that they won that neat item and now all they have to do is send out their check." You can include the ticket in a boilerplate email that you send out to everyone, customizing the item name, number, and cost including shipping. Most email programs allow you to create a draft that you can use over and over again, or you can simply copy the text of a previously sent message each time.

People's email inboxes are active places with messages streaming in from co-workers, family, and friends. On the subject line of your message, include both the item title and the eBay item number. The item number by itself may not mean much to the buyer. However, "Signed Joe DiMaggio baseball card" is sure to resonate. The item number is handy because recipients can cut and paste it into the *Item Search* field to get back to the listing, a frequently necessary step in the course of a transaction.

You've Got Mail

When creating a generic after-the-auction email to send to buyers, go out of your way to sound cheerful and courteous. Money is about to be mailed to you—what's not to be happy about? Here's a sample:

FROM: lostmymind@collectorheaven.com
TO: thenuttycollector@gottahaveit.com
SUBJECT: Heintz Art Metal Table Lamp eBay #4932987422

Hello:

Congratulations, you were the high bidder on my recent auction listed above. The final price for the item including priority mail shipping and insurance is: $ ——. I happily accept personal checks (I hold five business days only for clearing) or, if you prefer, a money order or certified check. Please send your payment to:

John Q. Seller
1234 Anyplace Street, Apt. 7A
My Town, USA 12345-6789

Thanks for your bids. I have many items up for sale, so if you could please include the item description AND number on your payment, or enclose a copy of this email with your payment, it would help me keep things in order. Please acknowledge that you have received this email by replying with your shipping information ASAP. Feel free to contact me with any questions.

Reminder: I have a three-day no-questions-asked return policy on every item. I do ask that you notify me by email within seventy-two hours after receipt of the item to inform me if you are planning a return. I will refund your purchase price when I receive the merchandise back. You have to pay for the return shipping and insurance. Let's not tempt fate.

We can do the feedback thing when you let me know the item has arrived and you are satisfied.

I appreciate your business,

John (lostmymind) Q. Seller

Tracking Down Email Addresses

To get the ball rolling, you need to get the buyer's email address. Just go to the listing and click on the user's name. If someone's email address and user ID are the same, an email template will pop up; type your message and you're done. When the person's user ID name doesn't double as an email address, eBay takes you through a quick verification process. At the end, click on the address or copy and paste it into the address line of your email program.

I Want a Cookie

When you ask for someone's email address, eBay gives you a cookie. Don't get excited—these are virtual cookies, not your favorite Toll House recipe. In Internet lingo, a *cookie* is a piece of text that can be held in your

Only on eBay

eBay customers transact more than $200 million in gross merchandise sales per month (as of July 1999).

computer's memory. When you use some sites, they place a cookie on *your* hard drive, where they can retrieve it later—but only when you're logged on to that site/service.

Why do they do this? So you can personalize your use of the site. Cookies remember certain things about you that help you complete functions. Some people worry that cookies are an invasion of privacy. Others feel that cookies actually protect them because the information is stored on their computer, not on the service providers' computers. You can set your browser to deny cookies and delete any existing cookies from your computer.

eBay uses cookies in three ways:

1 **To save time in retrieving email addresses:** When you ask for another user's email address, a small box appears at the bottom of the page with the words *Remember me.* By selecting this option, you create a cookie that eliminates the repetitive task of entering your user ID and password every time you make such a request. In fact, until you log off, wherever you come across a user ID on the site, the cookie will show that person's email in parentheses next to it. This is what's known as an *end-of-session cookie—* when you close your browser, the cookie is erased, requiring you to reactivate the cookie for each new session.

2 **To tailor advertising:** At least two companies that eBay employs— Link Exchange and DoubleClick—use cookies to manage the number of times they serve you the same ad. They do not have information on who you are, although they can measure the kinds of ads you tend to respond to.

3 **To evaluate partnerships:** If you arrived at eBay from one of its many Internet traffic partners, you might have received a cookie that tells eBay the link.

4 **For access to the "adult" area of eBay:** This is also a session cookie.

Temporary Parking: Escrow Services

When buyers and sellers feel the need for an extra level of security, they turn to an escrow service, a place where buyers can "park" their payments (for a small fee) before the money is released to sellers. Consummation of the deal might be contingent upon a final inspection or authentication process. Following are some buyer and seller rationales for using the escrow process.

eBay has entered into an agreement with i-Escrow, an Internet provider

Why Use Escrow?

buyers	sellers
Bidding on an expensive item and want to ensure the item is shipped.	Selling an expensive item and want to ensure funds are received before shipping.
Have questions about authenticity of item and want to inspect and verify before releasing funds.	Want to allow inspection of an item but want to secure by holding funds.
Want to use a credit card, but seller is not equipped to do so.	Want to offer the opportunity for buyer to provide credit card but are not set up for credit card sales.
Seller does not yet have an established track record on eBay, and buyer wants an added measure of protection.	Want to offer a way to overcome buyers' hesitation about purchasing an item and/or give credibility to their guarantee.

of escrow services, to facilitate users' access to services. i-Escrow charges 5 percent of the purchase price ($5 minimum), usually to the buyer. Fee payment can be negotiated between buyer and seller but should be done beforehand to avoid confusion. Here's how the process works:

1 During or after an auction, buyer and seller agree to use escrow and settle on who is responsible for fees.

2 To sign up with i-Escrow: A link is provided on the end-of-auction notice for those items where the seller indicates in the payment option that he or she will accept online escrow or the value of the auction exceeds $1,000. You can also access i-Escrow through *SafeHarbor* (see chapter 8, "*SafeHarbor* and Happy Trading").

3 Buyer sends payment (including fee, if buyer is responsible) for item to i-Escrow.

4 Upon notification of payment, i-Escrow notifies seller to ship the item.

5 If buyer approves, i-Escrow releases funds to the seller.

6 If buyer rejects, buyer returns item to seller.

7 Upon receipt of item by seller, i-Escrow returns funds to buyer.

SPECIALTY:

Depression Glass

eBay HANDLE: lkdt@glasscity.net   AGE: 45

HOW I GOT STARTED: I bought a rare jade-colored juicer for $12 and sold it for $1,200.

THE QUESTION I'M ASKED MOST: Why does this cost so much?

WHAT'S IRONIC ABOUT "DEPRESSION" GLASS: I make a full-time living from it.

THE BIGGEST CHALLENGE: Finding space for it all.

PEOPLE'S BIGGEST MISCONCEPTION: That all Depression glass is pink or green.

WHAT MY COLLECTION SAYS ABOUT ME: It's always changing, most of it is in boxes, and it gets spread all over the country. Vat do you think, Dr. Freud?

MY FAVORITE: Depends on which direction I'm looking.

THE PIECE I'M DYING TO ADD: Something small, perfect, rare, and cheap.

WHAT I TELL NEW COLLECTORS: Read, ask questions, have fun.

MY THREE BEST BIDDING TIPS: Buy what you like, buy what you like, buy what you like.

WHEN YOU THINK ABOUT IT: eBay has expanded the marketplace as dramatically as the telephone and daily newspaper probably did when they were new.

MY BEST FIND ON eBay: The enthusiasm and friendliness of my new customers.

Shipping News: Getting Out the Goods

The consequences of merchandise arriving damaged are more than heartbreak. Insurance claims have to be filed—if the item was insured—and deeply disappointed customers placated. Chances are the item is irreplaceable. Where are you going to find another great old Eider duck decoy for the price you paid? To avoid these kinds of disasters, learn to pack like a pro. And who better to help you with this daunting task than the pros themselves?

Packing Like a Pro

Savvy shipping starts with the right materials. Put together an inventory of supplies and tools that include the following:

- A stockpile of boxes in various sizes.

- Packing tape with a tape dispenser cutter and a minimum width of 1½ inches. Transparent allows you to tape over labels and still read the address.

- Sheets of corrugated cardboard for making protective sleeves, wrapping books, or using as dividers between multiple items shipped in the same box. You can flatten out old boxes to use for this purpose instead of purchasing new ones.

- Padded envelopes for shipping books, paper ephemera, and other flat items.

- Wrapping materials such as bubble wrap, padded paper, padded sheets (those blue diapers), newsprint, and tissue paper.

- Stuffing materials such as cellulose peanuts, shredded paper, and newspaper.

- Shipping labels.

- Return address labels.

Only on eBay

Five percent of all home-to-home packages shipped in the U.S. are for eBay purchases.

● A good pair of scissors and an X-Acto knife, or good jackknife.

● A postal scale if your volume warrants it. Make sure it has rate schedules for the U.S. Postal Service and UPS that can be upgraded when rates change.

● Stick-on notes to use as temporary labels.

● A medium- to wide-tipped indelible ink marker in a dark color such as red, blue, or black.

● A stapler for sealing padded envelopes.

Shop around for shipping supplies; they can be expensive, and real savings are realized by purchasing in bulk. Don't skimp. Get solid boxes that can take a beating and are large enough to pack things safely. Save money—and perhaps a tree or two—by recycling shipping supplies. Liquor stores, supermarkets, and office buildings throw out tons of boxes, some of them filled with peanuts, Styrofoam, and bubble wrap scraps. Find out from the office or store manager or custodian the best day of the week for you to drop by and grab a few. Also, you might want to reuse boxes from items you have received if you are both a buyer and a seller.

Size matters. Don't use a huge box for a small item just because it's the only one you have in the garage. The extra shipping costs could be more than the cost of purchasing the right-size box. As a rule, allow two inches of padding between your item and the side of the box and use stuffing materials that won't allow your item to shift in transit.

Ordering Supplies on the Net

Check out these Web merchants and compare their costs with those of buying locally or even at an office supply store:

● www.adpaq.com: Carries a full line of supplies—tape, boxes, padded mailers, peanuts—at decent prices.

● www.mylan.com: Specializes in bubble wrap, bubble wrap bags, and pads.

● www.movewithus.com: All kinds of boxes, wrapping materials, and supplies, including boxes for items like lamps.

● www.cleancarton.com: Features a broad range of items including "job lot" supplies at deep discounts (if you buy in significant bulk). Job lots are closeouts or overstocks of materials printed with company names.

Packing requires organization. Set aside several items to be shipped and pack them at the same time. This works especially well if you have a designated packing area—your own mailroom, as it were—where supplies are always out and ready for action. Think of yourself as a human assembly line; grouping like tasks together makes the job go faster than going through all the steps for one box, then starting over with all the steps for another. First, assemble a bunch of boxes in a row. Then go down the line, stuffing each one with protective material, the wrapped item, and more material. Pop packing slips into each open box. Finally, address and seal one by one. Here are some other tips to make the job easier:

- Do your packing in a large enough space so everything is handy and you don't lose the scissors under scraps of bubble wrap and tissue paper.

- When packing extremely fragile items such as ceramics or glass, the safest method is to double box them. Pack them in a box and then pack that box inside a larger one with plenty of stuffing material in between.

- First wrap the item in a layer of protective material such as bubble wrap or several layers of tissue paper. Be careful about what you wrap in old newspapers; ink can bleed off the paper onto an item.

- Prepack items so they're ready to go when payment arrives. Note: Mark each box in a corner or with a stick-on note indicating what's inside. It's a bummer to have to open things already packed because you forgot.

- Put a layer of clear tape over the shipping and return address labels to protect against loss or moisture.

The Art of the Invoice

Just as retailers include packing slips with shipped goods, you too should provide a little backup with your shipments. You can easily create a standard invoice in which you thank buyers, request that they email you that the item arrived safely, reiterate your return policy, urge them to notify you of any problem, and gently encourage them to leave feedback. Most important: Include the item number and description! Many sellers leave blank spaces on their packing slips and write in this vital information by hand. Also include your name, user ID, address, and email address.

For some sellers, the eBay packing slip has become another opportunity to express their persona. Their slips resemble artful hang tags or employ calligraphy, cartoons, and graphics. They might be printed on colored paper, several messages to a page, and then cut apart into individual slips. An invoice may be as chatty or as cryptic as you like. Some dealers use this opportunity to publicize their other auctions. In any case, the contents are direct and courteous. Here is a typical example:

> *Thank you for your winning bid and your swift payment. Your item is enclosed, and I hope you like it. If you have a spare moment, drop me an email and let me know that your item has arrived safe and sound. Don't hesitate to contact me if you have any questions. If satisfied with the transaction, please post some nice feedback for me. I will respond in kind. Regards, . . .*

With the boxes packed, you can either load up the car and head to the post office or call for a pickup. Like overnight couriers such as Federal Express and UPS, the USPS picks up for a fee. USPS packages must be Priority Mail, weighed and with postage affixed. Note: You are no longer allowed to drop packages in mailboxes. For security reasons, all packages over one pound have to be brought to the post office and given to a clerk, although you can weigh them and apply postage at home. When you call UPS for a pickup, you tell them the weight and destination of the package and they tell you the shipping cost plus fee, which you pay the driver.

Shipping and handling can become a full-time job in themselves. If you start doing large volume, it might make sense to hire a student to come in a few hours a day or week to pack and make the post office run.

Stamp Me—I Must Be Dreaming

The United States Postal Service (USPS) provides free shipping materials for Priority Mail customers. That's right—*gratis!*—and they ship directly to your door. Among the freebies available are Priority Mail boxes and envelopes (in a variety of sizes), rolls of tape (printed with the Priority Mail logo), and Priority Mail address labels. (URL http://supplies. usps.gov.) Obviously you have to ship Priority Mail to use these materials.

Handle with Care: Finding Info on Major Shippers

The Internet is a great place to get information on shipping costs and regulations. All the major shippers maintain sites:

● The United States Post Office:

On www.usps.gov you can get rates for domestic and international shipping, use rate calculators, order stamps and free shipping supplies, and find zip codes and zip plus 4s (a longer zip code that can speed your packages to their destination). You can verify delivery of packages through the site if you have purchased that service at the time of mailing.

● United Parcel Service:

www.ups.com has a rate calculator and information on pickups and deliveries.

● Federal Express:

www.fedex.com is a comprehensive site that has several tools for business. FedEx offers many varieties of automated shipping services for businesses of all sizes. Besides rate calculators and general information for small businesses, there is a survey form that directs you to the best services for your volume.

Only on eBay

You can help bidders get free estimates of shipping costs by inserting a link in your listing to eBay partner iShip.com, a Web-based shipping service for online buyers and sellers. Before filling out the *Sell Your Item* form, click on a link—located just above the title field—to *Free Shipping Estimates from iShip.com*. Step one is a form where you indicate carriers, whether you drop off or have pickups, the zip code you ship from, the approximate weight, and the amount of insurance you expect to purchase. You also have the option of having iShip.com add a handling charge (either fixed, as a percentage, or both) to the estimate bidders see. When the form is complete, press the *Preview what bidders will see* button. Then proceed to the *Create my iShip.com link now!* box. This takes you to a page with the HTML code. Copy this code and paste it into your item's description. When you preview your listing, the following should appear in purple as a link:

Click here to use iShip.com to view your shipping charges

Note: It's best to complete the iShip.com process *before* inputting any other listing information. However, if you decide to take advantage of this service as an afterthought, be sure to use your browser's back button to return to your completed *Sell Your Item* form. Otherwise, if you use the *Done return to eBay* button on the iShip.com form, you'll end up at a blank *Sell Your Item* form, and all your work will be lost.

● 135 ●

Closing the Loop: Leaving Feedback

Typically, you close the deal by leaving feedback for buyers after they notify you that goods have arrived and they're satisfied. Some users get this step out of the way as soon as they've shipped an item. In these cases they usually alert the buyer by email that the package is on its way and feedback has been left. They might also nudge buyers to reciprocate on the Feedback Forum, if they're so inclined, after the package arrives.

In the early days of the Internet, critics warned that consumers would never warm to the idea of buying things through their personal computers. The fear of fraud and concern about launching one's credit card into cyberspace, they argued, would stymie e-commerce. But those pundits underestimated human nature—and intelligence. People like convenience and choice. They like good deals. They like interacting with other people. They like to feel empowered, and they especially like experiences that reaffirm their faith in human nature. eBay provides all those things within a new kind of marketplace where trading on a global scale can happen person to person. After all, millions of users can't be wrong.

CHAPTER 8

safeharbor and happy trading

Although eBay is at its core a small town (or, perhaps more accurately, a global village), it is not utopia. Misunderstandings, complications, fraud, and unsavory business practices do crop up—just as they do in any marketplace. Creating a safe trading environment requires not only the participation of corporate entities like eBay and systems that provide "secure" transactions, but also the involvement of the community members who buy and sell. eBay's value system—people are basically honest and good—is noble. But those principles need a support system. *SafeHarbor* is that system and represents eBay's commitment to build the largest, safest trading community possible.

To the credit of eBay users, most disputes get resolved before harsh action is necessary. That explains why the number of formal complaints in eBay's first three years amounted to only a few dozen per twelve million items for sale. But when you need help, eBay is there. In this chapter we explain what constitutes a violation of eBay's policies and the penalties involved. We also give tips on trying to make things go right and, as a last resort, how to report bad incidents to eBay. Just remember, to quote that Osmond Brothers hit single from the 1970s (now worth $5.50 on eBay—$16.51 with a Japanese picture sleeve!), "One bad apple don't spoil the whole bunch. . . ."

Heading for *SafeHarbor*

When the wind howls and the seas are fierce, smart captains steer their boats to safe harbor. eBay has created its own *SafeHarbor*, a place to go when you need protection and help. eBay's *SafeHarbor* is not a physical place but, rather, a set of services and rules to calm the trading tempest. In this port you can

- Report suspicious activities for investigation.

- Access programs such as Insurance, User Verification, Escrow Services, and the Fraud Reporting System.

- Find information on prohibited or infringing items.

- Learn about eBay's privacy policy and methods of self-protection.

- Discover tips for making your buying experience more positive.

Suspicious Minds: Identifying and Reporting Bad Behavior

When something about a transaction or another user doesn't seem quite right, try to put your finger on what bothers you about it before reporting this "something" to eBay. The following infractions are serious offenses and can lead to suspension of a user. If the offending behavior doesn't fit these descriptions, perhaps there's just been a misunderstanding. The only way to be sure is to know eBay's policy, so read the following with care.

Fishy Feedback

As explained in chapter 2, "The Perfect Setup," *Feedback* is designed as an open forum to keep users on their best behavior. Positive feedback is like gold on eBay, which explains why some people might be tempted to manipulate the system in their favor—or to libel someone else. These specific offenses include

Meet eBay Ambassador Maria Keller,

SPECIALTY:
TV Memorabilia

eBay HANDLE: 1sommer   AGE: 44

IT ALL STARTED WHEN: I was thirteen back in 1968 and started saving *TV Guides*. I was convinced they'd be worth something someday. They were! Now I'm a charter member of Packrats Anonymous.

MY FAVORITE MEMENTO: The April 10, 1955, New York metro edition of *TV Guide*. It's the week and place of my birth, and I wouldn't part with that for anything. Well, make me an offer I can't refuse. . . .

WHAT MY COLLECTION SAYS ABOUT ME: I take pride in being a baby boomer. I recognized early in my life that we were living in most interesting times. Now that I've found eBay, I've been able to share my items with other baby boomers seeking to recall their childhoods.

ONE THING I COULDN'T HAVE DONE IN THE 1960s: Meet my significant other online, which I did in the early 1990s. I've also made some wonderful friends through eBay.

THE BIGGEST CHALLENGE AS A BUYER: Finding a bargain that's been overlooked by other eBaysians.

TO SELL ON eBay: Just know what you like. If you're enthusiastic about what you sell and write a killer description that tantalizes, buyers will pick up on your passion and want what you have.

PEOPLE ASK ME: How can you do eBay, be a PowerSeller-wannabe, give people great customer service in email and prompt receipt of their purchases, and hold a day job? Well, after doing eBay part time for eight months, I've decided to quit my job and do it full time!

ADVICE TO NEW COLLECTORS: Don't try to do it all. If you try to collect every edition ever issued, it's too much.

TO FIND A BARGAIN ON eBay: Watch the *Going, Going, Gone* section for items that have been overlooked for some reason. Don't use sniping software. If you want something badly, put the effort into watching it in the last minutes.

eBay BONUS: Trust. Discovering how the vast majority of people are scrupulously honest.

- **shill feedback:** artificially increasing a user's positive or negative feedback through the use of secondary registrations or associates.

- **feedback extortion:** demanding a certain action such as selling at a certain price if a reserve hasn't been met or threatening negative feedback.

- **feedback solicitation:** offering to sell or trade feedback or buy feedback for the sake of feedback itself.

Bad Bidding

Although some users complain about sniping, it's not illegal. However, other kinds of bidding abuses are prohibited:

- **Bid shielding (shill bidding):** using secondary registrations or associates to artificially raise the level of bidding (and subsequently canceling a bid) to protect a low bidder.

- **Bid siphoning:** emailing bidders in an open auction to offer the same or similar item(s) for below the current bid.

- **Auction interference:** emailing bidders in a currently open auction to warn them away from a seller or item.

- **Bid manipulation by using the bid retraction option:** bidding a high amount to find the maximum bid of the current high bidder and then retracting your bid and bidding a smaller amount above the high bidder.

- **Bid manipulation by use of an alias to register bids to gain a *hot* rating:** the deliberate use of secondary registrations or associates to artificially raise the number of bids to receive a hot rating, which is reserved for no-reserve auctions with at least thirty bids.

- **Bid manipulation (chronic):** bidding on items at auction without completing the sale, thus blocking legitimate bidders and hurting the sellers' ability to complete auctions.

- **Persisting to bid despite a warning from the seller that bids are not welcome:** sellers have the right to reject bids of any bidder based on feedback or a previous bad experience with an individual.

Slippery Selling

When people talk about their fear of fraud, they usually mean the following kinds of offenses:

● **Shill bidding:** deliberate use of secondary registrations or associates to artificially raise the level of bidding or price of an item.

● **Auction interception:** representing yourself as an eBay seller and intercepting the ended auctions of that seller for the purposes of accepting payments.

● **Illegally avoiding fees:** avoidance of fees through manipulation of the system.

● **Auction nonperformance (chronic):** selling items at auction and not completing the transaction after accepting payments.

Illegal Identity

Although people use all kinds of creative user IDs on eBay, behind each name there needs to be an email address, street address, and legitimate contact information. Offenses having to do with contact information and identity include

● **misrepresentation of identity (eBay):** representing yourself as an eBay employee or representative when you are not employed by eBay.

● **misrepresentation of identity (user):** representing yourself as another eBay user or registering using the identity of another user.

● **false, missing, or omitted contact information:** providing false information when registering.

● **underage usage:** registering as a user when you are under eighteen.

Miscellaneous Offenses

A few other types of behavior can also jeopardize the eBay community and the integrity of the site and are therefore prohibited:

- **Interfering with eBay's operations/site:** the deliberate use of software or other devices or engaging in any activity designed to interfere with the eBay site or its functions.

- **Sending spam:** sending unsolicited, commercial emails, including those to past bidders or buyers.

- **User-to-user threats:** threats or harassment made via email or telephone.

- **Publishing the contact information of another user on any online public area:** this does not include addressing users by their user IDs or handles in chat rooms.

- **Offering pirated software/bootleg tapes/illegal items for sale:** see later in this chapter a discussion of prohibited, questionable, and infringing items and in chapter 3, "The Quest for Amazing Stuff."

- **Use of profanity or patently vulgar language of a racist, hateful, sexual, or obscene nature in a public area:** although eBay believes in freedom of speech, such language goes against the spirit of the community.

The email address for reporting these offenses is safeharbor@eBay.com. When you make a complaint, provide as many details as possible, including any emails you have received (with complete text and headers), item listing number, or other pertinent information. You should quickly receive an automated email response from *SafeHarbor*.

eBay is committed to getting the situation resolved. However, understand that in some instances legal reasons forbid them from sharing the details or results of an investigation. Even though you may not have been notified, eBay may have taken disciplinary action against a violator of the rules.

Stake Your Claim: Insurance Against Fraud

Nothing gives comfort like the knowledge that you are insured against fraud. Every eligible eBay transaction is insured through Lloyds of London for up to $200 (minus a $25 deductible). You may be eligible for the program if you meet the following criteria:

● Both buyer and seller are in good standing on eBay (maintaining non-negative feedback ratings).

● The auction must be in accordance with eBay's user agreement.

● The final value of the auction must be greater than $25 (because a $25 deductible applies).

● Actual fraud has been committed.

● The buyer sent the money in good faith to the seller and never received the item.

● The item received is significantly different from the auction's description. (This insurance does not cover damage during shipping. Contact the carrier for information on their policies.)

● The buyer registers the complaint in eBay's Fraud Reporting System within thirty days after the auction's close.

If your experience matches the guidelines, you can start the insurance process, which takes four steps:

1 **Register your complaint:** Do this in the Fraud Reporting System (accessed through *SafeHarbor*) within thirty days of the auction's close. The seller will be notified that a complaint has been lodged.

2 **Try to resolve the complaint with the other user:** Continue to try to resolve the dispute with the other party for the next thirty days.

3 **Update the complaint status:**

● At the end of thirty days, return to the Fraud Reporting System to file or delete your complaint.

● If you file your complaint and are eligible for insurance, Lloyds sends you documentation for filing an insurance claim.

● If you delete your complaint, your complaint against the other user will be removed.

4 **Send your insurance claim to the Lloyds claim administrators:** After you have filed a claim, Lloyds claim administrators will contact you within thirty days to let you know the results of the investigation. The Fraud

Reporting System pages provide full instructions for submitting claims, supporting documents, and so forth.

Violations eBay Responds to Automatically

There are two kinds of infractions that eBay responds to automatically without a *SafeHarbor* investigation or complaint from another user or customer support representative. Known as *system-automated policies*, they are as follows:

1 **A user's feedback falls to a minus 4 rating:** In this case the system automatically disables the user's ability to list or bid on items and leave feedback. Note: This is a rating of "−4," not four negative feedbacks. If a person has twenty positive feedbacks and four negative feedbacks, her rating would be 16. (See chapter 2, "The Perfect Setup," for more on the mechanics of feedback.)

2 **Nonpaying bidders:** Users who win an auction but never complete the transaction are known as *nonpaying bidders*. When a seller requests a credit for a final value fee due to nonpayment by the bidder, eBay automatically sends a warning email to the user accused of deadbeat bidding. The user will receive two warnings before a suspension. On the third instance the user is suspended for thirty days. A fourth offense results in indefinite suspension.

It's the Law:
Prohibited, Questionable, and Infringing Items

eBay prohibits the sale of illegal or infringing items (items that are in violation of copyright, trademarks, or patents) and makes efforts to keep such items off the site. The staff of eBay cannot be at all places at all times. Every user plays a role in helping to keep eBay free of problem items. If you see an item you believe is illegal or infringing, notify eBay at ctywatch@eBay.com to kick off an investigation. You may also fill out a *Community Watch Report* under both *SafeHarbor* and *Community Standards*. If eBay finds the item in its database of illegal items, they end the auction immediately. Sometimes what's legal or illegal is not clear-cut. If there is a question, eBay reviews the laws and acts accordingly. (For a list of illegal items, see chapter 3, "The Quest for Amazing Stuff," or go to *Help* on the navigation bar, click on *Community Standards*, and see *Prohibited, Questionable, and Infringing Items*.)

eBay works closely with the *content* community—which comprises owners of intellectual property—to keep the site free of pirated items or those being sold in violation of copyrights, trademarks, or patents. It's easy to get confused about what can and cannot be sold in the area of intellectual property. Infringing items include the sale or distribution of *any* items not authorized by the intellectual property owner. Below is a partial list:

okay to sell or resell	not okay to sell
If you purchased a computer that came with software, you have a license for the software on that machine. You can sell the software only when you sell the computer with it.	Backup copies of any software or duplicates of software that came installed on a machine.
Books, records, movies, CDs, and the like that were purchased legally.	Copies of books, movies, CDs, bootleg tapes of concerts. Promotional or pre-release materials made specifically for publicity uses and not for resale/retail.
Game software, Sega, Nintendo, and Sony if purchased as a legal copy.	Multiple games on one CD, games that require a mod chip or other special hardware, backup copies of games, prerelease games acquired prior to the manufacturer's sale to the general public.

To educate eBay users and to help combat the sale of infringing items, eBay has set up the *Verified Rights Owners (VeRO)* program, a cooperative effort between eBay and the content community. eBay reviews listings reported by program members in an effort to eliminate infringing items, and it also relies on the help of users. Sometimes, eBay cannot end questionable auctions based on the report of a user, unless that user is actually the owner of the property. All listings that you suspect may be infringing should be reported to infringement@ebay.com. eBay will take appropriate action. It's a good idea to check the *Prohibited, Questionable, and Infringing Items* area for updates and detailed information on questionable items (under *Help*, then *Community Standards*).

Protecting Your Privacy

Privacy issues are one of the biggest concerns that Internet users have. Is Big Brother watching? Is an e-commerce site going to track all your purchases and sell that information? Will they use your email address for unsolicited emails? As you surf the Net, you will come across many legitimate requests for personal information. A simple eBay example is giving your address to sellers so they can ship you items you've won. It's sad but true that occasionally unscrupulous individuals will steal this information from unsuspecting users.

eBay's Privacy Policy

To build a bigger, safer Internet, many of the leading Internet sites have banded together to establish standards that articulate how they protect users' privacy and use information that is collected. eBay is a licensee of the TRUSTe Privacy Program, a nonprofit initiative whose mission is to "build users' trust and confidence in the Internet by promoting the principles of disclosure and informed consent." To comply with TRUSTe's guidelines, eBay has agreed to notify you of

- what information it gathers/tracks about you.

- what it does with that information.

- with whom it shares information.

eBay's privacy policy is accessible from the bottom of *every* page on the site. Here are a few choice points:

- eBay does not sell or rent any personally identifiable information about you to any third party. They do provide aggregate data—with no information that could be traced back to you personally—to advertisers and for other promotional purposes.

- eBay does not disclose email addresses. However, other users can obtain your email address. Of course, if your user ID is also your email address, there's no mystery in tracking it down. eBay takes measures to prevent robots (automated searching and information-gathering tools) from reading its pages and finding your email address.

eBay and its users do not tolerate spam. (See "Why Spam Ain't Kosher," page 35.) Therefore, without limiting the foregoing, you are not licensed to add an eBay user—even a user who has purchased an auction item from you—to your mailing list (email or physical mail) without their express consent after adequate disclosure.

When you read the eBay privacy policy, ask yourself, do you know as much about your credit card, favorite mail-order company, or magazine subscription service as they know about you? All that junk mail comes from somewhere, doesn't it?

Making Your Experience More Positive

You should take an active role in protecting your privacy when using the Internet. Following are some standard precautions you can use not only on eBay, but on other sites as well:

Where a password is required, use one with at least six characters containing both letters and numerals.

Create a password that can't be easily guessed by someone who has access to other kinds of information about you. For example, avoid your kid's name, birth dates, and so on.

Never give your password to others, especially through emails or message boards.

Change your password regularly; some people suggest as frequently as every thirty days.

When information is requested while you are visiting a site, check the URL in the address field on your browser to make sure you are still on the company's site before releasing the information.

Read a company's privacy policy before giving information.

If at any time you receive a pop-up request for your email address, Social Security number, credit card number, bank account number, telephone number, or password, exit out of it immediately. eBay, for example, never requests information in this manner.

● Never send your credit card via email (call or fax). Submit your credit card information online only if the data is encrypted using a secure server.

● Never download files unless you know what they are and who sent them. Computer virus and destructive programs that could cause your computer to divulge personal information are often transferred in cleverly disguised files.

When a Deal Goes South

Even under the best circumstances, problems occur. Unless someone is trying to commit outright fraud, most problems between buyers and sellers are resolvable with a little effort from both sides.

Sellers should understand that people are emotional about purchases. When a collector wins a piece he has been dying for, his anticipation builds as he envisions a package of goodies working its way to his doorstep. If the item turns out to be damaged, have condition issues, or be a reproduction instead of the original it was billed as, the disappointment is usually in direct proportion to the preceding excitement. (In other words, the recipient can be devastated.)

Of course, buyers need to appreciate the sellers' perspective as well. They hunt high and low to find merchandise, research and photograph it, write a description that they believe honestly represents the piece, and pack and ship it in a timely fashion. When a buyer accuses them of misrepresentation, they're very likely to take it personally. Everyone has a point of view. Problems occur and escalate when people jump to conclusions. As Uncle Griff says, "If you assume the worst, it becomes self-fulfilling."

The good news is that after the initial shock most people are open to finding a solution. This takes communication—something that email is not always conducive to. Email is convenient and fast, but it has shortcomings. Irony doesn't work. Neither does sarcasm. Even all those cutesy chat room punctuation faces (see "Talk the Talk" in chapter 9) can be misinterpreted. Does :(mean you're grumpy, angry, or just sad? Safer to stick with dignified, straightforward, even-toned language. "Remember that you may be looking at an email address, but there's another human being at the other end," says eBay's founder, Pierre Omidyar. "Better yet, exchange phone numbers and work it out before the situation deteriorates."

Both buyer and seller have to be open to reaching a solution. If either party chooses to be stubborn or belligerent, the odds of reaching a mutually acceptable solution are greatly reduced. Following are some common disputes and creative ways to approach them.

problem	seller response	buyer response
Buyer thinks the item has condition problems when it arrives.	Take the buyer's concerns seriously. Review your listing. Is it possible the buyer is right? Is your spouse right about your needing a new pair of glasses? If you stand by your listing, communicate that as diplomatically as possible. In cases where the buyer has a point, offer to either accept a return or partially refund the purchase price.	Send an even-toned email to the seller. Be specific about the condition issues that concern you and point out the differences between the item description and what you see. Don't hesitate to mention a possible resolution such as returning the item.
The merchandise arrives in need of repair. For example, the buyer finds that the old Nikon single-lens reflex camera that was in perfect condition when you last used it (eight years ago . . .) needs minor repair.	If it's worth it to you, ask the buyer to get an estimate for the repair and offer to pay or split the cost. Maybe you don't get as much as you had hoped for the camera, but it's sold and you don't have the hassle of taking it back.	Email the seller immediately upon discovering the problem. Do not assume that this was intentional. It's fine to request a return. Maybe you accept splitting the cost because you do want the camera and you got a decent price to begin with.
The item is seriously damaged.	Do whatever possible to support the buyer, including doing what's needed to file insurance claims. If the item was not insured	Notify the seller immediately. You need to determine if it was damaged in shipping or before it was sent. Work with the seller

(cont.)

	and the damage could be due to your packing, offer a refund.	to file claims or reach a financial settlement.
Buyer's remorse/buyer backs out.	You're not obliged to let people off the hook. Bids are binding. However, if it's not a big deal, contact the underbidder or accept a return. It's a good business practice.	Plead your case as humbly as possible. If a financial situation occurs that keeps you from completing the transaction, either ask to back out or propose a date on which you might be able to pay. In cases of remorse, you need to understand that the seller is in no way obligated to you.
Other problems.	Take the initiative. If you have a good idea, present it. Keep working at it. Sincere efforts from both sides to resolve a dispute normally end in success.	Take the initiative. If you have a good idea, present it. Keep working at it. Sincere efforts from both sides to resolve a dispute normally end in success.

On occasion, even everyone's best efforts can't resolve a problem. After exhausting all efforts, there are some other measures you can take:

Use arbitration: If you feel the need to go to a third party, many services are available. Check Yahoo's (www.yahoo.com) arbitration page for more information and service providers.

Post negative feedback: As a last resort, if no compromise can be reached, use the Feedback Forum to leave negative feedback. Do so only after you have exhausted all avenues, as you cannot take back a complaint posted in haste.

File a formal complaint: If mail fraud is involved—you paid for merchandise but received no goods—file a complaint with the U.S. Post Office or your state's attorney general's office.

Best Remedy Prevention

We all know the old saying "An ounce of prevention is worth a pound of cure." The same holds true on eBay, and by taking some basic steps and allowing calmer heads to prevail, you can reduce the possibility of a stalemate and increase the chance for a solution. The responsibility falls on both buyers and sellers to maintain civility. To avoid and/or resolve disputes:

sellers

Describe merchandise as accurately as possible. This is probably the number one cause of complaints and misunderstandings. Assume that buyers know nothing.

Respond to buyers' inquiries promptly, completely, and courteously. Spell out shipping and packing costs. Send emails when the auction ends, when you've received payment, and when you've sent the goods.

When responding to a complaint or problem, be understanding. Put yourself in the shoes of the unhappy buyer. Do not insult, blame, or otherwise belittle buyers by telling them they should have known better.

Believing a resolution is possible increases the chance that it is.

Ask the buyer, "What can I do for you?"

Remember, a negotiation is an exchange of ideas, not a contest to see who can yell the loudest.

buyers

Know your stuff and ask lots of questions—*before* you bid. Assume nothing.

Take the initiative to find out everything you can about an item. When the auction ends, don't necessarily wait for the seller to notify you. Be clear about how you intend to pay, the shipping method you prefer, and when the seller can expect payment.

When reporting a problem to sellers, be specific and justify your complaint. Do not make personal comments about their integrity or intelligence.

Believing a resolution is possible increases the chance that it is.

Tell the seller what you want—within reason.

Remember, a negotiation is an exchange of ideas, not a contest to see who can yell the loudest.

(cont.)

When an amicable resolution is reached, leave feedback and let the world know the buyer is a good customer, a credit to eBay.

When an amicable resolution is reached, leave feedback and let the world know the seller respects buyers, stands by her product, and works to resolve problems.

Escrow Services

A great way to avoid disputes before they happen is through the use of escrow services. The buyer makes payment through a third party that holds on to the funds until the buyer has a chance to inspect merchandise and accept or reject it. Depending on the outcome, the escrow service then releases the funds to the seller or returns the funds to the buyer. eBay has arranged for the availability of escrow services from i-Escrow. For details about the process, see "Temporary Parking: Escrow Services" in chapter 7, "The Bidding Is Closed—Now What?"

Who Was That Masked Man?: Reaching Out to People Beyond Email

If you can't seem to get a reply or if something comes up that would be easier to discuss on the phone, you can request a user's contact information (email address, phone number, city, state, zip, country, and company information) under *Search* (on the navigation bar) and *Find member*. eBay then sends an email to both the requesting and requested user with this information about *both* users.

In the early days of eBay, Pierre Omidyar personally fielded queries from confused or upset traders. Because the online auction process was so novel, it took a while for people to catch on to how things worked and how to behave. For example, folks tended to get panicky if a payment or shipment took a little longer than expected. They'd jump to conclusions, assuming they were getting ripped off. Pierre would counsel patience and encourage people to make "real" contact by calling each other on the phone. "Think about it," he'd say. "How many truly dishonest people do you know?"

CHAPTER 9

when you need a friend

More often than not, he'd hear back a week or so later that the matter was resolved and there was a perfectly good explanation for the misunderstanding. That experience, repeated over and over, confirmed Pierre's contention that most people are basically honest and want to do a good job. He also knew that people need support and help when learning new things, and thus eBay's multitiered support environment was born.

In fact, it didn't take Pierre long to realize that some of the best sources of tips and advice were other eBaysians who'd mastered the system. He established the first message board in 1996, where users posted questions and answers—and generally helped each other become more successful. These exchanges grew into marathon conversations, generating spin-off boards and chat rooms. Today, whether you need a quick answer or want to kick back and shoot the breeze, there's an eBay forum for you.

If the little gnomes who live in your PC aren't cooperating, check out the help and support available throughout the site. Members of the eBay staff are available to assist you with administrative, legal, and technical questions. There's usually a

Only on eBay

In the early days, one of the calmest and most knowledgeable voices rising above the din on the boards was that of Jimmy Griffith, a former mural painter in West Rutland, Vermont. With his avuncular musings, he quickly established himself as an authority on technical issues and matters of online etiquette. His early postings are the stuff of eBay legend, thanks in part to a wacky fictional persona he created for himself of a cross-dressing dairy farmer who lived in West Upperbuttcrack, Vermont, with his mother (despite her untimely death thirty years earlier). Uncle Griff, as he became known, personified not only the self-reliant, eccentric spirit of eBay (and Silicon Valley), but also the company's core value that good behavior inspires the same in others. As Griff says, "Uncle believes you can teach by example." Today Griff divides his time between Vermont and San Jose as eBay's customer support supervisor, coaching some two hundred representatives to guide users through the system.

knowledgeable soul or two hanging out in the *eBay Café*, the *Q&A* board, or one of the many topic-specific boards. Do-it-yourselfers can access massive amounts of online help loaded with valuable information. Finding answers is a matter of knowing where to look and whom to ask—and that's what this chapter is all about.

For Do-It-Yourselfers

Nothing builds self-confidence like solving your own problems. Many people are happy to bang away on their computers, practicing trial and error. However, if your problem is with *proxy bidding* and the auction you want to win ends in one hour, thirteen minutes, and twenty-two seconds, you want help and you want it now. Before you hurl your mouse out the window, this would be an opportune moment to notice the *Help* link that appears on the navigation bar. This is your gateway to solutions.

The *Help* link takes you to *Help Overview*, where you can start navigating the online help options. Just getting started? Try the *Basics* area to work through some of the issues and questions that are common for beginners. The *Welcome Wagon* (found under *Basics*) takes you on a quick "walking" tour and offers lots of links to additional information. Need to dig in more deeply? Cruise through the *Buyer Guide* or *Seller Guide*, *My Info*, and *Community Standards*. When you have questions about your account, need to change some information such as your email address, or forget your password, use *My Information*.

Through the link *More Basic Help*, you can access *Frequently Asked Questions (FAQs)*, which is an excellent way to seek answers. FAQs anticipate your needs and list the solutions as links. For example, under the heading *Registering*

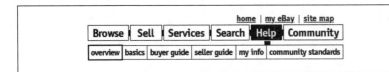

there are more than thirty questions, such as "How do I change my user ID?" "What should my user ID be?" "How often can I change my user ID?" Click on the question, and the answer appears.

In *Basics* you'll also find a link to *Glossary*, which contains definitions of words you might encounter while using eBay. This is an excellent place to expand your vocabulary. After a little practice you'll be speaking fluently on the boards.

At the top of the *Help* overview page, you can also search eBay's text documentation by writing a question in the box, such as, "What is a reserve auction?" The search returns documents relevant to your query. It's possible that despite all your efforts you can't find the answer to a question. On the bottom of some pages you'll see a link to leave a question for eBay. From here you can complete a form and get an email response from customer support in 24 hours.

The documentation of the site is useful even when you don't have a problem. Stop in at the FAQs or cruise the help documentation whenever you have a free moment and bone up on how eBay works. Becoming an expert and learning the rules helps you know your community and become a successful buyer and seller.

By the Boards

The Internet is a powerful way to bring people together, and eBay takes advantage of that power to provide customer service and to create peer-to-peer support. This all takes place on what eBay calls the *boards* (also known as chat rooms), two-way communication venues where people can post messages and respond to each other. The boards are an essential part of the community life—the true heart of eBay. If eBay is a small town, the boards are the town square or general store where you can catch up on the news and gossip and get an earful (or eyeful).

But how about the advice that proliferates from your fellow eBaysians—can you trust these people? For the most part, yes. Many of the regulars on the boards are longtime users who have benefited a great deal from eBay and view helping others as giving back to the community. They take pride in their

SPECIALTY:
Dolls

eBay HANDLE: jadoll   AGE: 63

THE BIGGEST CHALLENGE: Finding quality. I collect older dolls, but I like them to be MIB (mint in box). The dolls I sell on eBay are mostly new.

I'M AMAZED THAT: Novice collectors can't get past all the lace and ruffles, beads and feathers, on the new dolls. The doll is the face (and body), not the clothes.

DOLL DELIGHTS: My dolls are like my little friends. I love them like children or babies. They have personality—they move, smile, pout, talk, giggle, and cry. When I'm not looking, though, I'm sure they get into my candy because I sure don't eat the whole box myself!

WHAT MY COLLECTION SAYS ABOUT ME: I'm a child at heart. And a very greedy one.

MY FAVORITE: That would be my new (old) trunk doll—a tiny, 5½-inch French all-bisque who came in her trunk with her extra dresses, pillow, hankie, and her own doll. Tomorrow, who knows?

A DOLL I'D LIKE TO MEET: A Schoenhut wooden doll with spring joints.

I'VE COME A LONG WAY SINCE: My first doll that I bought as an adult—a very small plastic doll called a Pee Wee. I paid a whopping $2 for her.

MY BEST COLLECTING TIP: Buy the best you can afford, even if you have to make payments for a while. I'm a big believer in layaway.

WHETHER BUYING OR SELLING: Research! Decide what you want to spend (then bid a little more). And goodness knows I've sold things for way less than the value because I didn't know what they were.

FOR DOLL DETAILS: Check out the monthly doll magazines. If you like antique or vintage dolls, you need books and lots of them. On eBay's doll chat board, we've archived some good studies on various dolls.

DOWNSIDE OF eBay: I expected to clean my house by selling off what I don't need. Instead it's a bigger mess because I am always photographing, storing, and packing things for shipment.

BEST THING ABOUT eBay: I've owned a doll shop and antique co-op and sold at shows. eBay is so much easier—I stay at home, pack my things once (when shipping), and make more profit because my things sell faster.

work. Of course, eBay is an intricate place, and sometimes you might see some well-intentioned but misleading information. Not to worry: the boards have a self-righting capacity. If someone slips up, it's likely another eBaysian can set the record straight.

The boards fall into three categories: eBay customer service, peer-to-peer general, and category specific. Sleepless in Seattle? Work the night shift? Do your eBay shopping and listing in the predawn hours before you make the kids breakfast? No problem. The boards are up and running twenty-four hours a day, seven days a week. So if the spirit moves you, click in. On some boards, users vie to sound reveille and greet the new eBay morning and their comrades in collecting.

To find the boards, select *Community* from the navigation bar and click on *Chat* to get to a full list of boards. Then select a destination. Once you've selected a board, posting a message requires only the input of your user ID and password. Type your message in the box provided. If you are responding to a specific posting, start by typing in the name of the user you want to respond to: "Archrival—So you like to snipe, eh? Well, two can play at that game!"

When you want to see if anyone responded to your post and you don't want to scroll down through the entire board (which can amount to two hundred messages), use CTRL-F on your keyboard to activate your browser's *Find* box. Then type in your user ID and go directly to any responses.

The boards are busy. On the most active ones, messages get posted every couple of seconds, so reload often to refresh and see the latest. Be cautious and judicious in use of uppercase text. On the boards, as well as in emails, text in all caps is considered the equivalent of SCREAMING AT THE TOP OF YOUR LUNGS!

Only on eBay

In addition to Uncle Griff, another regular at the *eBay Café* is Aunt Flossie, whose mission in life is to exhort others to play nice. She's fond of quoting Ralph Waldo Emerson: "Life is not so short but that there is always time enough for courtesy." When eBay created the "user-to-user" Q&A board to supplement the *eBay Café,* she voluntarily and cheerfully answered questions asked by other users. Eventually she became the second member of the eBay Customer Support Team. The driving force behind the creation of the original *Support Q&A* board, where members could receive "live" customer support, she tirelessly and politely fielded countless queries about eBay, the Internet, and out-of-the-ordinary transactions. On the eBay Customer Support Team, she is known as Louise and serves as the liaison between customer support and product marketing while continuing to participate in community development.

Only on eBay

The people at eBay's main office know the importance of listening to community members. That's why they instituted the *Voice of the Customer* program. eBay regularly invites eight to ten customers to visit the main office in San Jose and share with employees in customer support, marketing, engineering, and other areas. "The participants in these forums have provided us with invaluable insight and perspective," says Matt Bannick, eBay's Vice President of Support to the Community. "We are confident that this helps us build a better eBay."

eBay Customer Service Boards

When you want the official eBay version of what's going on or how to do things, check out *Help* and *Community* on the navigation bar. In these areas you'll find boards staffed by eBay and special pages with informational updates hot off the server in San Jose.

Stump the Experts

Want clarification on how a Dutch auction works? Frustrated by getting outbid at the last second? Curious about policies regarding what is allowable in a listing? Customer support staff are here at the *General Support Q&A* board (under *Help*), ready to explain even the most esoteric of eBay functions.

Coming to You Live from eBay

When you're new to eBay (and maybe the whole world of computers), there's no such thing as a stupid question. Learning takes time, and these experts are ready to clarify and elucidate. The customer support staff provides help at the *Direct Support for New Users* board and are ready to help you negotiate all the ins and outs of eBay.

What Do You Think?

As the site grows, it is inevitable that changes take place. Many changes are instigated by user feedback. Want to sound off about some change in the system that irks you? Think something new is awesome and want to praise the genius of the site designers? Discuss the latest changes on the *New Features* board. Most of the discussion here is peer to peer, but it's not uncommon for eBay staff to stop in, take the community pulse, and thank users for their comments. Warning: Failure to stick to the topic at hand on this board can be considered site interference and result in a twenty-four-hour suspension even if the user's current bids and auctions aren't completed.

If you want to make sure the eBay staff sees your brilliant insights, send them to the *Suggestion Box* under the *Community* button on the navigation bar. The person who monitors the *Suggestion Box* makes sure ideas are routed to the appropriate eBay staff person.

Breaking News

System seems slow? Not available at all? Want to know what changes are in the pipeline? The *Announcements* board (under *Community—News*) is eBay central, where important news is disseminated. This is not a traditional board because you can only read messages, not leave any. Nonetheless, this is the most reliable, up-to-date source of information on the site and should be a regular stop on your eBay grand rounds. If you want to discuss an announcement or find out more, hit the *General Support Q&A* board or the *eBay Café* (read on).

For a more long-term look at what's going on in eBayland, click on the *Calendar*, which shows events where eBay will be represented in a given month. *Cool Happenings*, also found under *News*, provides links to special eBay events and features, from the Gallery to charity auctions.

Peer-to-Peer Support Boards

There are many ways to connect on eBay. The various boards and chat rooms enable you to hook up with collectors who share your interests, users who just want to be sociable, and sellers who might have exactly what you're looking for.

A Latte Fun

The *eBay Café* was the site's first chat room and where the eBay community began. It's here that Uncle Griff and Aunt Flossie started eBay's customer support movement. You can't get a cappuccino or a buttery

Only on eBay

Like a small-town newspaper, where covering hard news is secondary to chronicling the births and weddings, *eBay Life* distills the essence of eBay into a monthly newletter. You'll find amazing stories ("eBay Auctions Help Judy Stay Off Social Services"), trading tips, an events calendar, articles on collecting, and "Getting to Know Us," a column profiling eBay employees. Uncle Griff and Aunt Flossie answer questions ranging from feedback etiquette ("netiquette") to the meaning of arcane collectibles lingo. You can write them at unclgrff@eBay.com. There's an ongoing contest for the best *About Me* pages, and editor Arlene Brenner is always seeking stories. Share your greatest find or other eBay experience by emailing ebaylife@ eBay.com. Find the Newsletter by clicking *Community* on the navigation bar.

Only on eBay

croissant, but you can join your fellow eBaysians in discussing a broad range of topics. Located under *Chat* in the *Community* section, this spot is the cyberequivalent of Central Perk, the coffee shop on the TV show *Friends*. The regulars may not always exhibit the wit of Chandler Bing, but then you don't have to have Monica's cheekbones to get a seat on the sofa and join the party. (For more on the *eBay Café*, see page 235.)

Questions and Answers

Neighbor helping neighbor is the foundation of any strong community, and the *User-to-User eBay Q&A* board is the online version of borrowing a cup of sugar from the folks next door (even though "next door" might be in New Zealand). Your neighbors are here to get you acquainted with the 'hood. Think of them as proud townsfolk dying to share the collected wisdom and lore of their community. Pretty soon you'll be an old pro yourself, so come on back and share all you've learned.

Tech Talk

Like the *User-to-User eBay Q&A* board, the *Help* section's *Images/HTML* board is where eBaysians help one another through what many users find the most difficult parts of selling on eBay: posting pictures to their listing and using HTML. Some of the regulars, like Pongo, have been leaders in helping people master the HTML and images on eBay. Even if you're doing well with images and HTML, you might want to stop in and learn a few new tricks, like creating a link to your other auctions on eBay or creating an ad with a background color.

AOL Café

America Online is the largest of all the ISPs, and eBay has its own gathering spot for AOL users. As with the *eBay Café*, folks on the *AOL Café* share their experiences and discuss eBay and AOL issues.

If You Read This, All Is Forgiven

Sometimes you space out and lose a user's email address or forget to send payment right away. Then you realize that thirty days have gone by and you can't find the listing, since eBay purges completed auctions after that length of time. The *Emergency Contact* board is the place to post a message and plead forgiveness. With luck the other party will see your post and make contact. Don't forget to check this board for someone who might be trying to get in touch with you.

eBay International

These boards are eBay's council of world trade, where buyers and sellers from around the globe get together and discuss the intricacies and fun of trading internationally. No foreign-language skills are required (although some exchanges are in other languages), but if you can explain a Dutch auction in German, it will no doubt be appreciated. In addition to the *eBay International* board there are country-specific boards for Japan (messages in English and Japanese), the United Kingdom, and Canada.

A Board Just for You

Get ready to meet some serious collectors. eBay's *Category-Specific* boards are targeted toward many of the major categories. This is where you'll find your collecting soul mates: the people who actually understand what you're talking about when you explain the cold sweat you broke out in when you stumbled across that Atari 2600 game cartridge of Chase the Chuckwagon—in its original shrink-wrap! They are also usually more than willing to help you identify that two-handled thingamajig you picked up at a garage sale or help you evaluate that Superman comic book your son left in the closet when he went to college. These boards also function a little like the *Q&A* boards, with users happy to answer eBay-related questions or point you in the direction of help. You can access the category-specific boards through the home pages of the various categories or off the *Community* link on the navigation bar. (See page 162 for a list of *Category-Specific* chat rooms eBay has as of this writing.)

eBay Ambassador Jayne Best describes the kinds of friendships that can flower on these boards: "The best part of eBay is all the wonderful friends I have made through the doll chat board. I spend a lot of time there talking, and have met quite a few collectors in person. A group of us met at a doll show in Vallejo, California. There were sixteen of us there from as far away

eBay Chat Rooms

Advertising	Garage
Antiques	Glass
Beanie Babies	Jewelry
Books	Movies
Coins	Music
Comics	Photo Equipment
Computers	Pottery
Diecast	Sports
Dolls	Stamps
Elvis	Toys
Furbies	Trading Cards

as New York, and six states represented. It was so much fun, we are going to do it again, and we expect a bigger turnout."

The conversational thread in these chat rooms can take some pretty interesting and bizarre twists. As in face-to-face chats, the original topic is often left far behind as non sequiturs fly and people digress into whatever's on their minds. Sometimes the talk devolves into meaningless blather or "popcorn fights." On the book board, for example, users have been known to fret about the buzz getting banal—to which others have replied that if they want to see banal, check out the Beanie Baby chat. Admittedly Beanie and Furby chatter is ostensibly perky, but discussion occasionally turns serious, especially when the conversation turns to fakes.

Talk the Talk

To type is to chat. The Internet has spawned a new culture complete with codes of conduct and communication. The one or two times you did check in on the boards you saw people talking about *lurkers*. That sounds scary. And then there are those acronyms such as *LOL*—what does that mean? Live online?

Well, lurking is hanging out on the boards and watching but not participating in the conversation, and it's perfectly allowed. As Yogi Berra once said, "You can observe a lot by just watching." As for LOL, it stands for "laughing out loud," and it's one of the many shorthand codes that have evolved within chat culture to express moods that would be picked up from body language or sounds in spoken conversation—and to save some typing. Here are some common phrases you're likely to encounter:

WB	*Welcome back*
LY	*I love you*
OTF	*On the floor (laughing)*
ROTF	*Rolling on the floor*
ROFLWTIME	*Rolling on floor with tears in my eyes*
BRB	*Be right back*
AFK	*Away from keyboard*
:-D	*Laughing, or a big grin*
BAK	*Back at keyboard*
BTW	*By the way*
GMTA	*Great minds think alike*
IMHO	*In my humble opinion*
POOT	*Goodbye*
-)	*Smile*
:-(	*A little sad or grumpy*
;-)	*Wink, wink, know what I mean????*
:-X	*My lips are sealed*
CUL8R	*See you later*

Now, you can converse with the best of them.

Chat Room Policies

The boards on eBay are informative, helpful, and entertaining. Still, they are public and you need to abide by the rules eBay has established to ensure that some common decency prevails and the boards don't degenerate into mob hysteria or a free-for-all.

The following types of postings are cause for immediate post removal, warning, and/or suspension from the site:

- Posting contact or personal information about another individual without permission.

- Posting material containing profanity, vulgarity, hate speech, or threats of violence.

- Posting material (graphic or text) that is obscene or pornographic in nature.

- Using JavaScript, repetitive posts, or other actions that interfere with site operations.

⬤ Advertising your or others' merchandise, auctions, services, or commercial Web sites.

When a post is in violation of eBay's policy and removed, all posts submitted by that user will be automatically removed as well.

Using HTML on the Boards

The boards are HTML friendly. You can gussy up your postings with images and graphics such as colored fonts. You can post an image right to a board using the same HTML you use in your auction listing. This feature is helpful when you seek to identify an object or have its value assessed. However, because images can take a while to load, many people create a link to their images. The HTML code for that is as follows:

```
<a href="http://www.yoursite.com/mypics/pic.jpg">Click here</a>
```

Note: You replace the *URL* with the address of your image, and you can replace "Click here" with any text you like, such as "See my photo" or "View the whatchamacallit." See chapter 5, "Putting It on the Block," for more information on HTML.

Giving Back

"Personally, I have always believed in helping people become the best they can become," says Pierre. Thus the eBay Foundation was born. Prior to eBay's initial public stock offering, 107,250 shares of eBay common stock were set aside for the eBay Community Foundation. The organization made its first grants in 1998 and expects to continue to grow in the years ahead.

The foundation supports organizations and programs that

⬤ reflect the values and community orientation of eBay.

⬤ provide tools, hope, and direction to those who seek new skills.

⬤ teach the teachers, who in turn help people recognize the potential in themselves to improve their surroundings, their lives, and their communities.

⬤ are like eBay—clever, unique, passionate, and eclectic and have long-term implications and maximize the ability of the foundation to do good in the world.

Only on eBay

In its first two years, the eBay Foundation gave grants to the following organizations for programs that provide long-term and far-reaching benefits for the community:

- **Friends of Farm Drive:** To fund a summer program to teach at-risk youth computer skills in a neighborhood where drugs and gangs are rampant.

- **University Research Expedition Program (UREP):** To provide scholarships to send California elementary and high school teachers on UREP trips, where they will work side-by-side with university scientists and local residents in other countries on research projects investigating critical issues of environmental, human, and economic importance worldwide.

- **CHAMPS/ Project Team Work:** To help place San Jose State University athletes in public schools and community youth groups to serve as mentors and role models for youth who need academic, social and/or emotional support.

- **College Kids:** For programs that develop and support grassroots partnerships that help kids from low-income communities, grades 3–12, realize their potential to make it to college. The College Kids model brings resources into the community (mentors, college students, etc.) and strives to enable community members to become service providers and not just service recipients.

- **Home Care Companions:** To enable people living with life-threatening illnesses to receive sufficient, appropriate, and affordable health care in their own homes by training patients, families, and friends in basic home-care nursing skills.

- **Inn Dwelling:** For a shelter that assists underprivileged families as well as handicapped and elderly people in the Germantown area of Philadelphia toward self-sufficiency. Some of the many programs offered are related to budget and debt management counseling, educational opportunity, job and literacy training, and relocation assistance.

- **Parents Helping Parents, Inc.:** For programs that help children with special needs through mentor parenting, education planning classes, learning disability and attention deficit disorder classes, and children's neighborhood projects.

- **Project H.E.L.P. (High Expectations Learning Program):** For initiatives geared toward ensuring academic success for all elementary school students. This San Francisco–based organization's mission is to become a county, state, and national model for early academic intervention through parent involvement and teacher training.

- **Students Run LA:** To encourage underachieving students in Los Angeles county to set athletic goals for building self-esteem, self-control, and a sense of personal achievement—thus increasing their chances of staying in school.

Only on eBay

Application guidelines and current grant activities can be found on the *About eBay* area of the site, accessed through the *Community* link on the navigation bar.

Rosie the Role Model

Auctions have long been a fund-raising tool for non-profit organizations. Many groups hold silent or live auctions in conjunction with all kinds of fund-raising events. The organization's supporters donate the goods and services that are sold, and the bidding can be lively and fun. Organizations might have access to unique items created especially for the organization by an artist or donated by celebrities or merchants.

Now charities have another outlet to sell items—eBay. Several organizations have hopped on the bandwagon. Perhaps the most widely known are the auctions benefiting the For All Kids Foundation, Inc., which Rosie O'Donnell started in February 1997 to help support the intellectual, social, and cultural development of at-risk and underserved children across the country. Since its inception, the foundation has awarded more than three hundred grants to nonprofit organizations providing child care, education, health care, and other essential programs for children and their families in forty-one states and the District of Columbia. In the first six months of its eBay auctions, For All Kids raised more than $750,000 by selling memorabilia donated (and often signed) by guests on the *Rosie* syndicated talk show. Sure, Rosie has a built-in cadre of fans who support her auctions, but that shouldn't stop you or your favorite organization from starting your own. All it takes is good-quality merchandise and an investment of time.

Doing for Others

As an organization selling on eBay, you get all the benefits of any eBay auction, including an active community of millions of buyers and low overhead. eBay does not provide discounted or no-fee auctions to nonprofit organizations. Even so, with the inexpensive fees for sellers, eBay auctions are probably a more cost-efficient way to raise money than other endeavors such as direct mail and you can reach a whole new universe of donors with an eBay auction.

Nonprofit organizations should take the following steps:

● **Register a new user ID:** The organization should have its own user ID and not an individual's. Why? Because people might be leery of an individual claiming to be a tax-exempt organization. It's also probably a good idea to make the user ID an email address so people see you are open to questions.

● **Create an About Me page:** Use your page to state clearly your mission, where you're located, and how the funds raised on eBay are to be expended. Prominently display a phone number and the name of a contact person. You might even want to have a link to an annual report so people can see the size and scope of your organization. Make sure you include your current listings on your page. (See chapter 2, "The Perfect Setup," for more information on About Me pages.)

● **Provide proof of tax-exempt status:** Tax-exempt organizations have an IRS determination letter (commonly referred to as 501(c) 3, the section of IRS code that pertains to non-profit tax exemptions) that proves they are tax-exempt. Make this letter available on your About Me page and/or from a link on each listing.

● **Clarify tax deductibility:** Many people falsely assume that any money given to a qualified nonprofit organization is automatically tax-exempt. Tax deductibility is a complex matter, especially in auctions. Generally, if a patron buys an item or receives a service from a tax-exempt organization, only that portion in excess of the "fair market value" is deductible. Since an auction for all intents and purposes is the closest you can get to a fair market value, many items sold via auction would not be tax-deductible (this is especially true for items such as autographs or special works of art). However, sometimes buyers might qualify for a tax deduction. For example, let's say a non-profit organization puts up for sale a brand-new Pentium III PC with monitor and printer that was donated by a local merchant. The retail value of that PC package is $1,300. If the PC sold for $1,500, the buyer could possibly deduct $200. If it sold for $1,200, no part would be tax-deductible (although the buyer would have gotten a great deal, and the organization would be better off, too). Consult with an attorney, accountant, or fund-raising expert before making any claims about tax deductions.

● **Be even more zealous than usual in answering questions:** All sellers need to be responsive to potential buyers. Organizations should be doubly so. You are different from part-time sellers, and it's important to represent the good work that you do and the professionalism of the organization. Establish a response time for getting back to potential buyers within twelve or twenty-four hours, for example, and say so in your listing.

● **Include a receipt and letter with each purchase:** A letter of thanks from the executive director or board chair along with a receipt for the purchase should accompany every shipment. Purchasers can then use that documentation to figure out what part, if any, of their purchase they can deduct. (In general, the burden of proof falls on the taxpayer claiming the deduction, although organizations are required to provide receipts for donations in excess of $250.)

● **Don't reuse names:** It's tempting to reuse names of purchasers in future solicitations for your organization, such as in direct-mail campaigns or for upcoming events. Some people might consider getting solicitations as a form of spam (see chapter 2, "The Perfect Setup," for an explanation). If you plan to build a mailing list from your bidders, let them know in your after-the-sale email and offer them an opportunity to have their name removed from the list.

● **Promote your auctions to your donors or members:** Your current supporters are always a great audience to have bidding on your items. They are the ones who know your cause and want to support it. Find ways to create excitement about your auctions. For example, you could start three auctions every Monday evening at seven P.M. so people would know exactly when to get in on the action. Send a letter to supporters (or use your newsletter) with a list of the items you are going to sell and the dates they'll hit the block. Include an information sheet on eBay and how to register. If possible, designate someone on the staff or recruit a volunteer who is available to provide support to those not familiar with eBay. Have an "eBay night" and set up a few computers (connected to the Internet) and show people the ropes; they can practice bidding on your organization's items, naturally. If you have a bevy of great items, do a press release to the local papers about the upcoming sales or announce sale results when you reach a benchmark of $5,000, $10,000, or $25,000 and profile those individuals and local businesses that have donated choice goods.

● **Do everything else it takes to be a good eBay merchant:** Write good descriptions (include a paragraph or two about the charity), insert good photos, have a business plan, ship items quickly, and leave feedback.

● **Solicit goods and services from your supporters:** A steady flow of goods is the best way to raise funds, so be creative. Sponsor a spring-cleaning drive encouraging your supporters to go through their closets and give you good-quality resalable items (cameras, designer clothes, jewelry, collectible first editions, and so on). Write to local sports figures and encourage them to donate signed goods with a letter of authenticity. Make connections with local businesses to give you old PCs to sell when they upgrade and excess merchandise or returns, or ask them to provide Web space for your images and email accounts (get them to put links on their corporate site to your eBay About Me page). Make sure people know that they can take a tax deduction for donating goods. Give them a credit in your listing or on your About Me page so their good deeds get recognized. Provide letters confirming such in-kind donations.

● **Pace yourself:** One of the great aspects about eBay is that it's always available, so you don't have to sell everything at once. In fact, selling a few items a week could be done easily without too big a time commitment of staff or volunteers.

Charity Begins on Your PC Screen

If you're not involved with a charity, you can still reach out and help others in the eBay community. On eBay's *Giving* board, members can ask for assistance from their fellow users. Some people ask just for a few kind words, a prayer, or a birthday card for a shut-in or disadvantaged child. Others request clothes and financial assistance. Still others stage charity auctions, which you can access through *About Me* links. In particularly desperate situations you might best be able to assist by referring the people involved to an appropriate agency or social services organization. Bear in mind that the board is not connected in any way with the company and any messages are solely the opinion and responsibility of the person posting it. eBay members do have big hearts, and this board has served as a catalyst to help many people. But before you send money, it's always a good idea to contact the recipient and/or the person posting the request to get more details and make sure the need is legitimate.

PART FOUR

YOU ARE WHAT YOU

collect

Although people use eBay to trade lots of everyday merchandise such as computers, cars, clothes, and canoes, the majority of eBay addicts log on to trade collectibles.

So that's what the rest of **CHAPTER 10** this book is devoted to. If you happen to be among the .0000000001 percent of the population who didn't get the collecting gene, we sympathize—and urge you to seek professional help in coming to terms with this deficit. But we also urge you not to pass up the rest of this book. You might gain insights that help you better market to all those collectors on eBay. Who knows? You might also come to the realization that all those ashtrays you've stolen—borrowed!—from hotels over the years really do constitute a collection and, hence, make you a collector.

collecting your thoughts

Why Do People Collect?

Cruising through the categories on eBay, you're bound to come across whole galaxies of stuff that you never dreamed someone would pay good money for. And sometimes it's true: nobody would. But more often than not, the collectors come out of the virtual woodwork, upping the ante for a Troll or a sheet of Marilyn Monroe commemorative postage stamps or a baseball autographed by Ken Griffey Jr. What do they see in such stuff? Why does it move them? Why does an object speak to some people and not to others? Well, you might as well ask how salmon know which river to return to to spawn. They just know. It's in their genetic code. And so it is with collectors.

When collectors do try to articulate what motivates them, they may claim a love of history or art, the quest for knowledge, the thrill of discovery, a belief in preservation, or the need for self-expression. They may even admit to less altruistic

motives: object lust, obsession, greed, power, or control. Some psychologists say collecting is about compensating for a deep loss or even about sublimating the sex drive. (Whatever!) In the end, however, collectors collect out of passion—an uncontrollable ardor for a particular type of thing in its various forms and permutations.

What fuels this intense, overwhelming emotion? Some might argue that we are programmed to collect. After all, where does a child learn to sort through a pile of rocks and then take home a few "special" ones to store proudly in a box? Perhaps that behavior can be traced to a prehistoric hunter who amassed the best set of arrowheads, which bettered his chances of bringing down some prey for dinner. Or maybe the child just gets satisfaction from mastering her world and making connections among interesting objects.

Now that child has grown into you—the adult collector. Your family and friends might not get it. They think you're nuts as you slog through flea markets on rainy days, only to return home and immediately log on to check your eBay auctions. You detect the eyes of co-workers glazing over as you relate your latest eBay victory. Your mail carrier has made your house a special stop on his route since you bought that sniping software. But you're engaged in a noble crusade, a sport that is more exciting than the Super Bowl, the Triple Crown, the World Series, the Iditarod, and the Iron Man rolled into one. Yours is an individual (although not necessarily solitary) sport requiring guts, stamina, vision, alacrity, and sacrifice. The objective is to amass a significant collection. The rules are complex, arbitrary, and subject to revision at any time. But that's fine because you write them. Play begins with the first acquisition and ends, well, never.

Recently we have seen a boom in collecting and collectors. Although a strong economy has fueled the market, collectors abound in any economy, pursuing their passion despite great obstacles. They might make fewer purchases when times are lean, but they don't stop altogether. In fact, the bottom of a cycle is usually an excellent time to buy, and that's when many collectors go to town.

Ruminating over an auction in 1995 of Rudolf Nureyev's possessions, *New York Times* writer Elizabeth Kaye called collecting a "passion with a subtext, a connection to an identity." Perhaps collecting has gained momentum at the end of the twentieth century because it offers one of the last bastions of individualism. In our increasingly overscheduled, digitized, multimedia world, people feel their choices are becoming limited and their local character homogenized as chain stores and restaurants take over. Every town starts to look the same, every meal tastes like the next. But as a col-

Meet eBay Ambassador David Moser,

SPECIALTY:
Philately

eBay HANDLE: stamphick   AGE: 56

NUMBER OF YEARS COLLECTING STAMPS: Forty-five, since my grandmother gave me a stamp album for my eleventh birthday. I wasn't active for thirty of those years, but availability of material via Internet auctions rekindled my interest.

TO IDENTIFY STAMPS: You need to know about various printing processes, types of paper, cancellation devices, postal rates from different times, and when post offices opened or closed.

PEOPLE'S BIGGEST MISCONCEPTION: That the only participants are stodgy old men with no other life. On second thought, maybe that isn't a misconception.

HOW YOU CAN TELL I'M A COLLECTOR: All around my house there are lots of little envelopes full of stamps waiting to be properly identified and organized.

MY FAVORITE PIECE: A "Century of Progress" sheet of twenty-five imperforate one-cent stamps. The bottom right stamp has been cut out, and I often wonder who or why someone would do that to a fairly valuable souvenir sheet.

STAMPS I'M DYING TO ADD: The 1915 series of Kangaroo and Map stamps from Australia. Not particularly valuable, but difficult for me to find.

BEST BIDDING TIP: Search for material in unusual categories.

IF IT WEREN'T FOR eBay: I'd have to travel eighty miles to the nearest stamp shop or stamp club to sell my extras to finance my collection. I live in a rural area, where people collect more barbed wire than stamps.

MY BEST FIND ON eBay: The stamp chat board, which is frequented by many with expertise in every area of philately. There's no question so obscure that it doesn't get a quick answer, sometimes from world-renowned experts. Lots of camaraderie, too.

lector, you are master of your unique domain. You need not conform to anyone's idea of what's right or cool except your own. Your collection reflects the somebody you are.

Collecting vs. Accumulating

In this world there are collectors and there are accumulators. (In between there are decorators, but that's another story.) To the uninitiated, a gazillion tchotchkes may look like a collection, but a pack rat does not a collector make. Nor are collectors materialistic hoarders who never met an object they didn't love. (At least, not all of them are.) In fact, the occasional tough-love culling is an essential part of upgrading and building a collection.

So how to know when all that stuff you've been accumulating is actually a collection? For starters:

accumulation	collection
Random objects that have no discernible connection other than being owned by the same person.	Objects chosen carefully by design, by an overriding philosophy or aesthetic.
Quantity over quality.	Quality over quantity (although both are important).
Objects chosen to fill shelves.	Shelves built to hold objects.
If these objects could talk, they'd natter on to anyone who'd listen.	Items sing to you.
Eclectic is a word you often use.	Eclectic is a four-letter word to you.
If you like it, it stays.	What you eventually get rid of says as much about you as what you keep.

When Does a Collection Start? When Does It End?

To some people, a collection can't exist until enough items have been brought together to form a pattern. Others say that all it takes is one item. Collecting is as much a state of mind as it is a gathering of goods. Therefore a collection often begins as a nubbin of an idea. Perhaps you've been surfing eBay or roaming the flea market and, out of the thousands of objects, you find yourself inexplicably drawn to teapots. You find yourself stopping to pick up all shapes and sizes and give them the once-over. You think, These are kind of interesting. Now that you're aware of them, they seem to be everywhere. Prices are all over the place as well, and you notice some pieces are marked or signed while others are not. One day on eBay you spot a fine little porcelain number with an art deco motif and a German manufacturer's mark. You bid $35 and get it for $28.

Now if it ends there, be happy and enjoy the teapot. However, if you put your teapot on a shelf and it looks as though it needs some friends, a collection has been born.

How big your teapot collection grows depends on the parameters you set in terms of budget (will you start moonlighting to support your habit?); maker (only deco artisans?); style (one spout or two?); culture (what about those cute Japanese ceremonial iron teapots?); era (only those from the heyday of the British empire?); and so on. Figuring this out takes research and a trained eye. Your investigating might lead you to branch out to teacups and saucers. Will this collection ever be complete? That's up to you. But unless you collect in a category that has a finite number of items, it's likely you're in for the long haul. Welcome to the club.

Kids' Kollections

Given their inquisitiveness and frequently deep—although sometimes fleeting—passions, children are natural collectors. Creating and maintaining a collection builds self-confidence and teaches responsibility, initiative, and value. Typical childhood collections of fossils, model airplanes, or bottles often spark an interest in science, history, and other related subjects. Of course, kids need guidance in selecting items they (you) can afford as you make the rounds together of shows, flea markets, shops, and garage sales. To use eBay, they must wait until they're eighteen. But there are still ways for them to learn about their collecting area through the Internet. For example, www.collectingchannel.com provides background on thousands of areas. Who knows? Maybe that childhood passion will lead to a lucrative profession so your kid can support you in your old age.

It's Your Collection—Be as Weird as You Want

The first law of collecting is, Be yourself. Don't let anyone tell you what's right or wrong. Follow your heart and the rest of the world be damned. Sound like the narcissist's creed? Okay, a little—but only if you apply it out-

Only on eBay

eBaysian collections run the gamut. Some of our favorites:

- Bathing caps
- Ties
- Bubblegum wrappers
- Razor blade banks
- Telephone insulators
- Egg cups
- Rolling pins
- Toothbrush holders
- Old Maid card games
- Blue Chip and S&H stamp books
- Bowling shirts
- Doorstops
- Corkscrews

side the arena of collecting. This is one of the few areas in your life where you get to do whatever you want—as long as it doesn't land you in jail or bankruptcy court. You don't need to explain yourself. Just have fun with it.

The categories on eBay cover a lot of territory (see chapter 3, "The Quest for Amazing Stuff"), but many collectors have found that the fastest way to their heart's desire is through a customized search. That's because they're the inventors of their own specialty. It was only by accident that they discovered other aficionados who shared their interest.

Setting Parameters

Part of collecting is defining the scope of the hunt. Every acquisition has the potential to send you into a new direction or reaffirm that you're on the right track. As fluid as that may seem, most collectors set limits to prevent chaos. Here are some ways to organize your treasures:

Object type: By focusing on one kind of item in all its manifestations, you can create a highly structured set with great depth, breadth, and diversity. Part of the appeal of such collections is discerning patterns within a series of objects, such as several hundred walking sticks or glass marbles or modern first editions.

Theme: These tend to be the most eclectic of collections because they comprise anything that relates to the subject. For example, if you love airplanes, your collection might range from Wright brothers memorabilia to pressed-steel toy planes to commercial airliner swizzle sticks and barf bags—and perhaps a hangar to house all these goodies. The list of possible themes is limited only by your imagination. You can be as broad (Hollywood) or narrow (sterling silver spoons from Niagara Falls) as you like. These collections bring you into contact with a broad spectrum of collectors and dealers, making it all the more difficult to resist expanding the scope.

● **Era:** Limiting your sights to a particular period can make the hunt manageable and save you money. For example, if you're interested in vintage clothes but focus exclusively on flapper dresses from the 1920s, your collection might be stronger and more cohesive than a closetful of dresses "representing" every year since the Taft administration. Another way to go is to collect all kinds of distinctive items from a particular period such as the New Deal, the cold war, the 1960s, and so on.

● **Artist or factory:** Many collections revolve around a single artist or factory, or small groups of artists and factories that produce similar items. By acquiring pieces from a series or by reconstructing a complete line, you're able to develop a keen understanding of the material, its creators, and the manufacturing process.

● **Price:** The less you spend, the more you can buy, so sticking to a price limit is a good move for any collector. However, you'll have more fun if you identify a median price you're willing to pay and keep track of your purchases. For example, you decide that your median price for any item is $30 but then see a stunner for $52. You go for it, but remember that the next purchase needs to be under $18 so you don't blow your median. To win at this game takes discipline—it's easy to delude yourself that you've been "good" if you don't have your

Only on eBay

Are You an eBay Addict?

● You can remember every price you've ever paid in an auction.

● You can also remember every price you wish you'd paid.

● You and your Beanie Babies are homeless.

● You've checked the phone book for an eBayaholic 12-step program.

● You haven't spoken to your sister in a year, but you speak every day in the chat room to a collector in Finland.

● Your idea of a vacation is getting up from the computer and going out for dinner.

● You need a new TV, but you bought a postage meter instead.

● You find yourself waiting to buy groceries until five minutes before the supermarket closes so you can snipe at the checkout counter.

checkbook register or other record to refer to (see chapter 14: "Out in the Field").

Creating a structure can make a collection more meaningful. The discriminating collector might have to wait longer between acquisitions, but each addition becomes all the sweeter.

Getting Picky: Building and Upgrading

Many times a collection shifts directions or takes on new meaning as you pass milestones. Once a collection reaches twenty, fifty, or one hundred items, take a breather and review. Does every piece belong? How does your collection look after you put aside the bottom 20 percent? You might be surprised to find that you don't miss any of the items and that, in fact, the overall effect is not dissimilar to that of your aunt Fanny after she shed 20 percent of her poundage at Weight Watchers. Slimming down gives you a new outlook on life. Perhaps this is the time to upgrade—sell a few lesser pieces and use the proceeds to buy better ones.

All kinds of events make a collector take stock, but a new "best" piece— one that raises the level of the collection—prompts you to reevaluate. How does it compare to the others? Is it among its peers, or does this diva need to break out of the chorus? Your taste may also change as you gain experience and develop a greater understanding of quality. One of the joys of collecting is continually refining your taste and sharpening your eye. For example, a collector of simple landscape paintings might be attracted initially by their familiarity and accessibility. As he studies them, he develops a keener understanding of composition and technique. Eventually his early acquisitions seem cloying and clichéd as he gravitates to genre and abstract work. It's not that the new paintings are better. But he appreciates them in a way he never had or could before. Pretty soon the new work is crowding out the old-timers on his walls.

Over time, serious collectors develop instincts that help them see qualities in objects others do not. Because of their intense focus and boundless passion for what they collect, advanced collectors can become more knowledgeable than dealers and even auction houses. They translate this knowledge into an endless pursuit for the best items they can find.

Scanning one eBay listing after another to deduce a formula for the setting of prices is like trying to predict the weather by sticking your head out the window. You can tell it's sunny and warm

CHAPTER 11

the mystery of value

yet have no inkling a hurricane is on the way. Why do some items command high reserves while similar ones are lucky to get a single niggling bid? When bidders go into a frenzy over a seemingly mundane object, are they getting swept away in a freak phenomenon or do they know something you don't? How do you know what something is worth?

In an open trading environment like eBay, an object's worth is what someone is willing to pay. But just because something costs a lot doesn't mean it's valuable. Value is derived using a more complex set of criteria. For example, you have inherited your grandmother's wedding ring. She died before you were old enough to remember her, and it's the sole possession of hers that's made it into your hands. An appraiser might estimate its worth at $100; one would guess that it's infinitely more valuable to you for sentimental reasons. Collectors can use the same combination of tangible and intangible criteria to determine the value of an object before translating the amount into a bid.

Whether you're buying or selling on eBay, your success depends largely on your ability to judge value. In this chapter we show you some ways to determine the worth of an object.

Separated at Birth: No Two Collectibles Are Exactly Alike

One of the most exciting aspects of collecting is figuring out the quality and value of items. This depends on your ability to sort out the universe, a task made all the more challenging by the fact that seemingly identical items are rarely the spittin' image of one another. For example, let's consider a commonly collected product such as Roseville Pottery. The factory churned out line after line with various shapes and decorations. One might assume that every jardiniere in the pine cone pattern would be exactly alike. No such luck. For reasons such as fluctuating firing temperatures and glaze consistency, variations are widespread. While some pieces approach perfection—and are thus more valuable—just as many others are proof that factories have bad days. Serious collectors can tell the difference. These nuances are a critical component in every area of collecting. Of course, some flaws, like misprints in stamps, have the opposite effect and increase value. But that's one of the joys of collecting: the rules are almost never hard and fast.

Other factors that have little to do with quality can also affect value. For example, a painting might be a masterpiece but so huge that it can be installed only with the aid of a crane. Or it might be so tiny—say, a one-by-three-inch thumbnail sketch—that it generates little interest by serious collectors. In both cases the pieces are practically novelties and might never realize prices for comparable yet sofa-size paintings by the artist.

Another curious variable in value is region. Differences in taste and culture often make something that is valuable in one area of the country less so in another. Perhaps that will change, however, as eBay and the global marketplace expands.

With all this talk about collecting, you might wonder, What is the difference between an antique and a collectible? According to *Webster's* dictionary, an antique is a "relic or object of ancient times or of earlier time than the present, or a work of art, piece of furniture, or decorative object made at an earlier period and according to various customs laws at least 100 years old." A collectible, curiously enough, is "an object that is collected by fanciers; *esp:* one other than such traditionally collectible items as art, stamps, coins, and antiques." An item doesn't automatically increase in value the day it turns one hundred. Great examples of furniture from the 1950s routinely command higher prices than do some pieces from the nineteenth century. In fact, the word *antique* has come to be used rather loosely, although there are strict laws about the export of antiques and antiquities—the *really* old stuff—in many countries trying to preserve their heritage. Many dealers and sellers call anything they consider old "antique" and the rest "collectibles" (anything worth collecting) or "vintage collectibles" (to describe items old, but not really old). In both cases factors such as quality and condition affect value more than age does.

Eight Is Enough:
The Collectibles Checklist

There's no cartel establishing prices for collecting categories. After a while people who share the same passion recognize the nuances that make one piece hotter than another, and sellers set prices based on this conventional wisdom. Miles of books might be devoted to dissecting the fine points of a given antique or collectible—and we encourage you to consult them all—but you can also assess the value of any given piece by applying the following eight criteria.

Demand

It's Economics 101. The stronger the demand and the lower the supply, the higher the price. For example, furniture by Gustave Stickley is highly prized these days—but the number of original pieces in the world is finite. With a resurging interest in the Arts and Crafts movement, an increasing number of collectors are competing for an ever-shrinking pool of available items. His designs are so popular that they're now being reproduced, but those don't command as much money as the originals. However, should someone discover a warehouse or two full of old Stickley furniture that nobody knew about and then flood the market with them, prices might dip.

Rarity/Supply

If the demand is there, an item that's unique or in short supply might sell for more than one that's ubiquitous. But rarity alone does not give inherent value. A one-of-a-kind item is worthless if nobody's interested in it. For something to be collectible, there has to be enough of it around—what we call *inventory*—in decent condition to supply a budding trove or two.

Only on eBay

A pickle jar might seem the most prosaic of objects, but if it's the right pickle jar, it's a masterpiece to a collector—and worth considerably more than that bottle of baby dills in the fridge. In 1999 Richard Rushton-Clem of Lewisburg, Pennsylvania, spied an old pickle jar for $3 at a tag sale. He left the embossed amber jar on his windowsill for eight months before asking an antiques mall to sell it on eBay. The "early blown glass cathedral bottle" started at $9.99 and escalated quickly. Although he suspected it was special, Richard had no idea the eleven-inch jar, made in Willington, Connecticut, in about 1850, is one of the rarest of its kind—only five are known to exist. However, several collectors knew, and the fact that the jar was in perfect condition sent the bidding into high gear. The winner, a Pennsylvania doctor with a substantial bottle collection, prevailed over four other bidders (including someone with the user ID "Pickleman") and took it home for $44,100.

By the same token, items that are in plentiful supply usually have trouble attracting competitive bidders on eBay or stable price levels. That's good news for beginning collectors or consumers who just need a reasonably priced set of andirons or computer modem. But if you're a seller who snagged twenty-five identical signed photographs of Carol Burnett at the yard sale of her Burbank fan club president, you might want to pace yourself and not dump them onto the market all at once. Look up current and recent auctions of similar items; the more there are, the longer you might want to wait until the demand grows again.

Beanie Babies are one collectible that has refined the law of supply and demand by intentionally limiting the amount on the market. As soon as a new crop rolls off the factory floor, people are clamoring to get their hands on one, knowing that the (retail) supply will soon run out. Even when those Beanies show up on eBay, collectors know they're competing for a limited number. In fact, that's part of the appeal—being one of the relatively few in the world who own Spike, Princess, or Bongo.

Quality

The way a particular piece is made—the materials, technique, craftsmanship, and detail—all affect value. If you collect handmade objects such as glass, pottery, or art jewelry, you know that two supposedly identical pieces can have substantial differences. For example, you love the glass of world-renowned Finnish designer Kaj Franck. You know that while the factory made many copies of his designs, each piece was mouth blown and subject to variations, so some pieces are better than others. Your trained eye tells you when the color is right, the symmetry is there, and the technique is flawlessly executed. These factors constitute quality, and the higher the quality, the more the piece is worth.

Condition

No matter how high the quality, an item can be worth significantly less if it's in bad shape. Condition is about beating the odds. The more an object looks as if it's been sealed in a time capsule since it was made, the more it's worth. In fact, condition is the most significant factor affecting value.

Toys are a great example. How many kids do you know who leave a new toy in its box and stick it on a shelf for posterity? The typical MO is to rip off the packaging and proceed to bang, throw, kick, smash, chew, tear, spindle, and mutilate the toy beyond recognition—all in the name of innocent fun, of course. But just think of all those Barbies whose hair you butchered, the toy

Meet eBay Ambassador Jill Hirsch

SPECIALTY:
Beanie Babies and Plush Bears

eBay HANDLE: Jillze1@aol.com   AGE: 34

MY FIRST BEANIE BABY: Coral, the tie-dyed fish.

WHAT'S COOL ABOUT BEANIES: Their huge success and the variety of collectors, including men and women from kids to grandparents.

BIGGEST CHALLENGE: Getting the brand-new ones.

WHAT YOU NEED TO KNOW: How to tell the difference between real and fake and what is retired, common, and hard to find.

QUESTION I'M ASKED MOST: Why?

PEOPLE'S BIGGEST MISCONCEPTION: That it's a stupid toy.

WHAT MY COLLECTION SAYS ABOUT ME: I love bears.

MY FAVORITE BEANIE: Changes all the time. Right now it's my Erin and Cranberry Teddy Beanie Buddies (the larger version).

I'M DYING TO ADD: Germania, the exclusive German bear.

ADVICE TO NEW COLLECTORS: Start easy and try not to pay too much, especially for current pieces.

MY BEST BEANIE BUYS: Garcia, Coral, and Chops for $90 total. Their value now: approximately $385 total.

BECAUSE OF eBay: I've met great people by buying and selling things I never would have been able to otherwise—and made a *lot* of money.

MY BEST eBay TRANSACTION: The guy who trusted me so much that he shipped the item the day before I sent payment.

Mint to Be

Some long-standing communities of collectors have established grading systems and a common language to describe condition and its impact on value. Stamps are a good example where grades—"superb," "extra fine," "very fine," "fine to very fine" and "average"—refer to a stamp's centering and other conditions. "Superb" means the stamp is exactly centered on the paper and the opposite margins are equal and generous. Other factors used to clarify a stamp's history and provenance include the condition of the gum—which has its own grading system—and definitions of use such as "mint," "unused," or "used." These terms are not to be taken lightly. Before announcing that a collectible is in mint condition, check to make sure it really fits the universally accepted definition.

soldiers you decapitated, the Spirograph discs you used as mud pie plates. If you had them now in all their spanking newness, you'd be rich! Okay, if not rich, then very, very happy, because virgin vintage toys are highly sought after. Toys were made to be played with, so every time a pristine one surfaces in its original box or wrapper, it's a small miracle that collectors are happy to pay for.

The same goes for any other category on eBay: the less used something is, the higher the price. Collectors are darn picky. Take people who go for modern first-edition books. If a tome isn't in perfect condition (which means not even price clipped), it's not worthy of consideration. Why would only perfect copies be valuable? Because of their relatively recent vintage, modern books are accessible enough to render all imperfect copies worthless except as used books for reading.

A major condition bugaboo involves restoration and refinishing. Part of what makes some things valuable is their patina—the surface finish achieved through age. Attempting to "improve" such a surface can be a huge mistake (see page 188, "Consult Before You Clean"). In the case of furniture, it's better to have the original finish in not-so-great condition than the finest refinishing money can buy. Removing that "tacky" fake mahogany paint from a maple Queen Anne highboy can drive down the value by 40 percent or more.

Historical Significance

A relationship to a historical event or famous person can increase the value of an object considerably. The connection, however, must be provable. You can't just take someone's word that a fine piece of luggage stamped FDR was used by Franklin Delano Roosevelt and not Francis Deborah Ritter (whoever she may be). Put on your detective's hat and dig for real evidence. Among the clues to look for:

- **Engraved marks:** A plaque with a name or date commemorating some event or honor or an inscription to someone (of course, this can be faked but *look* real).

- **Lines of inheritance:** Maybe FDR bequeathed his alligator trunk to a family member.

- **Photo documentation:** A picture that shows the luggage by FDR's side as he boarded a train for Warm Springs, Georgia, would be pretty convincing.

- **Receipts:** Showing where the piece was originally made or bought; also bills of lading that prove, for example, that the piece was docketed on an ocean liner.

- **Books and magazines:** References and detailed accounts that place the object at a particular place or time.

To put these bits and pieces into perspective, seek out the advice of experts at historical societies, collectors' clubs, appraisers, and the eBay chat rooms.

Provenance

Any time you can trace an item's lineage and history of ownership—known as *provenance*—you increase its value. Just knowing where an item has been during its existence is relevant. And if you can prove its origin (for example, that it was purchased directly from an artist) or that someone famous owned it, you add to the item's mystique and proof of authenticity.

As eBay proves every day, people will collect anything. Your nice but otherwise unremarkable ceramic ashtray might attract its share of bidders. But if you can prove it was once owned by a celebrity, a megacelebrity, a dead celebrity, or—the big kahuna—a dead megacelebrity, you're likely to see an extra zero or two on the final bid amount. The hysteria surrounding the auctions of items from the estates of Jacqueline Kennedy Onassis and Princess Diana, among others, has helped increase the cachet of celebrity provenance. Whether that value will appreciate over the years remains to be seen. It all depends on whether anyone remembers or cares about these people in twenty, fifty, or one hundred years.

Consult Before You Clean

A collector we'll call Nouveau Nell had the stars in her favor the day she snagged an item listed on eBay as "1933 Tree Lamp—TIFANNIES!!!" for $250. Besides committing an egregious misspelling, which no doubt threw many Tiffany hunters off the trail, the seller clearly didn't know much about the lamp. When it arrived, Nell inspected the base with a magnifying glass and discovered the mark "HANDEL 33." Aha! This was a valuable lamp by the Handel Company Inc., a Tiffany competitor that went out of business in 1928. (The "33" probably referred to a production number.) The shade—copper-soldered stained glass— was slightly damaged, but she figured the base would clean up well. She went to work, scouring away a stubborn layer of greenish brown film. A few hours later the bronze gleamed like new. Feeling proud—and with visions of adding a few zeros to her investment—she took the lamp to a dealer for an appraisal. "What a beautiful lamp," the dealer said, and then shook his head. "It's a shame, however, that someone cleaned off the original patina. No collector would pay serious money for this piece—original condition is everything." Nell's lamp, which could have been worth thousands of dollars, was now worth only hundreds.

The lesson: Don't meddle with the metal (or any other material) before distinguishing plain old dirt from decades-old patina. That greenish cast on metal might have been intentional, as designers often patinated new pieces to make them look old. In any case, collectors prize *original* condition—even if it means a "dull and dirty" finish. The same goes for wood furniture: No matter how beautiful a piece looks after you've cleaned off that old varnish or paint, it's always worth more in its natural, if slightly decrepit, state. Before wasting your elbow grease, consult an expert or conservator.

Design/Attribution

In decorative and fine arts or manufactured goods, the maker is a significant factor in value. To determine how significant, you need to know the name of the person or company that produced the item and, more important, understand where the piece fits into that maker's total output.

Here's where specific knowledge about the artist or company is important. In the decorative arts, for example, it's not uncommon for a designer to create both mass-produced pieces (also referred to as *production pieces*) and individual or unique ones. When the designer is engaged in several lines like this, the individual pieces are usually of greater value. However, even production pieces might be done in a limited number or involve a complicated technique, adding to their value.

Items outside an artist's normal oeuvre, such as drawings by a sculptor, may be less valuable, but exceptions exist. For example, although Picasso was primarily a painter and his most valuable works are in that medium, he also produced ceramics and glass in sufficient quantities to create a demand by collectors for works in these media.

You can't always determine the value of a piece based on a comparable version—or, more accurately, what you think is comparable. Let's go back to the pickle jar (see "Only on eBay", page 183). Enough publicity surrounded that sale to create a mythology about the value of pickle jars. How many of us ever gave pickle jars a second thought until we learned that some are worth five figures? Undoubtedly many owners began thinking their perfectly average pickle jars were worth more than they had been the day before. After all, don't they look an awful lot like that Lotto-ticket-of-a-jar that was in the news? Sadly, that's not enough. Value is determined by your understanding the differences between items, not from assuming generalized similarities.

Material

Great artists take the most common materials—glass, clay, stone—and give them tremendous value by molding them into objects of artistic expression. Some objects, on the other hand, have intrinsic value because they comprise precious metals, stones, fabrics, or woods. Such items are sometimes subject to price swings when the markets go into motion. For example, if the scrap value of silver rises, all items made of silver rise proportionately.

Take two 14-karat gold rings, one by Tiffany and the other by an unknown, mediocre metalsmith. If you melted down both rings, they'd be of equal value per ounce—which only goes to show that without the other seven components of value such as design, condition, and so on, an object is only as valuable as its raw parts.

Distinguishing Price from Value

Market factors can affect price, so when something is hot, prices rise quickly. To a serious collector of Civil War items, for example, an infantryman's letters home will always have tremendous value, even though prices may rise or fall. Smart collectors buy objects with inherent and, preferably, unrealized value. That way, should the market go down (and it always does—

Car Collecting Caveats

In a few areas, such as antique cars, restoration—depending on the quality of the job—is acceptable and doesn't affect value. However, if you happen to find a "shiny like new" 1938 Buick with only ten thousand miles on it in your grandfather's barn, it will always be worth more than a restored version. To a collector's ears, the words *all original* sound like angels singing, "Hallelujah!" This field also adheres to an accelerated time line in describing the age of automobiles. A vintage car is twenty years old, but one that's just five years older is an antique.

see "The Price Cycle" in this chapter), the owner knows that the items will never become worthless.

Keeping Tabs on Prices

When shopping, don't hesitate to ask dealers the price of any item, especially if it's like one you already own. Taking into account condition and other factors, you can use this information as a rough indicator of the market. We say rough, because there's always a chance the dealer is utterly clueless and pulling prices out of the ether. More reliable price benchmarks can be found in the following:

- **Auction catalogs:** Over the last several years catalogs from past sales at large houses have become available at large antiques shows and on eBay. When possible, get catalogs with the "prices realized" list that is usually sent out after the sale. This shows the difference between the experts' estimate and the actual price, which can be substantial in either direction.

- **Completed eBay auctions:** You can easily do a search of auctions held on eBay in the past thirty days for any kind of item. Check these results regularly as a primary source of market information.

- **Collectors' clubs and newsletters:** Conventions are excellent places to gauge prices. Although some newsletters might track significant sales, most price info appears in advertisements and classifieds.

- **Your own market survey:** Cruise the markets and check prices everywhere you go.

Markups and Margins

Pricing can seem arbitrary, and at times it is. You might walk the floor of a large antiques show and find two items that appear the same and yet bear different price tags, one $65 and the other $300. Does this make the lower-priced version the bargain of a lifetime? Or is the expensive dealer over-shooting the market? The truth probably lies somewhere in between. Keep in mind that there is no true wholesale market for collectibles as exists for other commodities such as food, clothes, or computers. Wholesale becomes what the seller paid for it. The dealer at $65 probably found the piece for $30. The dealer who brashly priced the item at $300 most likely paid around $150. Neither had a clue what it was really worth.

When you see an item at a show similar to one you own for a lot more than you paid, don't start salivating. Take a deep breath and remind yourself that it's still sitting in that dealer's booth; no one has validated that price by paying it. You can ask any price for any item. Whether you get it or not is a different story.

There might be people in this world who love paying full retail price but we don't know them. All the collectors we know are born bargain sniffers: a dollar saved is a dollar pumped back into their precious collecting fund. So how do sellers set their prices? Some actually pull them out of thin air. This can work both for you and against you. In general, though, dealers rely on the following guidelines:

- **Precedent:** They've sold similar items in the past for the same price.

- **Strong client base:** They know their buyers and who's willing to pay slightly higher prices to ensure authenticity.

- **Knowledge:** They're experts, or think they are, in a given field and establish prices based on that real or alleged expertise.

- **Straight percentage:** Some dealers simply double or triple the amount they paid for an item. If they got a great deal, you benefit as well, despite the markup.

- **Fantasyland:** The seller affixes an outrageous multidigit price tag based on wild speculation or a misunderstanding of the facts. Caution: Don't don your Good Samaritan cap and try to set such people straight. They likely paid too much in the first place based on their own misguided perceptions. If you're at a show, wait until you're out of hearing to break into hysterical laughter. These kinds of encounters make great fodder for your favorite eBay chat room.

This diversity in the pricing of items is in reality a boon to the collector. It creates a wide-open marketplace that increases the likelihood of your finding amazing stuff at the price you're willing to pay—or less.

Trading on People's Mistakes

It's a sad but true statement, but most successful collectors build their collections on other people's mistakes. They know their stuff, so when they see an object that's incorrectly attributed, priced, overlooked, or listed in the wrong eBay category, they swoop in and snatch it up. That doesn't mean you have to go for the jugular every time. Neither does it mean you should gloat (it's not becoming). But don't feel guilty, either. You deserve to score every once in a while.

The Price Cycle

From the time she was a child in the 1950s, a foresighted friend quietly amassed a collection of toys from that era. Her most prized possession: a Mr. Potato Head from 1952, when he had a real potato as a head and was the first toy advertised on television. Few people seemed to share this passion, which was fine with her because it meant more selection, steady prices, and frequent bargains. Then came *Toy Story*, and seemingly overnight she found herself in a hot market filled with nostalgic baby boomers clamoring for the same postwar toys. Prices began hitting scary levels (at least compared with the garage sale scores she was used to). She was caught in a phenomenon of the antiques and collectibles market: a feeding frenzy. Various events and turning points in popular culture and history can move a market to such levels of hysteria:

- A blockbuster movie or the rerelease of an old movie (think *Titanic*, *Star Wars*, *Gone With the Wind*).

- The death of a beloved person or the birthday of a dead beloved person (think Elvis, Diana, Ol' Blue Eyes).

- A significant anniversary of a historic event (think Pearl Harbor, Woodstock, first man on the moon).

- An article or feature about an area of collecting on TV or in a major newspaper, especially if it reveals that a celebrity or other well-known arbiter of taste is interested in that area (think Demi Moore and her doll collection in *People*).

⬤ A major museum exhibit reexamining the work of a particular designer, era, or school (think the 1999 Charles and Ray Eames show at the Cooper-Hewitt National Design Museum).

⬤ A zeitgeist moment—the simultaneous realization by a group of unrelated people that something is worth collecting, which then escalates their buying in that area, prompting dealers to raise prices (think baby boomers and *Dick Van Dyke Show*–era furniture).

When a fever breaks out, proceed with caution. If you're a longtime collector and your area gets discovered, this may be the time to cash in and move on to new pastures—that is, if you can bear to part with your precious babies. At least consider selling some of your lower-end items. Your reject could be the centerpiece of another collection.

Frenzies in hot collecting areas have the unwanted affect of raising prices across the board regardless of the true value or quality of any individual piece. Everybody tries to get in on the action. Dealers snap up any piece they can in the hopes of making a killing. Consequently collectors who haven't done their homework pay extreme prices for mediocre objects. In a worst-case scenario, fakes come onto the market and many unsuspecting people get burned.

When prices get too astronomical and the flow of better pieces dries up, serious collectors drop out. Eventually the market starts to fall and dealers get stuck with items they've bought at a premium. It may be several years before the market bubbles up again.

This cycle happens over and over in the collectibles marketplace. How many of us are kicking ourselves for throwing away the baseball cards we had as kids? "If I'd only known, I could've retired young!" you say. Savvy collectors *do* know. You don't have to be a human Ouija board to anticipate trends and revivals. Just think about what's been popular in the past, what's enjoying a vogue now, and what's been underappreciated in between. Most of all, develop an eye for quality. Nostalgia is a potent commodity, and at the millennium people, especially boomers, are buying back their past at an astounding rate.

Where Passion Meets Price: Collecting as an Investment

The conventional wisdom about collecting is that you should buy things because you love them, not because they're a good investment. You often hear this from dealers who are trying to sell you something expensive. Do they say this because they care about your personal happiness? Not exactly. Chances are, they know that their price is already the top of the market and the piece isn't likely to appreciate much in the near future. They also know that whereas "investment" buyers look for undervalued pieces that will increase in value—and are therefore harder sells—passionate collectors are likely to fork over big bucks because their emotions are calling the shots. So when you hear a dealer say, "You should buy it only if you really love it," understand that it's a test. If you walk away, they know you're looking for value for your money. If you continue to stand there swooning, they know they've got a live one.

Of course, for dealers to pooh-pooh buying as an investment is hypocritical. After all, do they buy pieces for their health? An axiom of the antiques and collectibles business is that desirable objects escalate in value over time. Unless you have unlimited funds, you should be concerned about what your collection's worth in the long run. Should the day come when you want (or have to) liquidate, wouldn't it be nice to get more out of it than you put in?

Building a valuable collection is not a get-rich-quick scheme. Most items appreciate slowly, yet you can't count on a fixed rate of return, as in a savings account or certificate of deposit. Only in rare cases does a confluence of events send prices into the stratosphere overnight. When a fad or frenzy does hit, the evidence is usually anecdotal. There's no Dow Jones Industrial Average by which to gauge values on a daily basis. Auctions and eBay are the closest things to market barometers.

But as in the stock market, your goal is to buy undervalued items whose value appreciates over time. As you build your collection portfolio, look for individual pieces that are not only intrinsically valuable, but also add value to your collection as a whole. But don't put all your financial eggs into the antiques and collectibles basket. You run the risk of making purchases based on their investment value, not on their value to your collection. You also tend to rationalize every purchase because it's an investment. However, a collection won't necessarily see Junior through college or earn you an early retirement. Smart and successful investors diversify and put their money in a variety of financial markets.

In general, collectors should seek out items with prices that seem reasonable in relationship to all the factors that contribute to value. And they should buy things they're prepared to live with for a long time.

Here are some ideas about collecting as an investment:

● **Be ahead of the curve:** Anticipate items whose time
has yet to come. This takes instinct, research, and a lot of attic space.
Judging from the way items that were once ubiquitous and then passé
have been rediscovered decades later, you can acknowledge how
today's commonplace goods might be tomorrow's treasures. For example, most kids in the 1960s probably never gave a second thought to
discarding their copies of *Mad* magazine after reading them. After all,
an issue cost only two bits and a new one would always be published
in a month. But for the few devotees who stuck them in a trunk for a
couple of decades, those mags might bring a tidy sum today if they're
in pristine condition. Think of it as the Noah's Ark syndrome: everyone
might think you're nuts to be squirreling away those Michael Graves
teapots (unused, in the box) from Target, but a future generation might
look on them wistfully as icons of their lost childhood and thus trade
them with zeal on eBay.

● **Buy the best quality you can afford:**
Objects that were valuable to begin with tend to be more valuable as
time goes by. For example, William Morris's Sussex chairs were dear
when they were made, owing to their craftsmanship and influential
design. Small market murmurs notwithstanding, they've been going up
in value ever since.

● **Understand the twenty-year cycle:**
Nostalgia is generational. It's hard to wax nostalgic about days gone by
unless they were *your* days. In the 1980s people looked back to the
1960s; in the 1990s we've seen a return to objects and items from the
1970s and 1950s. By the middle of the first decade of the twenty-first
century, the 1980s will probably be hot again. This time frame also
applies to art. If an item can transcend the period in which it was made
and be desirable twenty years later, it has a good chance of growing
increasingly valuable as years go by.

● **Follow the life cycle:** To put it bluntly, every time
someone dies, new stuff replenishes the market. People build households throughout their lives, and despite their best attempts to purge
clutter, they accumulate more things than they know what to do with.
No matter how much they post on eBay, people don't unload all their
possessions at once. They wouldn't even if they wanted to, because

who knows when Uncle Bertie will come to dinner and expect to see that gravy boat he gave them as a wedding present but which they never appreciated (especially after they became vegetarians). People eventually pass from this earth, but their worldly goods stay—and find new owners through wills, garage sales, estate sales, auctions, charity, and so on. That includes Bertie's gravy boat (which turns out to be a classic piece by Danish silversmith Georg Jensen and worth a pretty penny).

● **Buy as close to wholesale prices as possible:** Although, as stated earlier, there is no traditional wholesale market in the antiques and collectibles world, you can still buy at wholesale-like prices. Know the going "retail" prices and hunt for comparable pieces lower on the food chain—that is, 50 percent (or less) of the normal asking price or auction estimate. To win at this game requires patience and a sharp eye. Even if prices don't escalate, if you ever need to sell you are likely to get your money back.

Ready, "Set," Go: Collectors' Series

Whereas many collectibles are items that were once used for everyday life, others are created for the sole purpose of being collected. These include collector plates, dolls, figurines, Christmas-related items, die-cast toys, and plush animals. In 1998 the market for these kinds of collectibles was over $10 billion.

While collecting annual plates or Christmas ornaments might bring personal satisfaction, be aware of the market. You're buying at the prevailing retail price, so when you go to sell it's unlikely that any prospective buyer will pay more than 50 percent of the original purchase price. Also, producers create enough of each collectible to meet anticipated demand. It's just as easy to overestimate demand and create way too many as it is to underestimate and not produce enough.

This is not to say that some of these things don't eventually increase substantially in value. Beanie Babies are certainly a testament to the potential. Remember that value is complex and not based on one criterion. If limited editions or annual series is where your passion lies, you might try building an after-the-party collection, where you buy a year or two after issue. You might be able to find items at less expensive or even closeout prices.

How Limited Is a Limited Edition?

The National Association of Limited Edition Dealers along with the Collectibles and Platemakers Guild have adopted the following definitions for limited editions:

- **Original:** One of a kind created by the artist.

- **Edition limited by number:** A reproduction of an original, the edition limited by a number preannounced at the time the collectible is announced. Each piece may, or may not, be numbered.

- **Edition limited by time:** A reproduction of an original, the edition is limited by time—in other words, yearly or annual edition, subscription, or commission with preannounced deadline date for production and no preannounced number limit for the edition.

- **Edition limited by firing days:** A reproduction of an original limited by a number of announced firing days.

- **Open edition:** A reproduction of an original with no limit on time of production or the number of pieces produced and no announcement of edition size.

- **Sold out or closed:** No longer available from the producer. (Sold out applies to both numbered-limited and time-limited editions.)

- **Retired:** No longer available from the producer, and none of the pieces will ever be produced again.

- **Suspended:** Not available from the producer—production suspended.

Collectors can always spot each other on eBay. They're the sellers who wax poetic about the fine points of a piece, eagerly imparting historical footnotes to validate its authenticity: "Cracker Jack acquired the Checkers Company (of Shotwell Mfg.) in the twenties. . . ." They're the bidders who beg for more details, often flummoxing hapless sellers who know little about their wares: "Is the vase's pontil polished or rough?" And they're the category surfers who can't help themselves from correcting a fallacious statement in a listing: "FYI—this comb patented 1903 can't be Bakelite because thermosetting plastic resins weren't *invented* until 1909. Perhaps it's celluloid, which was developed in 1869. . . ."

CHAPTER 12

becoming an expert

The greater your expertise, the more fun you have as a collector. eBay offers many ways for people to grow not just their collections, but also their knowledge base. You can add to the dialogue by soaking up everything out there about your area. That means immersing yourself as if you were learning a foreign language. In this chapter we provide numerous ways for you to take the plunge.

Mastering the Details

Ever notice the way perfectly low-key, even reticent, people metamorphose into deliriously happy chatterboxes the second you ask them about their collections? It's as if you pressed a button marked "everything you ever wanted to know and more," for suddenly the person goes into resident-expert mode. Details and asides—an item's history, date of manufacture, artistic significance, where and when it was purchased—all flow from the collector's lips into the ears of anyone with enough patience (or little choice but) to listen. As it turns out, this stuff is usually pretty interesting, because collections are about not just the objects themselves, but also what they represent. And that has a lot to do with people like you and what makes you tick.

One of the most wonderful aspects of collecting is the journey. As beautiful or unusual as an object may be, the more you know about it, the more fascinating it becomes. Learning about its origins, its creator, how it was made, and what it was used for can take you all over the globe and into pockets of history and culture you never dreamed possible. As you put the puzzle together, you discover amazing connections and levels of meaning. Hey, you think, this stuff is really cool! No wonder you can't wait to blab about it to anyone who expresses a flicker of interest.

Getting to the point where you can blab intelligently takes time. No collector starts out an expert, and no expert knows everything about an area. Learning is a lifetime occupation—thank goodness. Expertise comes from being immersed in the field and doing research of all kinds. The payoff: mastery of the market—the self-confidence to sort through thousands of objects and select only those that matter—resulting in collections that are interesting and valuable because they're well documented and researched. If luck is opportunity colliding with preparation, you make your own luck as a collector. The passion to collect comes from somewhere deep inside; the skills of a great collector are learned.

Training Your Eye—and Ear, Nose, and Fingers

Getting into top form as a collector is like building a set of muscles. If you've been a couch potato and then wake up one morning, buy a shiny new mountain bike, and ride eighty-two miles that day, you'd be lucky to ever walk again. However, if you ride a couple of miles the first few outings and increase your distance a little each time, toning up seems painless. The same goes for ramping up a collection. You can't learn everything in one stroll through an antiques or collectibles show. You need to set a goal and work up to it.

You also need to engage and train all your senses. You probably already practice many of the following exercises without even thinking about it. Making them second nature is what distinguishes the amateurs from the pros—and the collectors from the accumulators.

● **Touch test:** Pick things up (use your judgment here if you collect cars or stone statuary) and run your hands over them. Are they smooth, rough, silky, cold, greasy? What's the weight? Close your eyes and lock in that feeling. Practice this technique in the field and at home with your own pieces.

● **Examine inside and out:** Remember the adage "The back tells more than the front" as you scrutinize objects for artist's signatures, design details, factory stamps, and other clues to authenticity. Sometimes printing and marks are tiny, so keep a magnifying glass handy. Compare these clues with those in books or on clearly identified pieces so you can spot flaws and bogus marks as well.

● **Compare objects side by side:** Line up several items and note their differences and similarities in terms of form, size, technique, color, and materials. Do they bear any telltale signs of a particular manufacturer? How else are they related, at least in your mind? You might be surprised to discern themes.

● **Look for fakes:** If you collect in an area where fakes or reproductions are prevalent or new versions of standard designs are still in production, you can learn from those as well. What's different? What are the dead giveaways? Develop a list of criteria; one or two obvious clues might not tell the whole story. For example, in an area such as furniture, where styles come and go, distinguishing between an eighteenth-century original and a nineteenth-century reproduction can be tricky.

● **Sort and re-sort:** Group your collection according to size, shape, color, period, maker, and other variables to help you understand how they relate to each other. Are some colors better than others? Are particular shades within, say, the red group more vibrant or consistent? Is one form superior to another? What pieces don't you have that would complement these objects?

● **Spot from a distance:** When at an antiques or collectibles show or flea market, see from how far away you can tell if an object is the real deal. The more you know, the more you can trust your instincts. You soon find yourself zeroing in on objects that feel "right" even though you've never seen them before. That's your research paying off.

● **Rate objects:** On a scale of 1 to 10, evaluate objects in your collection or for sale based on shape, decoration, technique, color, and condition, or criteria you create. You might notice that some items rate high in all categories while others have only a couple of points going for them. Ask other collectors and dealers their criteria for greatness. Although condition is usually the most important criterion, keep other quality points in perspective. Just because you've never seen a blue piece before doesn't mean it's rare or good. The best additions to your collection are those that rate high on your entire checklist.

● **Ask questions:** Engage knowledgeable collectors in conversation about the field. Many are happy to share their mastery of the details. Others, however, consider their knowledge proprietary information and don't appreciate being pumped for tips. Respect that they've invested countless hours acquiring their expertise. You might even be flattered that they regard you as competition. Dealers, on the other hand, are often forthcoming with information, including sources, if they detect an opportunity to make a sale.

● **Create a top ten list:** Go through your favorite book on your area of collecting and pick the ten pieces of your dreams. Why those? Can you define their appeal? Look for those characteristics in pieces you buy.

● **Go to museums:** Seek out museums with collections like yours or with related items. For example, if you collect axes, you might learn about medieval models by viewing suits of armor at a major museum or by checking out an exhibit at a historical society or small museum specializing in farming or timber. You might be pleasantly surprised to discover that your collection outclasses the museum's in terms of quality, scope, or display.

● **Stay open to change:** Why does a piece that once delighted now bore? Why have you relegated the former centerpiece of your collection to the closet? As you work to become more knowledgeable, your taste grows more sophisticated. That doesn't mean you're turning into a snob. But often, early acquisitions constitute the most accessible styles while later additions reflect a deeper understanding of the field—and a more profound insight into your collecting psyche.

● **Show it off:** Display your objects not only out of pride, but also to learn. After a while you're bound to notice new aspects and make new connections among objects. Rearranging items from time to time further enables you to see things in a new light.

● **Have fun:** If all this becomes a chore, you've gone too far. Mastering your collection is a self-indulgent, personal growth experience, so enjoy it!

Immersing Yourself in the Market

The best source of information is the marketplace: flea markets, antiques and collectibles shows, auction previews, live auctions, and, of course, eBay. All these venues offer countless items for your examination and the opportunity to trade war stories with your doppelgängers—committed collectors (or perhaps collectors who should *be* committed).

In the course of perusing these places, you naturally find items you want but can't afford. They can still teach you a lot. Inspect them to figure out why they command such prices. Ask sellers to tell you what they know. Before long you'll find you know more than most of them—and you'll be able to capitalize on their ignorance by purchasing items they've naively underpriced.

Auctions are terrific places to get an education. Before a sale, you can inspect items and quiz the experts. Afterward, the catalogs make great reference materials, especially if they're for specialized sales. You might assume that auctions at major houses such as Sotheby's, Christie's, and Butterfield & Butterfield (which is owned by eBay) are just for big shots, but they sell a range of items at many price points. In any case, they are a good barometer of current prices and trends. See chapter 3, "The Quest for Amazing Stuff," for more on Butterfield & Butterfield and eBay's Great Collections.

Research, Research, Research

Your collection will never be more than a hodgepodge unless you take the time to research and document it. Besides increasing your satisfaction, these efforts pay off in smarter purchases and, most likely, a more valuable collection.

Much research takes place in the field as you're frequenting auctions, shops, and shows. But smart collectors also rely on books, photographs, articles, catalogs, warranties, receipts, and ephemera to round out their knowledge. Astoundingly, many so-called collectors don't have one book on their area and rely on the speculation and misinformation supplied by others. Certain myths—for example, that you can determine the quality of any piece of glass by the ringing sound it makes when tapped or that signed items are automatically more valuable then others—have lives of their own and get perpetrated even though resources to debunk them are readily available.

Meet eBay Ambassador Diana

SPECIALTY:

1960s and 1970s Toys and TV Memorabilia

eBay HANDLE: DiKansas   AGE: 35

PEOPLE WHO COLLECT THIS STUFF ARE: "Tweeners"—people born in the early 1960s, between the baby boomers and the Gen-Xers.

HOW TO GIVE A TWEENER WARM FUZZIES: Mention the words Silly Putty, Clackers, Liddle Kiddles, Wacky Packages, Wizzers, Tipit, Baby Go Bye-Bye, Creepy Crawlers, Ertle, Flower Fun, cap guns, Crissy dolls, Pez, ThingMaker, Breyer horses, Hot Wheels, Lincoln Logs, *Star Trek*, *Star Wars*, *Brady Bunch*, *Flying Nun*, *Charlie's Angels*, *Partridge Family*, *Gilligan's Island*, *H. R. Pufnstuf*, *Green Acres*, *Little House on the Prairie*, *Bionic Woman*, *Starsky & Hutch*, *Waltons* . . .

THE BIGGEST CHALLENGE: Finding items in mint condition with their boxes— and without teeth marks.

WHAT MY COLLECTION SAYS ABOUT ME: I had a wonderful childhood.

I WISH I'D NEVER GIVEN AWAY: A Baby Go Bye-Bye doll with a battery-operated buggy, which I had as a child.

WHERE I FOUND A NEW ONE: On eBay after looking for ten years.

HOW eBay HAS CHANGED MY LIFE: We home-school our three children, so it's hard to fit in time for a hobby. I can do eBay at home without disrupting the family schedule. Other hobbies that I enjoy require that I find a baby-sitter—and they don't generate an income as eBay can.

THE BEST THING ABOUT eBay: It's open twenty-four hours a day, and there's no dress code.

HOW TO GET GRUMPY HUSBANDS PSYCHED ABOUT eBay: Tell them you'll buy lacy teddies (and wear them) with 10 percent of your eBay profits. That makes hubbies very, very helpful.

Collectors of the arcane may find little or no documentation. They must rely on their analytical ability, instinct, and self-taught expertise. They become the trailblazers, amassing a collection significant enough to illustrate the definitive book in that specialty.

Hitting the Books

Behind every great collection is a reference library. Some collectors' libraries in themselves are highly valuable. We're not talking about price guides (more on those later) or mainstream surveys spanning Mesopotamia to the present. Rather, you want to ferret out books, no matter how esoteric, that mention the items or period you collect. The more pictures the better. If you learn only one factoid from a publication—for example, the average number of pieces an artist produced in a year—it's worth adding it to your shelf. Each nugget of intelligence gives you an edge in the marketplace and prevents buying bloopers.

Many of the books you need are probably out of print. Become a familiar face at your local used-book store and library sales. Pore over the tomes offered by book vendors at shows. The Internet now brings the entire world of new and used books to your doorstep. You can find great books on eBay by cruising your favorite categories and searching the entire listings. Many good reference books are rare and thus cost considerably more, even secondhand. Some people will drop $300 on a new piece yet balk at spending $45 for a book on their favorite subject. If only they realized that a good reference library is better than a buyer's protection program.

Besides books created just for collectors, also hunt down the following:

● **Exhibition catalogs:** Galleries and museums often print programs that accompany group shows and single-artist retrospectives. These provide period overviews, information on specific works, biographical sketches, and lots of pictures. You can back-order museum catalogs from prior shows. Gallery catalogs are usually printed in limited numbers but are worth finding because they often hail emerging areas long before the "establishment" recognizes an artist or a style. In addition, some galleries now sponsor annual shows in certain media (glass, ceramics, textile arts, and so forth) that feature the best and the brightest of the moment. Such documents, especially a series of them, are incredibly helpful in tracking leaders, styles, and trends.

● **Manufacturers' catalogs:** Illustrated catalogs and brochures are as good as time machines that show you entire lines, including prices, as they were first produced, so you instantly understand where your pieces fit in. (Try not to feel too wistful upon seeing that your $50 piece once cost $5 new.) These documents sometimes also provide model numbers, variety and sizes of production, dates, and, in rare cases, the quantity produced. Their usefulness has led to the reproduction of period catalogs in some areas of collecting.

● **Period books:** In certain fields, such as furniture, decorative arts, cars, and toys, industry yearbooks and compilations are a tradition. These annual snapshots document products, factories, designers, and trends. Some read like a *Who's Who* of an industry, others review the year, and still others function as advertising annuals.

● **Old magazines and journals:** Because most periodicals focus on short time periods (the week, month, or quarter), they provide a contemporary perspective that can seem quaint years later. Still, magazines, especially specialized ones, are often the first to identify trends and new faces before they become known to the general public.

● **Auction catalogs:** The larger the sale and the house, the better the vetted descriptions and usually the photos. A large secondary market has sprung up for such publications, but the most useful ones contain the auction house's "prices realized" list from after the sale.

For book collectors, condition and edition are important factors in value. For your purposes, however, the value comes from what's between the covers. Worn copies go for less money, but treat any additions to your reference library as an investment. Protect even dog-eared copies with dust jackets. You never know when you'll outgrow a book and want to resell it on eBay to another collector.

A Picture's Worth $1,000

Finding your piece in a book is almost as exciting as finding the actual piece. Books verify your collection and knowledge. Any time you can truly document the authenticity of a piece and point other collectors to a common reference, you increase its value. However, just because information appears in black and white doesn't mean it's infallible. Authors can make mistakes or have inadequate research. Sometimes new information turns up after publication. That's why the most valuable part of any book to a collector is the pictures.

You might be searching on eBay when you come across an interesting object that confounds you. A dash to the bookshelf confirms your hunch, for there it is on page 72 of that odd little book you picked up last month. Seeing the piece published makes you realize its true value and saves you from wild speculation.

The Truth About Price Guides

Miles of books on antiques and collectibles clog the bookstores of the world, and their quality ranges from bare-bones vanity publications to stunningly illustrated coffee table–size boxed sets. Despite their pictures—always a plus—many such books lack the scholarly rigor necessary for credibility. This is particularly true with price guides. While a guide might list an item for a certain amount, those figures are often based on limited auction results, which themselves can be skewed because of regional factors or current events. What's more, the constant fluctuations in prices and demand make guides go out of date almost before they're off the press. As such, most are useful only as crude barometers of value and demand. Exceptions are guides, found mostly in the area of fine arts, which give actual sales results from all over the world.

A Look Online

There's plenty of help on the Internet when you want to learn more about specific areas of collecting or research value. Active collectors maintain many of these sites in their spare time. This is just a pupu platter of what's out there:

- **The Roseville Pottery Exchange** http://www.inch.com/ ~kteneyck/roseville.html#magnolia "Dedicated to helping the public spot reproduction (fake) Roseville Pottery."

- **The *Mad* Magazine Cover Site** http://www.collectmad.com/madcoversite/

Only on eBay

The peak times on eBay are one P.M. to eleven P.M. PST—when many eBaysians hit the site after a long day at the office or the kids are safely tucked away for the evening. Sunday is also a busy day for the listing of new items and the ending of auctions started the previous week. If you find that pages are poky to load, try logging on before or after prime time.

index.html   What, me worry? Not about finding information on this mainstay of American satire. This site has it all, including scans of covers from day one and a price guide. A copy of *MAD*'s first issue in very fine condition is worth $5,000. Who knew?

The Essentials of Book Collecting

http://www.lucasbooks.com/collect.html   This site covers such topics as how to read an entry in a book catalog, condition issues affecting nineteenth- and twentieth-century books, and much more.

Lisa's Postcard Page

http://www.geocities.com/Heartland/Meadows/2487/   Among the helpful pages are a postcard history, a glossary of collecting terms related to postcards, and tips for preserving your collection.

World of Cast Iron Cookware

http://www.mrpotatohead.net/   What were the companies that specialized in cast iron cookware? Find out and see images of some of their wares and a brief history of casting.

Periodicals

Magazines on antiques and collectibles provide important information on three fronts: trends and specific collecting areas, listings of upcoming shows and auctions, and advertisements from dealers, antiques malls, services, and businesses that cater to collectors.

Here are some top ones:

eBay Magazine: Co-published by Krause, the world's largest hobby publisher, this magazine debuted in September 1999 and is geared toward helping collectors get the most out of eBay. Filled with news, tips, and insights for the Internet and eBay communities. www.krause.com/ebaysub or www.eBay.com; 888-486-5478.

Antiques and the Arts Weekly: Many dealers consider this weekly, known fondly as *the Bee*, the best publication on antiques and collecting in New England and the mid-Atlantic. It also includes many feature articles and ads for shows. Diehards turn first to the back—which contains page after page of auction listings. www.thebee.com; 203-426-3141.

● *The Antiques Trader Weekly:* A weekly listing of classified ads covering a wide swath of the antiques and collectibles markets. Its show and shop listings and advertisements are national, making this a great resource for those of you who get around the country. (It's owned by Krause, the co-publishers of *eBay Magazine.*) www.collect.com.

● *Maine Antiques Digest:* A treasure trove of advertisements and information about goings-on. Don't be fooled by the name—it's not only about Maine, although its primary focus is the East Coast. www.maineantiques.com.

● *The Magazine Antiques:* This is the land of traditional antiques and art. A four-color glossy, the magazine has been a standard-bearer for years. 800-925-9721.

● *Echoes:* Billing itself as the "magazine of classic modern style+design," just a few years ago, this magazine was little more than a black-and-white compilation of ads. As a testament to the strength of twentieth-century design, *Echoes* is now a thick four-color glossy chock-full of editorial and ads. To complete your library on favorite designers, you can order back issues or publications from the *Echoes* bookstore—a catalog insert. www.deco-echoes.com; 508-428-2324.

Beyond these, freebie regional publications can be found at shops, malls, and events. The quality of the editorial is typically so-so, but the ads are a treasure map to area vendors. In a similar vein, local Yellow Pages provide a roundup of sources at a glance. Whenever serious collectors find themselves in a new city, their first move is to check the Yellow Pages for local shopping opportunities. The next great antiques mall might just be down the road.

To collect is to shop. Although eBay has profoundly changed the collectibles market (and consumer commerce in general), it will never replace the myriad places where antiques and collectibles **CHAPTER 13** have traditionally been found. Terrific merchandise enters the market at many points, which means that venues ranging from garage sales and thrift stores to swanky shops and specialized shows will probably always have their place. This chapter gives an overview of the market and the kinds of places that should become part of your regular tour as you hunt for new acquisitions—and items to resell on eBay.

where the action is

Making the Rounds

The land of antiques and collectibles is as big as the earth—and as full of unknowns as the universe. Even your friends at the psychic hot line can't predict where and when your next great find will happen. As a general rule, the closer you can get to the source of items—the place where they first come onto the market—the more likely you are to score objects at decent prices. That's why so many people spend countless hours combing flea markets, garage sales, shows, and auctions.

There's no question that eBay is impacting these traditional venues. Walk around any flea market or antiques show and you'll overhear comments such as "My new computer comes tomorrow. I *have* to go on eBay—everyone else in my group shop already has." They might cite eBay as the benchmark for price or rarity. Sometimes dealers shut up hagglers by saying, "You've got to be kidding—I can get more for it on eBay!" Undoubtedly knowledgeable eBaysians are also making purchasing decisions out in the field based on their ability to buy a similar item for a better

SPECIALTY:

U.S. Naval Postal History

eBay HANDLE: Sarge   AGE: 53

I'VE BEEN COLLECTING: Twenty-two years.

THE PIECE THAT GOT ME STARTED: A real-photo postcard showing USS *Oregon* moored in San Diego Bay and postmarked aboard the ship in June 1915. I was intrigued by the postal marking—round, but with the ship's name in it. And it cost $1!

THE CHALLENGE: Finding mail in decent condition—with clear, complete postal markings—sent by sailors and marines serving in unusual or scarce U.S. Navy ships from anywhere in the world.

WHY THIS STUFF IS COOL: It's an education in politics, geography, and history. I've turned the corner from the days in high school when I hated history.

TO BE AN EXPERT: You need to know a bit of naval history, where to find information *not* known, and how to present findings so that new discoveries are accepted.

PRIDE OF MY COLLECTION: The cover (envelope), dated 2 December 1941, mailed by a marine serving in the USS *Arizona* and who was killed in action five days later.

QUESTION I'M ASKED MOST: What do you *do* with this stuff?

PEOPLE'S BIGGEST MISCONCEPTION: That it's the letters I want to read. Not true! The letters, as a rule, shed little information about a ship, where the ship was and why, especially during the war years when mail was censored.

TO COMPLETE MY COLLECTION: I need a cover dated 6 December 1941, mailed from a U.S. Navy ship home-ported at Pearl Harbor.

HOW eBay HAS CHANGED MY LIFE: I quit my other job as a consulting placer mining geologist.

price on eBay. (The art of negotiation, however, is far from dead—see chapter 14, "Out in the Field," for tips on working the markets.) Part of being successful as a collector is understanding the subtleties and differences among various venues.

Garage and Tag Sales

Garage sales are as American as, well, two-car garages. Tag sales usually refer to indoor sales, and the pickings tend to be of a slightly higher grade. Either way, the garage/tag sale hound lives for the weekend, when most such sales are held. They especially swoon when several families combine forces and their castoffs are spread out willy-nilly over the garage, driveway, and lawn. You just know that somewhere amid all that flotsam is a treasure.

Some of the best bargains in the world can be found at these sales—you can't get better direct-from-the-source prices, even for used stuff. Of course, it's bad form to haggle on an item priced at $1.50 if you know it's worth $500.

Shopping garage and tag sales isn't for everyone. It takes stamina, as great items are found only by plowing through tons of junk. Competition is stiff; expect to cross paths with professional antiques dealers, decorators, and pickers, not to mention sale hoppers who make it a social occasion. Big yard sales draw crowds, and the opening moments (when you should be there) resemble feeding time at the alligator pit. Some pros go get early editions of the classifieds so they can call on sellers hours or even days before the sale. However, not all sellers appreciate early birds. If they really wanted to see you before breakfast, they'd throw in a cheese Danish with every purchase.

Estate Sales

Nothing gets the blood running like the phrase "Everything must go!" or "Selling to the bare walls!" Such enticements often indicate an estate sale, where the entire contents of a home are being sold because someone has passed away, was moved to a nursing home, or is substantially downsizing for some reason. Professionals who know the market usually promote and handle such sales. Therefore scoring a bargain is more of a challenge, but not impossible. After all, the goal is to move the merchandise by a given deadline, so there is some wiggle room. Be prepared for substantial competition, both at the start of the sale and toward the end, when the vultures swoop in for last-minute markdowns.

Thrift Shops

When things don't sell at garage, tag, or estate sales, they often get donated to charity for a tax write-off. Some people just prefer to skip the hassle of selling their junk and take the tax deduction. The charity then sells the goods in its thrift shop to fund programs. The occasional gem can be found amid the aluminum frying pans and curled-leather shoes, but you have to dig. Thrift shops are stereotypically musty, crammed, and disorganized, so it pays to be a regular and know what days new donations get put out. In recent years a few big-city charities, such as Housing Works in New York City, have upped the ante by creating stylish, clean spaces filled with designer clothes and cleverly displayed merchandise. (Attracting high-caliber donations is easier in a city where many people are affluent and few own cars and thus garages where they might have sales.) Still, dedication is the key to happy hunting.

Consignment Shops

Consignment shops play an important role for people who want to get rid of desirable items but can't be bothered with selling them. They consign their unwanted goods to a shop, which receives a percentage (usually 25 percent to 50 percent) of the proceeds when the item sells. To ensure a steady turnover of merchandise, most shops limit the length of time that goods are held for sale. When that period expires, consignors must pick up the item. In some cases ownership reverts to the shop if the consignor fails to return. Some shops start automatic markdowns after a predetermined time. Not much haggling goes on because the proprietors don't own the merchandise and have an agreed-upon price with the consignor.

Note: Dealers sometimes take items on consignment for people they know, and it's not uncommon to hear a dealer say, "I don't have any flexibility on the price because it's on consignment."

Flea Markets

The great churning engines of the antiques and collectibles world are flea markets, where large quantities of inventory flow in and get pumped into new hands on a regular basis. Dealers often dump entire estates at many of the better-known markets (such as the Rose Bowl market in Pasadena, California; the Annex Market at Twenty-sixth Street in New York City; and the historic Lakewood Antiques Market and Scott Antiques Market in Atlanta). These venues are like giant, ever-changing exhibits at historical museums, except that you get to pick up and examine all the artifacts and even take some home.

Find a local market and work it regularly. As you become familiar with the usual dealers and their wares, you'll be better able to spot items that haven't shown up before. Don't be scared away by people who say prices are too high at this or that market. The bargains are there, especially if *you're* there at dawn or as the dealers are packing up for the day.

Independent Shops

Hitting the back roads and stopping at country antiques shops—found in old barns out back and in farmhouses where the proprietor lives upstairs—is the quintessential antiques-hunting fantasy. Somehow you always think you've stumbled upon some forgotten corner of America where you're sure to find a pair of Duncan Phyfe chairs overlooked by the local rubes. Well, nowadays the owners of such shops are just as likely to be selling on eBay as to tourists, but that doesn't mean poking around these unique shops is less fun. These dealers are very close to the sources of the best local merchandise. Having the owner on hand also makes for great opportunities to sharpen the old pencil and haggle.

Antiques Malls and Group Shops

At first glance, the typical antiques mall or group shop might look like nothing more than miles of glass vitrines filled with bric-a-brac. In fact, these are rich veins to mine, as the dealers who rent booth and cabinet space keep them well stocked with new inventory. They're also an efficient way to shop since you can cover fifty, sixty, or more dealers under one roof.

Depending on the place, some dealers pay monthly rent (usually subtracted from their monthly proceeds). Some malls are co-ops, where dealers work the floor helping customers. Other shops charge rent and a small commission on each sale. The quality of the goods varies from excellent to not even garage sale worthy (sometimes under the same roof). Most malls offer a 10 percent discount for dealers or have a dealer price coded on price tags. Normally, to get this discount you have to have a business card or resale number or tax number that verifies your status as a dealer. You can also haggle at malls. Remember, though, that the items are owned by specific dealers and not the folks at the cash register. If you have a question or want to make a lower offer, most malls are happy to pick up the phone and contact the dealer for you. Don't bust people's chops about inexpensive items, but if you find something that's great but overpriced, make an offer. If the mall can't reach a dealer, just to sweeten the pot they may offer you the dealer discount even if you don't have the credentials. If not, leave your offer and phone number. The mall can ship the item later if the dealer accepts.

Malls often feature sales, so if you're buying ahead of the curve, you might be able to wait until it's marked down. Check back the last week of the month. Booth rent is probably due the first. If they haven't sold enough to make their rent, dealers might be motivated to make a sale.

Antiques Shows

Antiques shows remain an excellent place to purchase items and learn about the market. Many people falsely assume that shows are overpriced. Some, like the Winter Antiques Show at the Park Avenue Armory in New York City, do feature rarities that sell for more than $1 million. But believe it or not, that doesn't mean every piece in the show is so extravagant. Besides, high end is not the same as overpriced.

Shows abound around the country and vary from small twenty-dealer events to the megahappenings such as "Atlantique" City in Atlantic City, New Jersey, in the fall and spring and Palmer Wirfs & Associates' annual summer show at the Expo Center in Portland, Oregon. Both feature more than 1,500 dealers! There are probably one or two regular antiques shows a year in your vicinity.

You can shop an antiques show in the same way you would eBay: high and low. Not all antiques show dealers know exactly what they have, so it's possible for you to score even at heavily attended shows like the Triple Pier Expo, which happens every fall and spring in the heart of New York City. Keep in mind that a lot of preshow deals take place between dealers during setup. Dealers have even been known to favor particular shows less for the sales potential than for their own buying opportunities.

Inevitably, when the show does open, veteran buyers have been waiting on line for hours. You should be on that line, too—unless you've already attended an early buying session offered by some antiques shows. For a specified time before the show opens at the regular admission price, eager buyers can pay a premium (two to four times the regular cost of admission) to shop. One good purchase easily amortizes that cost. In addition, some antiques shows have benefit previews where charities—or sponsoring organizations such as museums—have galas on the night preceding the show's opening to the public. The dealers are all in attendance, hawking their wares to the patrons. Anyone willing to pay the freight can get in, and many serious collectors and dealers view these shindigs as *the* highlight of the buying season. Tickets can be expensive: $75 and up—way up—depending on where you live. One good thing about galas for buyers and collectors is that frequently the patrons are not necessarily interested in the stuff for sale. They're there to socialize. You can shop while the swells, oblivious of the buying opportunities around them, sip bubbly and blow air kisses. More good news: Your ticket price helps a worthy organization and may be partially tax-deductible.

Shopping the shows can be nerve-racking. There you are in a sea of humanity, circling like a shark that smells blood. There is so much stuff and so much you want. You may feel pressured to buy out of fear that someone higher on the collecting food chain will snap it up if you don't. Stay cool. Most buying mistakes are made when you forget to listen to your inner voice and don't your due diligence.

Unfortunately, on some days it's possible to come away from some shows, even the granddaddies of them all, without a single purchase. But it's not a total loss. Use it as a learning experience. Inspect tons of items and comparison shop.

Specialized Collectibles Shows

Nothing gets dedicated collectors' mouths watering like a show where all dealers are targeting their interests. Of course, you're also competing with your fellow collectors, so be sure to practice your best fake smile ahead of time.

By creating a huge mass of inertia, specialized shows create a vibrant marketplace and an unparalleled opportunity to comparison shop. You will likely see numerous examples of similar items and be able to hold them, inspect them, and quantify differences in quality, condition, and value. High demand is partially mitigated by extensive supply, and price shopping and haggling is a must. These shows often include learning opportunities such as lectures, demonstrations, and exhibits of significant collections. Dig in!

Only on eBay

The summer of 1999 marked the first On the Road eBay Tour—which traveled the antiques and collectibles show circuit from coast to coast. Or, as they say on eBay, "From our home page to your hometown!" One RV headed east from California, while another was westbound (more or less). Some of the highlights included Bonnie & Clyde Trade Days in Arcadia, Louisiana, and the National Scout Memorabilia Conference at the Tropicana in Las Vegas. Along the way, eBay Ambassadors meeted and greeted, shared tips, and hooked up users to the Web site.

Auctions

As you know from using eBay, auctions are one of the best places to buy—if you like the chance to snag bargains and experience an adrenaline rush. However, live auctions and eBay trading differ substantially, so learning the lay of the land is important. For openers, the business of auction houses is to sell items for other people (although in some instances they sell merchandise they own outright or in which they have interest) and get the best price they can for their customers who consign items for sale. Their motivation for high sales prices is not by any means altruistic. Auction houses make their money by a commission charged to the consignee and a premium paid by the buyer, both based on a percentage of the sale price.

Varieties range from country auctions to the specialized connoisseurs' auctions of high-quality art and objects. The latter can be done in two ways:

● **Cataloged:** The auctioneer or house experts create a catalog or printed listing of every item in the sale. There is no standard form. At minimum, catalogs have a description of the item, an estimate of the sale price, and the lot number. At fancy houses, catalogs come complete with full-page color photos, intricate descriptions, provenance, and related literature. A catalog by itself does not guarantee that objects are correctly attributed or authenticated. Many auction houses offer whole or multiple estates for sale at once, and they have just a week or two between auctions to list items, so invariably they make mistakes. However, the bigger auction houses have experts who research individual pieces before cataloging them and often provide authenticity guarantees.

● **Uncataloged:** At, say, the classic country auction, lots may or may not even have numbers. Stuff just comes up for sale, and the auctioneer makes a statement on the spot about what the item is or appears to be: "Here's a nice rocking chair. Who'll get things going with $5?" There can be great deals and boatloads of junk. You may have to wait hours for your item to come up for sale, although it's not unheard of to put in a request for a particular item to get moved up. (However, this will never happen in an auction where every item has a lot number.)

An auction of seven hundred or eight hundred lots can mean a grueling day for all involved. Some houses do you the favor of grouping like items together, so, for example, all oil paintings will be sold at the same time. In any case, you can usually get a reliable estimate about what time a specific lot will come up for bid so you don't have to hang around all day.

Most houses allow *left* bids or phone bidding. Left bids are very similar to eBay's proxy bidding: you leave a written bid of the maximum you are willing to pay, and the auction house bids for you until you hit your maximum or win with a lower bid. Phone bidding allows you to take part in the actual auction from a distant location. Normally you arrange with the auction house to be at a certain phone number and are called a couple of minutes ahead of the lot. You may have to leave a deposit for a left bid or phone bid. For tips on shopping at auctions, see chapter 14, "Out in the Field."

Swap Meets

In most parts of the world swap meets are synonymous with flea markets—a gathering for the sale or barter of objects. Sometimes swap meets are literally places where collectors swap items as opposed to selling them. For example, the Brick Collectors Association, International, holds regional swap meets where members trade bricks for bricks—not bucks—because they don't want anyone to feel excluded from collecting these historic artifacts for lack of the almighty dollar.

Clubs

It seems that no matter what you collect, there's a club for

Collector Connections on the Web

The World Wide Web is rich in resources that might be helpful to you. Here are a couple worth checking out:

- **www.collectingchannel.com:** A provider of content to eBay on various areas of collecting, collectingchannel.com has articles and advice in all major collecting categories and links to many other excellent sites.

- **www.collectoronline.com:** A full directory of more than eight hundred clubs related to antiques and collectibles. This site also provides links to clubs that have Web sites as well as to price guides and other resources.

it: the National Association of Milk Bottle Collectors, the American Hatpin Society, the Barbed Wire Collectors Association, the Charlie Tuna Collectors Club, the Comb Collectors Club International . . . You get the idea. Members generally pay a fee to belong, entitling them to newsletters, price information, and bulletins on conventions and shows. The best way to find out whether there's a group for you is to ask around in the chat rooms on eBay or search the Internet. For other specific sites, see "Collector Connections on the Web."

Special Sources for Established Dealers

No doubt, as you've wandered the shops, malls, and shows, you have wondered, Where do they get these great things? Dealers mostly likely will just say, "Everywhere." That may sound flaky or cagey, but it happens to be the truth. For them, everywhere includes a few special sources:

● **Pickers and scouts:** It's a happy day for most dealers when their favorite picker or scout pulls into the driveway with a full load of new finds. The true middlemen of the antiques and collectibles market, pickers and scouts scour the countryside, going door-to-door if need be, to track down fresh, unusual merchandise. Their goal is to find items they can turn over quickly for at least a twenty percent to forty percent markup.

● **General public:** Shop owners benefit from walk-in traffic when ordinary people bring in their items. While lots of people bring in junk, they also hand over some incredible finds because they don't realize what they have. At nearly every show people seek out dealers to sell to on the spot or show pictures to. They usually look for dealers with merchandise similar to what they're trying to get rid of.

● **Buybacks:** Say a happy customer buys a nice watch from a reputable dealer and five years later is bored with it or needs some cash. Often she will head back to the person who sold it to her. Many dealers are amenable to buybacks and trade-ins. If it was good enough to buy once, they are usually happy to buy it again, especially if the market trend has been up for that particular item. Some dealers even offer buybacks at the time of sale.

Unless you want to set up a shop or become a dealer, these markets are hard to tap into. Try putting an ad in your local newspaper or other journals' classifieds, advertising to buy antiques or specific kinds of items. It doesn't obligate you to buy anything anybody brings you, but who knows what goodies might appear. If you can ever come face-to-face with a picker or scout, let him know you are a buyer for certain types of items. If he does look you up, make sure you buy something, anything. He's not likely to come back if you're not serious.

SPECIALTY:

Breyer Horses

eBay HANDLE: Ms. Kitka   AGE: 32

THE HORSE THAT GOT ME STARTED: The glossy palomino Family Arabian Mare, which I got when I was five and is my favorite to this day.

WHAT'S COOL ABOUT BREYER HORSES: They're a lot less messy than real horses. But they still take up a lot of room.

TO RECOGNIZE A HORSE OF A DIFFERENT COLOR: You need to know what year what color came on what horse and in what finish.

PEOPLE'S BIGGEST MISCONCEPTION: Breyer horses are for little girls.

I'M HOT TO TROT FOR: The glossy dapple gray Belgian.

SELLING TIPS: Advertise correctly, be polite to even the most obnoxious people, and pack well.

NEW COLLECTORS SHOULD: Go to the shows.

HOWEVER, WITH eBay: I can now trade from my living room and not pay ridiculous show table prices.

As you build your collection or buy items for resale, the goal is always to get the best price possible. First you must know the market (see chapter 12, "Becoming an Expert"). Then it's a matter of being a skillful negotiator, a good judge of people, and utterly charming. In this chapter we share the secrets of successful buying, from haggling with dealers to bidding at live auctions.

CHAPTER 14

out in the field

Marketplace 101

No matter where you're buying—eBay, antiques show, auction, or flea market—you need to develop some good buying habits. Before you even *ask* a price, you should run through a few quick mental exercises:

- **Take a guess:** Before you look at the tag or inquire about the price, guess—realistically—what you think it is.

- **Set a firm maximum:** Set a firm upward limit price. Bring a sidekick—someone who will literally give you a good one in the shin if you get grandiose.

- **Judge harshly:** Inspect every item carefully no matter how good the deal appears. An unbeatable price can make you blind to chips, cracks, restoration jobs, or other condition problems.

- **Practice patience:** Unless an object is truly unique (doubtful) or extremely rare (ditto), you're smart not to pounce on the first one you see. Chances are you'll soon come across a better example in better condition and at a lower price. Antacids can make the wait easier.

Dealing with Dealers

Being a dealer is hard work. Most dealers are small entrepreneurs who must constantly bring fresh merchandise to market without the aid of marketing studies, focus groups, national ad campaigns, or expense accounts. They may have an affinity for the objects they sell, but dealing is not a hobby. Dealers still have to eat, put a roof over their heads, take vacations, pay for college, and hopefully retire (if dealing isn't already their retirement activity). As independent operators who don't have to fill some sales quota, they have flexibility in the prices they ask. But don't expect them to give away items and don't confuse haggling with a life-and-death struggle. This is not about world peace.

Cultivate relationships with dealers as you would with any business partner. In return, you may receive great merchandise, tips, information, and friendship.

Haggling with the Best of Them

You would never go into the local Wal-Mart and ask the manager if they could "do a little better" on a box of laundry soap. But in the antiques and collectibles world, bartering is a way of life. Perhaps it's a throwback to the days of the open-air bazaar. Or maybe it's because prices on used stuff naturally vary depending on the condition, provenance, and other factors. (See chapter 11, "The Mystery of Value.") In any case, dealers and buyers are well versed in this tango. Not surprisingly, a number of dealers prepare for this dance by adding a few extra bucks before the band takes the stage.

Many people are intimidated by negotiating; it's unknown territory with hazy rules. Overcoming fears and anxiety comes with time and experience. Ingredients for a successful negotiation include two parts self-confidence, three parts expertise, one part luck, patience as needed, and a dash of class.

Forces at Play

Haggling and negotiating are more art than science. Many things affect how a final price is reached, not the least of which is the chemistry between the buyer and seller. Successful shoppers are chameleonlike. They change their approach depending on the dealer instead of expecting dealers to adapt to them. Here are some forces working for and against you that may affect the outcome of a negotiation:

● **How long the piece has been in a dealer's inventory:** Dealers, like any retailer, need to keep the merchandise moving. If an item has been hanging around for, say, five or six months without generating much interest, a dealer might get antsy. Of course, unless the dealer mentions it, the only way you might sense that a piece has overstayed its welcome is if you've been checking up on it. (That's why it's important to visit your favorite hunting grounds regularly.) Maybe you thought the price was too high the first couple of times you asked. There's no need to remind the dealer of your past inquiries or that the piece is becoming a permanent fixture. The dealer knows—and, besides, talking down the merchandise is bad form (see "Mood Breakers" later in this chapter).

● **How well a show is going:** At shows and flea markets the first priority of dealers is to cover their overhead costs such as booth rent, labor, and travel. At a slow show where they haven't made their expenses, they may be in a bargaining mood (or just crabby—either way, tread carefully). How do you know a show is slow? Note the number of attendees—especially those walking around with shopping bags—"Sold" signs, and sales taking place. Eavesdrop; dealers are big talkers. Ask them casually, "How's it going?" (However, asking the dealer you're negotiating with is a bit obvious.) Be alert to conditions that affect sales, such as weather. Rain can kill an outdoor flea market but pack an indoor show. On the other hand, too beautiful a day can work against either as buyers head for the beach.

● **How long till the next show:** Even for dealers who sell in shops or on eBay, shows usually boost the cash flow. So if they have an upcoming hiatus from the circuit, they might be motivated to make a deal. Is it toward the end of the season or just before a holiday? You might say, "I like your stuff. When's your next show?"

● **The state of the market for that kind of item:** In a hot market, there's little flexibility. Dealers are confident that just around the corner is another buyer who'll meet their price.

● **The dealer overpaid:** When dealers pay too much for an object (for example, higher than prevailing retail value), they're often reluctant to sell it for less than their purchase price. They might say, "I paid more than you're offering," or they might even quote the actual price they paid. But just because they made a bad deal doesn't mean you have to. Unless the dealer is willing to cut her losses, you're better off moving on.

Laying the Groundwork

Always negotiate from strength. Even though the dealer has the merchandise you covet, only you know the magnitude of your desire and the price at which you are likely to utter the magic phrase "I'll take it."

First things first: inspect the item for condition, evaluate the significance to your collection, and establish the price you'd pay for your collection or resale. How does the piece score based on your criteria for shape, form, color, and so on? Give the piece your undivided attention, but do not show the faintest glimmer of excitement. (You can pass out with delight later.) Dealers are watching you, sizing you up and trying to figure out your interest. Offer a mild, professional compliment about the object's condition or other positive attribute—just enough to flatter the dealer without making yourself look overeager. Gushing platitudes about how wonderful an item is tells dealers they've got a live one—they won't be as inclined to haggle. However, icy detachment won't win you any favors, either. Ideally you want to send a message that you are intrigued but savvy.

Price Check, Aisle Six

Asking the price of something you don't intend to buy is perfectly legitimate. Many people do this to gauge the worth of items they already own. Others inquire just for sport. However, don't raise false hopes by asking for a *best* price unless you are seriously interested.

Getting to Sold

The first critical volley is getting the dealer's *asking* price. If there's no price tag, you have to ask. Watch dealers closely when getting quotes on unmarked items. Do they name a price immediately? Or do they think it over for a few moments? Some dealers make prices up on the fly or try out different prices on different people when they don't know the value. Even though this is shoddy on a dealer's part, you can still work with the dealer to find the right price through the negotiation process.

Everything's Negotiable

You want the object, and the dealer has quoted you a figure. Your next move depends on the distance between the dealer's price and yours. Here are three classic scenarios for arriving at an agreement.

Meet eBay Ambassador Cherie Carrol

SPECIALTY:

Used Books

eBay HANDLE: usedbooks (what else?) AGE: 35

I'VE BEEN IN THIS FIELD FOR: Twenty-plus years.

HOW IT ALL STARTED: I just loved reading, and before I knew it the books were taking over the house.

I'M NEVER BORED BECAUSE: The supply of books is endless—the collecting can go on forever.

YOU NEED TO KNOW: How to identify first editions and research values.

PEOPLE'S BIGGEST MISCONCEPTION: That all old books are valuable.

MY FAVORITE: A first edition of *Love Not the World* by Watchman Nee.

THE LIST OF BOOKS I'D LOVE TO OWN: Is a mile long.

ADVICE TO NOVICES: You may not always be able to find a first edition in perfect condition. Start with whatever you can find and then upgrade when better editions become available or affordable.

THE WAY TO BID: Research the value of a book (by searching for other copies of it on eBay) and decide how much you're willing to pay so you don't get caught up in a bidding frenzy. Wait until the last minute and snipe.

MY BEST eBay FIND: All my friends on eBay's book board.

A GREAT DAY: I sold a book for $76. My investment: $0—the seller threw it in for free since I'd bought so many others.

THE BEAUTY OF eBay: It doesn't feel like work, but the income says it is. Now we have a little extra to spend on fun.

Off to a Great Start

You see a great tin Hire's root beer advertising thermometer in perfect condition. It has no price tag. You decide you'd happily pay $135. "What's your asking price?" you say. The dealer replies, "I was asking $110." You are already a winner!

You could now offer 20 percent less ($90) without insulting the dealer, who will probably counter with something like $100. Done deal.

But if you like to live dangerously, you might ask, "What's your best price on this piece?" The dealer now has to size you up and decide what it's worth to her. Suppose she says, "Give me $80 and you can have it." You might think, Wow!—but don't dare say it aloud. Pause, look the item over again as if you're giving it serious thought and haven't quite made up your mind. Then say nonchalantly, "Okay, we have a deal at $80." You play it cool so the dealer doesn't feel as though she gave it away; the only thing worse than buyer's remorse is seller's remorse. Of course, it's likely she paid $25 for the thermometer, so she's pretty happy, too.

We're Close

Now you find the greatest little hooked rug, a must have. The dealer has a price tag of $650, significantly more than the $525 you want to pay. Think about what the dealer might have invested in the piece. If it's between $300 and $350, she might take your $525 happily. You want to be careful here, because if you ask for her best price and she says $575, that may be the end of the negotiation. Try putting all your cards on the table—say, "It's a nice rug, I'd like to own it, would you take $500?" Such an offer leaves some wiggle room, and it's not offensively low—only 23 percent off the asking price.

The dealer will likely make a counteroffer. Suppose she says $550. You can try splitting the difference, but be decisive. Say, "If you split the difference and let me have it for $525, I'll take it right now." A great forehand into the dealer's court.

Even if the dealer's first counteroffer is $575, you should still put your $525 on the table. You might get turned down or countered with $550. Don't sweat it. Thank the dealer nicely and go about your merry way, knowing that the door is still open.

Because you *will* be back. After further analysis you might conclude that paying $540 would be acceptable. The dealer is thinking, too. She just turned down a firm offer of $525—maybe she shouldn't be so quick to blow off a real buyer. Time your return strategically. The end of the day is best, especially if it's the last day of a show. Your sale could be the difference between a good show and a great one. Inspect the rug again. Do you like it better this time? If not, reconsider whether you want it at all. If so, that's a good sign. Negotiation should proceed swiftly.

You make the first move, saying, "I really do like this rug. I could go $540." The dealer might very well accept. You've shown a little flexibility, and now you are only a few dollars apart. If the dealer tries to bump you, stick to your guns. "I just can't pay any more." Emphasize the "I." It's not about the rug, it's about what you can give for the rug. If the dealer won't budge below $550, you lose no face by either meeting the price or walking away.

Way, Way Apart

When you and a dealer are far apart on a figure, there isn't a lot you can do except give it the old college try. You find an English biscuit tin that's interesting but not perfect. The dealer is asking $350, and you think that based on others you've seen it's worth only about $160. Ask what his best price would be. You might be surprised when he knocks half off, but don't be. Why would a dealer do this? Perhaps he paid about that much, and the tin has been gathering dust ever since and he just wants to unload it.

Of course, the dealer might respond with $300. At this juncture you respectfully say something like "Sorry, I couldn't pay that much for it." Act as though you're about to move on, but don't be so hasty that the dealer doesn't sense that you're open. He might not counter but ask what you had in mind. Now, exhibiting extreme diplomacy, say, "I don't want to insult you, but I collect these tins, and for similar ones I've paid about $165 plus or minus a few bucks." The dealer might just shake his head and shrug. But if he's smart, he'll concede that he doesn't know much about English biscuit tins and engage you in a conversation to learn a thing or two. If that happens, you've got the upper hand and you're likely to get the tin for a reasonable price.

Note: If you see an object in a booth of the dealer who specializes in such items, assume that she knows more than you do until evidence to the contrary emerges.

Buying in Bulk

It happens all the time that a dealer has more than one item that catches your eye, creating the possibility of a bulk purchase (or, as your uncle Bernie calls it, "two-for-one money"). For example, you strike the mother lode for your *Forrest Gump* collection when you stumble across a dealer with a Bubba Gump Shrimp hat with original tags, a first edition of the novel, and

A Tax Break for Dealers

By registering for a resale permit or certificate (commonly referred to as a *resale number*), you can exempt yourself from paying sales tax on items purchased specifically for resale. In other words, such purchases would be considered wholesale (dealer-to-dealer) sales. You need to register with your state, so contact your state department of taxation for more information. Note: Sales tax is governed state by state. It is usually no problem to use a tax or resale number from one state to claim an exemption on a purchase in another state. These are general guidelines. Consult a tax attorney for more information.

an original movie poster. As always, before you get to the price, evaluate each piece and the price you can pay individually. This benchmark helps you figure out the economy of scale for the group. Get the dealer's asking price for each piece, then ask if she can do better if you buy more than one or even all of them. Now you can proceed based on the schemes outlined above, depending on how far apart you are in price.

There are some other twists to keep in mind. Maybe the individual and group prices are too high, but you really want one of them. The solution: Buy all three, sell two, and use the profit to reduce your investment in the piece you want to keep. If you work the markets with a friend who collects, pool your buying power. You can even buy three pieces, keep one apiece, and sell the other, splitting the proceeds. Before you know it, you might have a partner in the business.

Mood Breakers

For a negotiation to be successful, everyone has to be in the right frame of mind. The last thing you want or need to do is put dealers on the defensive or injure their pride. We hate to sound negative, but don't forget these don'ts:

● **Don't criticize the merchandise:** Dealers are not sitting around waiting for you to pass judgment on their goods. You may disagree with their assessment of the quality of their items, but bite your tongue. Who are you to come in and tell them that their item is no good? And if it is no good, why the heck would you want it, anyway? If you want to purchase a piece that's damaged and the dealer hasn't put an "as is" sticker (the common way to indicate damage) on it, politely inquire if the dealer has noticed what you see. Don't assume the dealer is trying to pull the wool over your eyes. Dealers pack stuff and move it over and over again. Things get hurt along the way. An honest dealer who didn't see the damage is likely to cut the price substantially or even refuse to sell it.

● **Don't mention that you saw a similar piece at another dealer's booth for less:** The dealer likely knows about the piece and thinks, justifiably so, that his is better quality or in better condition and therefore worth more. What are you doing haggling with this dealer if someone has the exact piece for a better price?

● **Don't criticize the asking price:** If a piece is overpriced, it's overpriced. Avoid showing your disappointment in the dealer's error. You have to use your wits, charm, and guile to get it at your price.

● **Don't assume you'll get a better price by paying cash:** Your message could be interpreted as "Take my money under the table and pass on your tax-fraud savings to me." Reputable dealers pay their sales and income taxes as all upstanding businesses do. Asking them to act otherwise is an insult. Some states have been cracking down on sales tax payments by vendors at antiques and collectibles shows and have enforcement officers working the floor. The dealer might think you're setting a trap.

Maximizing Your Auction Action

It's easy to become a good auction buyer. Here are some tips to get you started:

● **Inspect, inspect, inspect:** All auctions have presale previews and inspections. You should *never* bid on anything unless you've inspected it. Don't be tempted when a great item you haven't inspected comes up for sale and seems to be dying. Assume it's failing to generate interest because everyone else has looked at it and knows that it's damaged or seriously flawed.

● **Bid early:** Would-be snipers exist at live auctions, too. They think, erroneously, that sneaking in at the last moment increases their chances of winning the day. Rarely is this a successful strategy. People are going to bid to their maximum and couldn't care less when some-one joins the fray. In fact, latecomers sometimes lose out altogether, while early bidders have a frequent advantage. At crowded, busy auc-tions, auctioneers speed through lots, and items often get sold in an instant while you take a sip of coffee. A common occurrence is a bid-ding war between two people in the same part of the room. Everyone focuses on the drama, including the auctioneer, and may not see a third bidder trying to horn in on the action. The lot sells when the auc-tioneer brings down the hammer. Bidding early or first tells the auc-tioneer you're interested, so she'll keep coming back to you. Even if you drop out, the auctioneer may give you a last "just in case" look before the hammer. Once you're targeted as an active buyer, the auc-tioneer will keep an eye on you throughout the day.

● **Research:** Throw a couple of your favorite reference books in the car before you head out. After you've looked things over and decided what's interesting, spend a few minutes hitting the books to help confirm your suspicions and fix an amount you're willing to pay.

● **Set your limit before you bid:** Know what you want to pay before the lot comes up for sale, and do not exceed it. You don't want to get caught up in the moment and bid out of spite or just because you think one or two bumps might prevail. You never know how far your opponents might be willing to go, and when they drop out, you could end up owning a piece for a lot more than you bar-gained for.

● **Come up with a list of runners-up:** At a good sale there will be substantial competition for many items. Sorry to say, you may not get everything you want. You need to think on your feet based on what you win and the prices you pay. Make a list or indi-cate in your catalog (without letting prying eyes see) the items that interest you and your maximum price for each one. Pace yourself, especially if the item of your dreams is late in the lineup or you find yourself on a winning streak early on.

● **Hang in there:** Auctions are the opposite of "hurry up and wait." In fact, you wait and wait and wait and—boom!—your item is on the block. Before you know it, it's over and, winner or not, you must wait some more for the next lot you're interested in.

● Don't worry about bidding by mistake:

You've heard the story about the $3,000 itch—a fellow scratches his ear during an auction and winds up owning an object for $3,000. Such tales are the urban legends of the auction world. Auctioneers can usually tell the difference between someone bidding and brushing lint off his shoulder. Don't, however, jump up and wave to your best friend in the middle of a sale. And when you do bid, raise your hand or paddle high so the auctioneer can see you. If it's important to you that no one knows you're bidding on auction, leave a bid or arrange to bid over the phone. You can also have someone bid on your behalf. Be extremely clear about the maximum you're willing to spend.

● Understand the buyer's premium: Most

auction houses charge buyers a premium, which is a percentage of the hammer price. You need to calculate that fee into the amount you are willing to pay. If you bid $700 on an item at an auction with a 10 percent premium, you will have to fork over $770 (plus applicable sales tax).

● Read the fine print: Every auction should make avail-

able (usually in the catalog) the conditions and terms of the sale, including fees that sellers pay, buyers' premiums, statements about authenticity or guarantees, bidding increments, how auctioneers bid in reserve auctions and handle left bids, and other rules governing the sale. Make sure you understand them completely before bidding.

● Become a regular: If you live in proximity to a regular

auction, make previewing and attending auctions a part of your regular routine. Auctions are fun social events—and educational, too.

Beyond Negotiating: The Law of Averages

Serious collectors are sensitive to the value of each and every object added to their collection. Although you do need to evaluate each new acquisition on its merit and price, you should also apply the law of averages.

You, for example, collect salt and pepper shakers. Generally you can get most pairs for under $25. You go to a show and right away find a cute pair of reclining banana people. You snap them up for $11. Later that day you come across an oddly adorable set of a barber shaving a pig for $22—quite reasonable for shakers in such flawless condition. The collecting gods are with you. At the last booth of the day you find a classic: Betty Boop and Bimbo in a wooden boat that screams to be added to your subsection of cartoon characters. However, the dealer's best price is $38. High for you, but not outrageous for such a splendid pair. You start thinking about ways to make up the difference in the coming week (only two cappuccinos instead of five . . .), while your collector soul shouts, "Go, baby, go!" You know, as most collectors do, that regrets rarely come from items you paid too much for—they come from the ones you left behind.

Of course, it's possible to rationalize anything. Still, this last set of shakers won't actually stretch you if you consider that the day's expenditure for all three pairs would come to $71—or an average of $24 per pair. Right at your limit. The law of averages is on your side. Over the long haul you can use this approach to keep your spending on track while splurging occasionally to upgrade your collection.

Finders Keepers: Shopping Etiquette

Even though we joke about collectors going overboard, the fact is that sometimes even the most gracious people let their passion get the better of them. Perfectly timid souls can get downright pushy when they get a bead on a particular gem. And although you do need to be assertive to score the good stuff, you also need to abide by these unwritten rules of the road:

● **No hijacking:** You are one step behind someone who picks an amazing item you were headed right for. The interloper asks for and is quoted an excellent price as you stand there stuttering like Porky Pig. What do you do? Nothing, except back off. You must wait until the first prospective buyer makes a decision. Don't hang over the person's shoulder or send any signals that you're interested in the piece—which might make her want it more. Feign interest in another object or booth until your competitor has moved on—hopefully without the object.

● **Keep your opinions to yourself:** Never offer advice to strangers who are contemplating a purchase. Even if asked, you should be noncommittal and say something like "I really don't know anything about these kinds of items." The most serious offense is to offer unsolicited advice. If you think people are so interested in your opinion, become a politician. Buying and selling is a personal matter, and unless you're with someone who needs or wants your advice, it's

Only on eBay

Early on, the *eBay Café* (see page 160) was a cozy place for community members to congregate. But, eventually, the community began to add on to its virtual civic center in the form of ad hoc sites voluntarily created by eBay members. Here are some sites created to inform, support, and entertain the locals:

● The EEEC (www.pongo.com/lockout/index.html)

Like any town, eBay can experience rare, freak natural disasters—floods, earthquakes, power outages. To provide shelter for those in need, the community created the *Emergency eBay Evacuation Center.* Thus, when the Powers That Be interfere with their ability to meet at the Café, residents meet at the *EEEC.*

● The Queen's Roundroom (www.pongo.com/guestbooks/1-roundroom)
The King's Room (www.pongo.com/guestbooks/wheelie)

The community generally tends to make decisions democratically. For example, the Café was known as the *Bulletin Board* before residents banded together and demanded that eBay rename their civic center. But this town also has its self-proclaimed royalty. Members frequently pay homage to the Queen and to her husband, the King.

● The Dungeon (www.pongo.com/guestbooks/1-roundroom/dungeon.html)

Offending the Queen—misspelling her name or calling her by the wrong name, for example—means incurring her wrath. Violators are sent to the *Dungeon* and must beg the Queen for their freedom. If you're lucky, she sets you free.

● The Chapel (www.pongo.com/guestbooks/2-chapel)

Online "religious" ceremonies are performed at the *Chapel,* complete with organ music. And Father Griff is always available for confessions.

● Rich's Archives at the Zoo (www.twaze.com/the_zoo)

To appropriately archive conversations and other noteworthy events at the Café, *Zookeeper Twaze* and the town's historians have built town libraries.

● Pongo's Hints (www.pongo.com/tutorials/aweb-images)

At these sites, community members can ask their neighbors for help with difficult online auction issues such as adding graphics to an item's description. eBay's community members are good neighbors. They once built a computer from donated parts for a user who wanted to spend more time with the coffee klatch. The recipient was then able to go online at home (not just at work) to spend her weekends at the Café.

likely that strangers will rarely care what you think. Don't delude your-self into thinking you're being helpful by praising a piece of merchan-dise. The dealer is more likely to resent you as a buttinsky.

● Don't ask the price of a piece that's on hold or already sold: The price agreed on between a buyer and a seller is confidential. Don't even inquire as to the asking price. No self-respecting dealer is going to tell you, anyway. Your only hope is to subtly look for a price tag, although they typically are removed immediately. You don't want anyone else knowing what you paid, do you?

● Be fair: There is no imaginable reason not to treat people with dignity. Be tolerant of other people's cultural and ethnic backgrounds, worldviews, and styles. Diversity is what makes the world of collecting so fascinating.

● Be a good sport: The marketplace can be fiercely competi-tive. Sometimes you win, sometimes you lose. Do both with grace.

Tricks of Trading

If you have a duplicate piece in your collection or one that you've tired of, you might take it to a show or dealer, where you can apply it toward the purchase of another piece you really want. Don't worry or be shy about ask-ing a dealer to trade. Dealers are always looking for merchandise they can turn over quickly at a profit, so they're usually curious to see what you have to offer. Just don't try to pawn off low-quality or damaged items.

Guesstimate the object's retail value—a fair price that you would pay. Divide that amount in half to get a rough wholesale price. This figure is also your trade price. If the price is less than you paid, either wait and sell it on eBay or think about taking a loss in the pursuit of upgrading.

Successful trades can take place only with a dealer who has something you want and who would be able to sell the piece you are looking to trade. To figure out what would make the deal attractive to the dealer, put your math genes to work. Follow these steps:

1 Get the dealer's asking price and reduce it by 33 percent. This number represents the dealer's probable investment (about half the asking price) plus a small profit. Every dealer is going to look for some profit, even in a

trade. For example, if the dealer's asking price is $100, subtract $33 (33 percent) and you've got a price of $67.

2 If your item is worth more than the price as just calculated, your goal is to trade for the item plus get some cash. No dealer should be averse to making a good buy. However, don't try to milk the value of your piece. For example, suppose the dealer's asking price is $100 and you've estimated that $67 would be reasonable compensation for him, but you've set a trade price for your piece of $95. If you wind up trading your item for his, plus he gives you $20, that's a good deal even though that in effect means only $87 for you. Never mind that the dealer will probably mark up your old piece to at least $190. You probably couldn't have gotten that much for it, and now you have a nice new piece and a twenty you didn't have before.

3 If your item is worth less than the amount calculated in step 1, you're going to trade your item plus pay cash to the dealer, which the dealer probably prefers. The dealer's item has a $100 price tag, and your trade price is $30. You goal is still to get the new piece for around $67, which is a reasonable amount that's less than the asking price. Start by offering your item plus $30. Move up to sweeten the pot until you can agree on a price.

All this fancy premath is to give you the advantage when the trading begins. The dealer looks at your item and asks, "What are you looking to get out of this item?" Never ask dealers to make you an offer. They won't do it. Calmly and confidently present your scenario: "I was thinking my item plus $30." The dealers now make their own esoteric math calculations. They may very well grant a higher value to your item than you did. If they balk, hit them with your logic. "I think a good price for my item is $30 to $35, and I'm willing to throw in another $30." Still no interest? Raise it to $35. Dealers who can see a profit in the deal will give you a green light.

It Happens to Everyone: Buying Mistakes

Everyone who has anything to do with antiques and collectibles has made a few mistakes along the way. If they say they haven't, they're lying. But buying a piece that's inappropriate, damaged, or even fake is not the end of the world. In fact, even if you can't return the item, you can learn a great deal from the experience. (In the future, however, make it a practice to get the dealer's return policy in writing whenever you make a purchase.)

First, learn by analyzing where you went wrong. Did you fail to inspect properly? Teach yourself what to look for. Did you speculate wildly, convincing yourself an item was rare and valuable when it was common and of average value? Base your judgments on experience and knowledge. Did you make several mistakes in a row? Take a breather from buying and just browse for a while, looking at *a lot* of stuff and learning. Did you buy something that doesn't fit into your collection? Before you go shopping, form a clear idea of the kinds of things you want to add to your collection. (For tips on setting parameters and refining your collection, see chapter 10, "Collecting Your Thoughts.")

As for recovering from a blunder, you have a few options. Try first to see if there's a practical use around the house for the heartbreak object. Can you store umbrellas in it, put it in the kids' rooms, use it in your workshop or garden, let the dog sleep on it? Perhaps you can resell it and recoup some of your investment. Of course, you must be completely up-front about its flaws and price it accordingly. Finally, there's always the thrift shop, where you can take a tax deduction and someone else can fall in love with your mistake.

PART FIVE

PUTTING IT ALL

together

When does the *Planet of the Apes* lunchbox auction end? Did you leave feedback for that buyer whose check arrived in record time? Did he leave feedback for you? How much did you bid on that ruby red pickle castor?

CHAPTER 15

Yikes! As an active eBaysian you sometimes feel as though you need a Ph.D. in organizational management—or better yet, a workshop with a staff of elves.

Of course, being successful on eBay is a good problem to have. But keeping track of your burgeoning eBay empire is not difficult. In this chapter we show you how to get organized using tools offered by eBay, as well as simple spreadsheets you can create yourself.

My eBay

Every registered user can create a *My eBay* page, which is like an omniscient butler that helps you manage all your eBay activities. In one fell swoop you can view the current status of items you're selling and have bid on, recent feedback you've received, and your account status, among other things. Links to your favorite categories can also appear, allowing for speedy navigation.

Setting Your Preferences

Access *My eBay* through the link at the top of every page or via *Services* on the navigation bar, which brings you to the setup page. Here, you personalize your *My eBay* page by checking off a few selections. Nothing you select is cast in stone—you can make changes anytime.

First you set the *Display Options*. This determines the information that you'd like to appear on your *My eBay* page. Options include *Favorite Categories*, *Recent Feedback*, *Account Balance*,

Only on eBay

Your eBay user ID can reflect your passion, alter ego, or sense of humor. Or it may be an inside joke or sentimental homage. Whatever the etymology, here are a few user names ya gotta love.

toadthedog
hotspark
dazyaday
gotitnow
queenxeno
toysnark
donkeymom
saddlesore
franks-for-the-memories
ickycritter
realjob
snufftin
gardyloo*
tvlampboy
zooman
piginthecity
hairgoddess
mr.imperfection
no.name
oldpossum
wheezy
stumpy27
ponyboy1
monkeyfuzz

*A medieval warning cry when it was customary to throw slops from the windows onto the streets.

Seller List (items you are selling), and *Bidder List* (items you have bid on).

Your *My eBay* page shows up-to-the-second activity. You have the choice of also showing activity on completed—up to thirty days—auctions as well. It's a good idea to have past items appear for a week or so as a reminder to send checks, post feedback, and otherwise complete transactions.

Note: Volume buyers and sellers might find that too many days of completed auctions makes it hard to find what's going on at the moment. In this case try limiting your *My eBay* page to three days of past auctions (just enough time to make sure contact is made with buyers or sellers and that the process is well under way). Then create searches for seller and/or bidder for your user ID that include past auctions. Use these searches to review incomplete transactions. You can even print them out and add a few columns by hand, such as *Check Received*, *Check Cleared*, *Item Shipped*, and *Date*.

Once you've selected your past auctions period and display options, the *Seller/Bidder List* options offer the opportunity to further customize the appearance of these two lists. You are programming the computer to deliver the information in an order that makes sense for you. Here are the options:

● *Item Title* (lists auctions in alphabetical order).

● *Starting Price* (lists auctions in ascending order, lowest to highest).

● *Current Price* (auctions listed in ascending order, lowest to highest).

● *Reserve Price* (descending from highest reserve sellers list only).

● *Quantity* (descending from auctions with the most items for sale).

SPECIALTY:

Collectible Records

eBay HANDLE: stratplan   AGE: 67

RECORD THAT FIRST CLUED ME IN TO COLLECTING: Elvis extended play album (EPA) 2-1515 of *Lonesome Cowboy* and three other songs. I acquired it in 1981.

WHAT'S COOL ABOUT THIS SPECIALTY: A vinyl record is a piece of history, especially now that compact discs have taken over.

THEY AREN'T ALL THE SAME: Just because the title is *Blue Suede Shoes* by Elvis Presley doesn't indicate if it's a rare Sun label recording worth $1,000 or an ordinary RCA version. There are many types of records—promotional, not for resale, foreign produced, and special colored vinyl—and the value varies widely.

WHAT I TELL NEW COLLECTORS: Check feedback, send emails, and wait for answers before bidding. If it seems too good to be true, it probably is.

FEEDBACK TIPS: Review negatives for sour grapes and be cautious on bidders with a changed identity (sunglasses) or few feedbacks.

BEST SELLING TIP: Be honest—people hate liars. If the record is scratched, worn, has a torn sleeve, or whatever, say so. Always follow up promptly by email when you ship the item and then check to see that it was received.

MY BEST eBay TRANSACTION: A computer part for a friend. The manufacturer had gone out of business, and a dealer was closing out brand-new stock.

WHAT MY COLLECTION SAYS ABOUT ME: I stick with the oldies and goodies.

home | my eBay | site map

| Browse | Sell | Services | Search | Help | Community |

| overview | registration | buying & selling | my eBay | about me | feedback forum | safe harbor |

▸ Never be outbid again! Check out our new eBay a-go-go service.
▸ Review mockups of new item pages. Tell us what you think.

[Search] tips
☐ Search titles **and** descriptions

My eBay!

cork 321

My Favorites

Collectibles: Clocks, Timepieces: Wrist Watches
Current ‖ New Today ‖ Ending Today ‖ Completed ‖ Going, Going, Gone

Jewelry, Gemstones: Jewelry: Costume: Designer, Signed
Current ‖ New Today ‖ Ending Today ‖ Completed ‖ Going, Going, Gone

Books, Movies, Music: Books: First Editions
Current ‖ New Today ‖ Ending Today ‖ Completed ‖ Going, Going, Gone

Photo & Electronics: Photo Equipment: 35mm
Current ‖ New Today ‖ Ending Today ‖ Completed ‖ Going, Going, Gone

Click here to change your favorite categories.

My Feedback (2)

Recent feedback about me:

03/30/99   (434) ☆ (praise)
15:07:55 PST Fast payment and great communications. A WONDERFUL eBay client! A+++++

03/25/99   (76) ☆ (praise)
14:55:30 PST Good communication, prompt payment, Thank You!

See all feedback about me
Review and respond to feedback about me
See all feedback I have left about others

My Account

As of **08/12/99, 22:26:32 PDT**, my account balance is: **$1.50**

Full account status: since my last invoice - entire account (takes a while; please be patient)

Up to the minute accounting of all credits, debits and current balance for your eBay accounts. Accounts are not created until the first credit or debit is posted, so even if you have already created your account, no information will be here until the first account activity.

Fees & credits - Payment terms - Use a credit card for automatic billing - Credit request - Refunds - Make a one time payment

Items I'm Selling — See details...

Item	Start	Current	Reserve	Quant	Bids	Start	End PDT	Time Left
3 pieces signed 1970's art glass NO RESERVE								
155968229	$29.99	-	-	1	-	08/31/99	09/10/99, 16:59:42 PDT	8d 2h 24m
Tin fire truck w/extendable ladder NR								
155979883	$15.00	-	-	1	-	08/31/99	09/10/99, 17:15:44 PDT	8d 2h 40m
Item	Start	Current	Reserve	Quant	Bids	Start	End PDT	Time Left
Totals: 2	**$44.99**	**$0.00**	-	**2**	**0**	-	-	-

Green indicates items that would sell if the auction were to end now.
Red indicates items that would not sell if the auction were to end now.
Click on an underlined column heading to sort in either ascending or descending order.

Add an item - Tips for sellers - FAQ - After the auction

Items I'm Bidding On — See details...

Item	Start	Current	My Max	Quant	Bids	Start	End PDT	Time Left
Classic Hubley cast iron racer w/ driver								
152757882	$10.00	$10.00	$100.00	1	1	08/25/99	09/01/99, 14:14:51 PDT	6d 23h 44m
Item	Start	Current	My Max	Quant	Bids	Start	End PDT	Time Left
Totals: 1	**$10.00**	**$10.00**	**$102.50**	**1**	**1**	-	-	-

Green indicates auctions in which you are currently winning. The totals in green exclude Dutch auctions.
Red indicates auctions in which you are not currently winning.
Note: Dutch auctions do not use the color coding.
Click on an underlined column heading to sort in either ascending or descending order.

Search - Wanted page - Tips for buyers - FAQ - After the auction

● *Bid Count* (descending from the listings with the most number of bids).

● *Starting Time* (ascending from most recent listings).

● *Ending Time* (descending from auctions closest to ending. Note: This is the default selection).

Once your choices are made—via check-off boxes—and your user ID and password are put in, press *Enter*. Note: You can also sort the lists directly on your *My eBay* page by clicking on any of the header words.

From the page itself you can further customize what you see. If you select the link to *Favorite Categories* in the lower portion of the category section, you are able to choose up to four categories to appear on your *My eBay* page. The categories you select appear with links to the listing menu options of *New Today, Current, Ending Today, Completed,* and *Going, Going, Gone.* This makes it a snap to stop in and check out what's happening in your favorite haunts.

Navigation

Think of My eBay as your personal site map. It features numerous time-saving links under each heading as well as options for viewing listings that can be accessed only through this page. Some of the links you should check out:

● See All Feedback About Me: My eBay always shows you your three most recent feedbacks, but this link takes you to your entire feedback history. This includes your *eBay ID card*—a score box showing your recent tally of positive, neutral, and negative comments.

● Review and Respond to Feedback About Me: Look up all your feedback at a glance. Then click on the *Envelope* icon to reply. Your response will then appear after the comment in question.

● See Feedback I Have Left for Others: Very handy if you can't remember whether or not you left someone feedback.

● My Account: A running total of your current account balance is displayed. Links to your account for the last two months or in its entirety. This is a time-saver from having to go to the account status forms. After a heavy day of posting or auctions ending, you can view your running tab with eBay. Another advantage is seeing exactly when eBay has charged your account or your payment has been received.

● Items I'm Bidding and Items I'm Selling: On the right side of these heading bars is a *See Details* link that brings you to a synopsis page. Miniversions of the listings show the header (*Seller, Bidder, Current Bidding Status*) of the listing. Perform all the usual functions here, such as *Bid, Leave Feedback,* and *Send E-mail.*

As a bid management tool and to help you keep pace with the market, *My eBay* can't be beat. Because all auctions you bid on remain listed for as long as you specify (up to thirty days after the auction ends), you can see where prices go on items you don't win. Depressing though that may be, it's good information to have.

One cool feature is that *My eBay* displays the status of your bid. When you're winning, the listing appears in green. When you're losing or the reserve has yet to be met, it appears in red. This ability to track the status of auctions you're bidding on is one reason to bid early in an auction so it shows up on your *My eBay* page.

My eBay works in concert with the proxy bidding system and displays your maximum bid to help you know how fast your competitors are creeping up on you. Note: Some browsers don't always refresh *My eBay* every time you return to it—they load from a saved version on your hard drive—so information might not be 100 percent current. Click on your browser's refresh or reload button to get the latest information. Also, check the setup of your browser; there might be an option in the preferences to always update the page when you open it. (AOL users will find this in the *www* section of their preferences under the *advanced tab and settings* option on the temporary files menu.)

Only on eBay

"We started selling on eBay about two years ago with one trading card," says eBay Power Seller Ed Robinson, whose primary category is now knives. "Now we are running over four hundred auctions a month. We have worked a small hobby into a family business."

Making Changes

Want to slice the data in another way? No problem—just use the *My eBay* link on any page and set your new preferences. To save these changes, be sure to create a new bookmark or replace in your Favorite Places.

Simple Spreadsheets You Can Create Yourself

If you intend to move beyond selling a few items to buying merchandise specifically for resale, you'll have to start keeping some records. If you go into business, you might be responsible for sales tax (see chapter 14, "Out in the Field") and business-related income tax. It's advisable to get expert tax advice because, for example, if you work out of your home, you might also be eligible for tax deductions related to your business.

Simple spreadsheets are a great way to start. They're flexible and easy to create, change, and update. If your computer came with any kind of office automation program—such as Microsoft Office or Microsoft Works—it includes a spreadsheet program.

Spreadsheets are automated charts that are set up along two axes: rows going down the sheet and columns going across. You decide what information goes in the rows and columns based on what you want to track. You can set up formulas so the spreadsheet automatically tallies totals, profits and losses, and percentages for items you buy and resell. The key to using these programs is keeping up with your inputting. But many are compatible with templates for writing invoices and generating reports. If you decide to take the next step and use a software package for small businesses, the data in these spreadsheets is usually easily uploaded. "My eBay Sales Results" (opposite) is a sample of a simple spreadsheet you can use to track eBay activity. This tracking system will help you keep your sights on the big picture and your average profit margin. It also gives you a historical record of what sells well and what doesn't.

It's a good idea to track expenses (beyond inventory costs) as well so you know whether you're running a profit or nickel-and-diming yourself into the hole.

"My eBay Expenses" (page 250) is a sample expense spreadsheet. A spreadsheet is only a tracking system. You must also keep all paper receipts in an organized fashion as backup for tax purposes.

my eBay sales results

Item #	Description	Purchase Date	Purchase Price	Sale Price Including Shipping	Sale Date	Gross Profit	Profit as Percent
99-001	Art Deco Inkwell	1/3/99	$45.00	$80.40	1/15/99	$35.40	79%
99-002	Chanel Perfume Bottle	1/6/99	$3.50	$15.70	1/15/99	$12.20	349%
99-003	Roseville Vase	1/8/99	$65.00	$134.00	1/18/99	$69.00	106%
99-004	Heisey Candlesticks	1/10/99	$50.00	$103.73	1/20/99	$53.73	107%
99-005	Unsigned Oil Painting	1/15/99	$35.00	$100.40	1/25/99	$65.40	187%
99-006	Porcelain Doll	1/18/99	$30.00	$40.40	1/25/99	$10.40	35%
99-007	Leather Handbag	1/18/99	$10.00	$25.40	1/25/99	$15.40	154%
99-008	Orrefors Vase	1/20/99	$35.00	$80.40	1/30/99	$45.40	130%
99-009	Biscuit Tin—English	1/20/99	$25.00	$57.40	1/30/99	$32.40	130%
99-010	Hall Teapot	1/30/99	$35.00	$72.90	2/12/99	$37.90	108%
99-011	Early Wire Hanger	1/30/99	$15.00	$31.20	2/17/99	$16.20	108%
99-012	Signed Elvis Photo	1/30/99	$60.00	$148.20	2/18/99	$88.20	147%
99-013	Advertising Ruler 15"	2/1/99	$2.00	$7.49	2/19/99	$5.49	275%
99-014	Tomato String Holder	2/1/99	$22.00	$49.50	2/20/99	$27.50	125%
99-015	Gunsmoke Lunchbox	2/1/99	$57.00	$90.70	2/20/99	$33.70	59%
TOTAL			$489.50	$1,037.82		$548.32	112%

my eBay expenses

Postage	Amount	Date
Shipping/FedEx	$15.00	1/22/99
Shipping Mail Boxes Etc	$33.05	1/25/99
Shipping/USPS	$16.20	1/30/99
Shipping/USPS	$15.75	2/25/99
Subtotal	*$80.00*	
Supplies		
Boxes and Tape	$15.00	1/15/99
Bubble Wrap	$30.00	1/18/99
Subtotal	*$45.00*	
Travel and Subsistence		
Gas L.A. Show	$9.57	1/8/99
Meals L.A. Show	$18.00	1/8/99
Subtotal	*$27.57*	
Miscellaneous		
Admission L.A. Show	$10.00	1/8/99
Book on Roseville Pottery	$25.00	1/25/99
Subtotal	*$35.00*	
Total Expenses	*$187.57*	
Total Expenses & Purchases	*$677.07*	◀ This is the total outlay for merchandise and expenses.
Sales	*$1,037.82*	◀ This is the total brought in from sales.
Income/Expense	*$360.75*	◀ This is the difference between purchases and expenses and sales income. A positive number equals a profit.
Net Profit	*35%*	◀ This is your profit after all expenses, expressed as a percent.

Try this exercise: Get out a calculator and traipse around the house, punching in the value or price you paid for every item in your collection. As the total creeps—or zooms—up, think about

CHAPTER 16

documenting the goods

how you'd feel if disaster struck and every piece vanished. How many pieces would that be? Many collectors reach a point where they have more objects than they can recall. Even if you have a photographic memory and can remember every piece you've ever bought (and what you paid), try telling that to an insurance adjuster. Certainly some of your pieces are irreplaceable, but if you were robbed or Mother Nature turned your house upside down, wouldn't you at least like to have the money to start over again? That's why taking the time to document your collection is so important. Once you set up a system, which we show you how to do in this chapter, all you have to do is update it every time you acquire a wonderful new addition to your precious collection.

Creating an Inventory

A solid inventory starts with a list. This can be as simple or as detailed as you like. For each piece, write down the following:

- Name of object.

- Date purchased.

- Place purchased.

- Item description (keep it short, but make it so someone who isn't familiar with your area of collecting can figure out which item you're talking about).

- Purchase price (keep all receipts).

● Estimated value (could be greater than purchase price if you got a steal or adjusted over time as the market shifts).

● Significant features (signed, purchased directly from artist, provenance, and so on).

● Condition (use the common nomenclature, if there is one, from your field of collecting).

● Date sold or traded (so anyone knows it's gone from your collection) and the price realized.

The easiest way to guide people through your collection is to use a numbering system. Try to avoid a multiple-digit system decipherable only with a secret decoder ring. A chronological ordering system satisfies most needs. Some people keep track of when an item was added to their collection by appending a year to the number, such as 99-001 or 001-99. If possible, and if it won't damage the item, affix the number to the item to make connecting the item to your inventory even easier.

If you want to go beyond pad and paper, you can enlist modern technology to create a more detailed and complete archive. Being consistent in your methodology makes it easier to keep your records up-to-date. Here are some ways to handle the information:

● **Videotape your collection:** If you have access to a videocamera, either set it up on a tripod and shoot a few seconds of tape on each object, or do a slow walk-through, panning the walls, shelves, or other locations where your collection is displayed. With either style, give your best Howard Cosell–style running commentary. This constitutes an oral inventory of descriptions, provenance, and value. Show details of any important feature such as signatures or labels. Create a miniset with a ruler or yardstick in the scene so every item's size and perspective is recorded.

● **Create a spreadsheet:** You can set up a spreadsheet in less than an hour and then spend only a few minutes inputting new acquisitions as needed. Spreadsheets enable you to keep a running total of the value of your collection. If you collect in different categories, you can create a category field and then periodically sort your collection by category or any other field, such as price or date purchased.

● **Shoot with a digital camera:** If you have pur-
chased a digital camera to use for selling things on eBay, use it to take
pictures of your collection and store them on your hard drive. Use the
pictures in conjunction with an inventory spreadsheet or database and
match file names with inventory numbers or create an inventory sheet
and drop the digital image into a word-processing document (see sample later in this chapter). There's no film, so there's no added expense
to keeping this kind of documentation.

● **Snap photos with a regular camera:**
Whenever you have a few extra frames on a roll, use them up by shooting some more pieces. After the pictures are developed, jot down the
descriptions on the back.

● **Set up a database:** Many office software packages come
with rudimentary database applications. Microsoft Office, for example,
includes Access, which is pretty easy to teach yourself. You can create
a program to track your collection with easy data entry forms and run
reports based on that information.

● **Use off-the-shelf software:** Collectors now have a
choice of several software packages for inventorying their collections.
Evaluate them carefully before you purchase. Software doesn't necessarily save time if you have to input a great deal of data or the program
is unwieldy. A spreadsheet or your own small database can be created
in the same amount of time or less than it takes to learn new software.
These systems generate lots of fancy-looking reports. Do you need that
or only a good solid list? Collectors' software is advertised at most big
shows and in antiques and collectibles periodicals. Many companies
offer a sample disk to get a sense of the look and feel of a program; it's
a good idea to take these for a test drive.

If your collection crosses many categories or is obscure, esoteric, or his-
torically significant, provide additional documentation. Write down what you
know about each item and indicate reference materials that offer more
details on the object. Include a list of experts in the field.

Treat inventory data as you would any valuable information or papers
and provide for its safekeeping. Follow the processes used by computer
operators and make backups—or copies—of data. Keep copies in a separate
location. If your basement computer room floods, you'll be thankful to have

Here's a simple inventory sheet created on a word processor with an image from a digital camera inserted (most word processing software has an insert or import function). You can create and store the basic form as a blank template.

Inventory of the Collection of
Ima Collector

Inventory number: 99-124

Item description: Art glass bottle form vase, 7 1/4" tall, signed S. J. Herman 1964

Date purchased: 5/16/99

Place purchased: 26th Street Flea Market

Purchase price: $75

Estimated value: Variable—this is an emerging market and should increase in value considerably in the next few years. Still probably 2 to 3 times what I paid for it.

Significant features: An early example by a well-known artist from the American studio glass movement (American working in England), which had its genesis in the early 1960s.

Relevant documentation: His work and biographical information found in most reference books covering glass during the periods 1960–1980. See *Contemporary Art Glass* by Ray and Lee Grover and *Contemporary Glass* by Suzanne K. Frantz.

Condition: Excellent.

Date sold or traded: N/A.

a set of disks with your digital images in a plastic box on an upstairs closet shelf. Notify at least one trusted person of the data's whereabouts should someone other than you need access to the information.

Here are some ways to safeguard your information and data:

- Back up computer-based data every time you update an entry. If cumbersome, make a point to do it weekly or twice a month. The key is sticking to it.

- Store videotapes in a cool, dry place and duplicate them periodically.

- Make a second set of prints and store them—with the negatives—in a cool, dry, separate place.

- Occasionally make an extra copy of any paper documentation.

Insurance

No doubt you'd be deeply pained to see your collection literally go up in smoke. And while the chances of this happening are slim and money cannot heal the emotional wounds of a loss, an insurance settlement really does take the sting away by helping you recoup your investment.

Perhaps you already have a homeowner's or renter's policy that covers your collection. However, chances are your collection is only *partially* protected by these policies. Not all insurance policies are alike, so you should read the fine print and consult with an insurance expert—usually your broker—to make sure that your collection is actually covered. In fact, having a good broker is an important part of having insurance. They know you, your collection, and how to work with insurance companies.

Insurance policies come with lots of exclusions—things or events that aren't covered. Policies are also riddled with confusing terminology such as deductibles, scheduled and nonscheduled items, and replacement costs. Unfortunately people often think they're covered when they aren't. For example, say you have a great collection of cookie jars you've been building for the last ten years. Your homeowner's policy has the value of your collection aggregated in the total contents of your home. One Thanksgiving your uncle Harold, who's never been the picture of grace, trips on your son's baseball mitt, stumbles into the bookcase, and knocks your prized Professor Ludwig Von Drake cookie jar off a shelf, sending the piece crashing to the floor. On Monday you call your insurance company and are unceremoniously

Meet eBay Ambassador Linda Miller

SPECIALTY:

Antique and Vintage Jewelry

eBay HANDLE: victorian-lady   AGE: 48

THE PIECE THAT GOT ME STARTED: At an antiques show in Baltimore fifteen years ago I fell in love with a 1920s filigree ring. It was the beginning of a wonderful addiction.

NO WONDER I LOVE OLD JEWELS: One of my ancestors was a pirate who ran with Blackbeard.

IT HELPS TO KNOW: About metals, styles, and eras pieces came from, as well as how to spot repairs and reproductions. There are many wonderful books to learn from, but handling and experience are the best teachers.

MY SECRET WEAPON: A jeweler's loupe. Out in the field, always look over pieces carefully before buying. Damaged pieces are hard to get rid of.

WALKING ADVERTISEMENT: I wear whatever piece suits me, whether it's Victorian or funky art moderne from the 1940s. People always stop me when I wear a silver charm necklace with antique photos of my family, including my grandmother as a flapper, my great-grandmother with her children, and my dad as a little boy.

PEOPLE MISTAKENLY THINK: That this hobby is expensive. So untrue. Jewelry doesn't have to be gold or diamonds to be charming. It can be gold-filled or brass, but the wonderful thing is that it was made one hundred years ago.

MY BEST eBay TRANSACTION: I once sold a mourning locket to a lady whose three-year-old son had passed away. She wanted to put a lock of his hair inside. It made me cry, but I was so delighted to send it to her.

HOW eBay HAS CHANGED MY LIFE: I bought a computer three years ago to write my résumé and find yet another boring, bloodsucking job. Instead I found a way to make a living from my own home. I think I've died and gone to heaven.

informed that "breakage" is excluded. "But I thought I was insured," you protest. Oh, you are, the company tells you, if your house burns down. This seems unfair, considering that the odds are higher that you'll drop a piece than incinerate it, but that's how many policies work. Other common exclusions include off premise theft, floods, and earthquakes.

To get the kind of coverage you need, you may have to provide a list of items to be specifically included in your policy with a value associated to each. In the world of insurance, this is known as *scheduling*. That means you pay for the insurance based on the kind of item and its value. Rates vary for different reasons. Jewelry is expensive to schedule because it's small, pilferable, and easy to lose—and it's the kind of item that robbers go after first. Paintings are fairly inexpensive to insure, as they hang on your wall and rarely get moved and are usually threatened only by total catastrophe. Costs are calculated per $100 of coverage. For example, it costs $0.60 per $100 of coverage to insure a musical instrument. Therefore it would cost you $9 to insure a $1,500 instrument (15 x 0.6 = 9). Below are some approximate costs for insuring various types of items in New York City (rates vary by geography, so this is only a guide):

Cameras	$1.80
China/Crystal/Glass	$0.46 first $1,500; $0.21 in excess of $1,500; breakage add $0.15
Coins	$1.75
Jewelry	$2.80
Silverware	$0.60
Stamps	$0.60
Fine Arts	$0.46 first $1,500; $0.21 in excess of $1,500; breakage add $0.15

At first blush this may seem expensive. Note, however, that the rates for just covering the contents of your home may actually be higher per $100 than scheduled rates (make sure your broker investigates the differences). Scheduled rates should reflect replacement value while contents may be subject to depreciation, making scheduling your collection a better deal.

Don't forget the furniture. Maybe you've decorated and furnished your house from flea market finds and auction buys, and some of those pieces have substantial value. Consider scheduling these as fine arts instead of

Only on eBay

The first night George Anne ventured into the *eBay Café*, she started chatting about Jadeite glassware with an eBay user named Janney. George Anne mentioned that she'd grown up in Nebraska and South Dakota, which turned out to be similar to Janney's background. As they corresponded, they discovered that not only were they about the same age and the mothers of toddlers the same age—but they were also *cousins*. It turns out that their grandmothers were sisters. George Anne's grandmother died in 1936, leaving a three-year-old daughter to be raised by George Anne's grandfather's side of the family. George Anne's mother was kept away from her mother's family and grew up feeling like an outcast. "I have since learned from Janney and her mother that my mother has always been wanted and loved by my grandmother's side of the family, and they did everything they could to try and get her to live with them," says George Anne. "My mother has spent sixty years not knowing this. I didn't even know that my mother's sister had a daughter, so I would never have gone looking for her. Ever since Janney and I first corresponded on eBay, our relationship has been nothing but wonderful. She's filled in so much about my past that talking to her is like having a huge piece of our family puzzle dropped in my lap."

including them in your general contents. It's going to be harder to replace that nineteenth-century French armoire than it is the dishwasher.

Appraisals and insurance go hand in hand. Whether or not you require an appraisal depends on your insurance carrier. Most carriers require an appraisal or bill of sale for items over $5,000, while others begin at $25,000. Some companies require an appraisal for every item. Take the extra step of sending a copy of your bills or appraisals to your broker in addition to the insurance company as a safety net if your copy is destroyed or lost. A few insurance issues to ponder:

● **Covering your computer:** Now that you've geared up to buy and sell on eBay, consider getting your computer equipment scheduled in your homeowner's policy, especially for replacement value, as the equipment depreciates quickly. If you plan to be in business, think about expanding your coverage to include software and data re-creation.

● **Receiving reimbursement for non-scheduled items:** Some items may be considered contents in your homeowner's or renter's policy. Normally there is a small limit (amount you can recover) for unscheduled jewelry less a deductible.

● Deciding when to revalue items: Every five years or if you request an increase in coverage.

In the unfortunate circumstance that you have a loss and no insurance, contact a tax expert. Some losses may qualify for personal tax considerations.

Appraisals

The time has come to get your collection valued for insurance, tax purposes, estate planning, or divorce. Before picking up the Yellow Pages and calling AAAA Acme Appraising—the first one listed—there are some things you should know.

Being out in the field hunting down items and seeing the variety in the market, you are aware of the serendipity of value and how items sell for different prices on any given day. Well, appraisals can also be all over the place, depending on who reviews your collection. You need to take charge of the appraisal process.

Anyone can claim to be an appraiser; there are no state or federal licensing laws or governmental certifications. In response to the wide-open nature of the appraisal business, organizations such as the International Association of Appraisers and the American Society of Appraisers were created to certify members through education and testing and maintain standards and ethics. Even so, certification by a society doesn't guarantee a fair evaluation. You need someone who is knowledgeable in your collecting area, with no other interest at stake except providing a quality service to you.

Questions for the Appraiser

According to the International Association of Appraisers, these are some of the questions to ask when considering engaging an appraiser to value your property.

● What qualifies you to appraise my property? Besides having formal education in appraisal theory, principles, procedures, ethics, and law, the appraiser should be up-to-date on the latest appraisal standards, be familiar with the type of property you want appraised, and know how to value it correctly.

● Do you belong to an appraisal society that tests its members? There are many appraisal organizations, but only a few require members to take courses and pass tests before being accredited. Membership in such an association shows that the appraiser is involved with the profession, has peer recognition, has access to updated information, and is subject to a code of ethics and conduct.

- Have you been tested? Do you take continuing education classes? If the appraiser claims membership in a group that trains and tests its members, be sure to ask if she has personally gone through those procedures. Some organizations grandfather members into high membership status without testing because they were members before certain rules took effect.

- How will you handle items outside your specialty area? No appraiser should claim expertise in everything. A good appraiser knows his or her limits and is expected to consult with other experts when necessary.

- What is your fee, and on what basis do you charge? Do not hire an appraiser who charges a percentage of the appraised value or *contingency* fee. These practices are clearly conflicts of interests and may result in biased values. The IRS will not accept an appraisal done with such fee arrangements.

- What will the appraisal report be like? You should receive a formal, typewritten report that presents the information you need in a complete and organized way.

Collector, Appraise Thyself

Unless you are required to get an appraisal, consider doing your own value analysis. After all, you probably already have an idea what your item is worth. The question is, do you know exactly *what* it is? For example, do you just know it's an Arts and Crafts buffet—or a signed Stickley Arts and Crafts buffet with original finish? Such nuances make a big difference. Consult books, dealers, museum curators, and the appropriate eBay chat room for advice on authentication and identification. To determine a value, you have to compare your item with similar ones. Your goal is to find at least three to use as comparisons. That's what a professional appraiser does.

Make sure to adjust the value of your items based on differences between yours and the ones you use for comparison purposes. A refinished buffet is going to be worth less than yours. A buffet descended through the Stickley family is going to be worth more.

Auction houses are a great way to get estimates of an item's value. Most houses give free estimates at no obligation. Call and speak to an expert or bring photos of the object. Auction sales estimates are not an exact science. Ask whether they have a history of selling similar items and if they have sold any recently. Even the experts among experts can't always predict how high a price an item might sell for. A Massachusetts auction house recently gave a pre-sale estimate of $25,000 to $30,000 for an eighteenth-century Pembroke table manufactured in Charleston, South Carolina. It sold for $266,500, which only proves if you get two or more collectors in a room, the sky's the limit.

You Can't Take It with You

If you're married to your collection, it's probably till death do you part. However, when you go to the big flea market in the sky, your collection of two thousand shaving mugs stays behind. Don't assume your family will be thrilled to inherit this hoard of barberiana. They may not share your passion, and it could be a burden and emotionally wrenching for them to deal with objects they identify so closely with you.

Coming to Your Town: The *Antiques Road Show*

It's hardly a coincidence that the collecting market is booming and the most popular show on PBS is the *Antiques Road Show*. The program travels the country, and wherever it lands it encourages folks to bring in their cherished items to expert appraisers to answer the big question: What's it worth? If the *Antiques Road Show* comes to your town, pack a lunch, because it's a long day waiting to find out if that weird and wonderful item you inherited from Aunt Mildred is worth anything. The show is a great source of entertainment as well as a fount of information about the general value of things. If you're lucky, you may even get your item appraised on the air.

It may seem morbid, but discuss the future of your collection with your family while you're still around. Perhaps it would be best to make arrangements for them to sell your collection after you're gone. Your loved ones might use the proceeds to upgrade *their* collections. If you don't sell before you die, leave explicit instructions for your family about the contents and value of your collection, as well as where to go to find the right buyer.

Don't forget your collecting friends. You may have an item or two they'd prize. Make arrangements to bequeath such items, knowing the pleasure your object might bring to another aficionado.

Going Public: Donating to an Institution

If you've truly amassed a collection of historical significance or have museum-quality pieces, think about donating your collection to a public institution. Don't assume a museum of fine art is going to welcome your donation of 150 antique apple parers, even if it is the best collection in the country. Keep in mind that by accepting your collection, the institution is accepting the costs of preservation and storage in perpetuity. You may have to shop around for a suitable museum or library to accept your gift. Your collection, however, could add to the "core" of an institution devoted to apples (or tools).

Start by writing the president or executive director of the institution, unless you know of a curator in your area of interest whom you can approach directly. Be explicit about wanting to make a donation. As you describe its scope and depth, be honest. These folks are experts, too, and they'll know if you've got the goods.

The donation will create some tax issues for you, so consult a tax expert. A lawyer will also be necessary to hammer out the terms. Even though you love every item, the recipient organization may not need *every* one and will want to reserve the right to sell some pieces. Any rights to sale should be specified, or you should know the museum's policy on selling donated items. Also specify how the collection should be handled if the institution closes, especially if there is an endowment associated with your gift.

Trailblazing a Library

No matter what your background and financial status, your passion can produce a collection of great significance. In 1984 Roger Wendlick got hooked on collecting rare books about the Lewis and Clark expedition with his first purchase, a 1904 edition of the journals of Meriwether Lewis for $695. By the time he was done, he had amassed more than one thousand books, maps, newspapers, and other documents. His prize possession: a first edition of the journals—printed in 1814 in Philadelphia—of which only thirty are known to exist in their original binding. He bought the books on layaway and paid off the total from his earnings running a backhoe. Wendlick's hard work paid off. In 1999 his collection was partially purchased and partially donated to Lewis and Clark College in Portland, Oregon. The proceeds will enable Mr. Wendlick to retire comfortably, happy in the knowledge that his sharp eye and deep appreciation resulted in a collection that historians will pore over for years to come.

BROWSE
- **Categories**
  Antiques
  Books, Movies, Music
  Coins & Stamps
  Collectibles
  Computers
  Dolls, Figures
  Jewelry, Gemstones
  Photo & Electronics
  Pottery & Glass
  Sports Memorabilia
  Toys & Bean Bag Plush
  Miscellaneous
- **Featured**
- **Hot**
- **Grab Bag**
- **Great Gifts**
- **Big Ticket**
- **Gallery**
- **Category Overview**
- **New Today**
- **Ending Today**
- **Completed Auctions**
- **Going, going, gone**

SELL
- **Sell Your Item Form**

SEARCH
- **Search for Items**
- **Search for Members**
- **Personal Shopper**

HELP
- **Help Overview**
- **Basics**
- **Buyer Guide**
- **Seller Guide**
- **My Info**

eBay site map

HELP *(cont.)*
- •**Community Standards**
- •**General Support Q&A Board**
- •**Direct Support for New Users**
- •**User to User eBay Q&A Board**
- •**Images/HTML Board**

SERVICES
- •**Services Overview**
- •**Registration**
  Register now
  Confirm registration
  I forgot my password
- •**Buying and Selling**
  MANAGE MY ITEMS FOR SALE
  Revise my item
  Add to my item description
  Change my item's category
  Feature my item
  Fix my gallery image
  Promote your listings with link
    buttons
  Cancel bids on my item
  End my auction early
  Relist my item
  Upload many items for listing
  POWER SELLERS
  SERVICES
  SELLER ACCOUNTS
  Check my seller account status
  Make payments toward my
    account
  Place or update my credit card
    on file with eBay
  Request final value fee credit
  Cash out your credit balance
  BUYER TOOLS
  Retract my bid
  Insurance

Escrow
Send a Gift Alert message
- •**My eBay**
  Change my User ID
  Change my password
  Change my registration informa-
    tion
  Change my email address
  Change my notification prefer-
    ences
- •**About Me**
- •**Feedback Forum**
  View a member's feedback
    record
  Leave feedback on a member
  Review feedback you have left
    about others
  Review feedback others have left
    about you
  Make feedback changes public
    or private
- •**SafeHarbor**
  Free insurance
  Escrow services
  Authentication
  Investigations

COMMUNITY
- •**Community Overview**
- •**News**
  Announcements
  Cool happenings
  Latest buzz on new features
  Calendar
  Letters to the founder
- •**Chat**
  CHAT ROOMS
  The eBay Café
  The AOL Café

Discuss eBay's Newest Features
Wanted Board
Emergency Contact
eBay International
CATEGORY-SPECIFIC CHAT
Advertising Collectibles
Antiques
Barbie Bulletin Board
Beanie Babies
Books
Coins
Comics
Computers
Diecast
Dolls
Elvis
Furbies
Garage

Glass
Jewelry
Movies
Music
Photo Equipment
Pottery
Sports
Stamps
Toys
Trading Cards
•**eBay Life**
•**Library**
•**Charity**
Giving Board
•**eBay Store**
•**Suggestion Box**
•**About eBay**

ANTIQUES
- **General**
- **Ancient World**
- **Architectural**
- **Books, Manuscripts**
- **European**
- **Folk Art**
- **Furniture**
- **Medical**
- **Metalware**
  GENERAL
  BRONZE
  COPPER
  PEWTER
  SILVER
  SILVER PLATE
- **Musical Instruments**
- **Primitives**
- **Prints**
- **Science Instruments**
- **Textiles, Linens**
- **Toleware**
- **Woodenware**
- **Antiques (post-1900)**
  GENERAL
  FURNITURE

AUTOMOTIVE
- **Collector Vehicles**
  GENERAL
  ACCESSORIES
  COLLECTOR CARS
  PARTS
- **General Vehicles**
  GENERAL
  ACCESSORIES
  CARS
  TRUCKS
  RVS

eBay category overview

PARTS
MOTORCYCLES
General
Harley Davidson
Japanese

BOOKS, MOVIES, MUSIC
•**Books**
GENERAL
AUDIO
CHILDREN
General
Big Little Books
Classics
Early Readers
Fairy Tales
Non-Fiction
Little Golden Books
Mystery, Adventure
Mythology
Picture Books
Series
Young Adult
EDUCATIONAL
Business, Finance
Computers, Internet
Encyclopedias
Homeschool
Language
Medical
Physical Sciences
Reference
Science/Technology
Self-Help
Textbooks
FICTION
General
Adventure
Horror

Humor
Military
Mystery
Romance
Sci-Fi
Western
FIRST EDITIONS
NON-FICTION
General
Arts, Entertainment
Auto/Biography
Collectibles
Cooking
Geography
History
Hobby, Crafts
Home & Garden
Hunting, Fishing
Military
Paranormal
Poetry
Price Guides
Religion
Travel
Vehicles
Western
PULPS, CLUB EDITIONS
PAPERBACKS
RARE
SCHOOL ANNUALS
•**Magazines**
GENERAL
ANIMAL
BUSINESS
CATALOG
CHILDREN
COLLECTOR
COOKING
CRAFTS, HOBBY

HOME & GARDEN
HORROR, MONSTER
HUMOR
ILLUSTRATED
MEDICAL
MEN
MOVIE, TV
NEWS
PULP
SCIENCE & NATURE
SCI-FI
SPORTING
TECHNICAL
TRAVEL
TRUE CRIME
WOMEN
•**Music**
GENERAL
CDS
General
Big Band/Swing
Blues
Children's
Comedy
Classical
Country
Dance
Disco
Folk
Holiday
Instrumental
Jazz
Latin
New Age
New Artists
Opera
Pop
Rap/Hip-Hop
R&B/Soul

Reggae/Ska
Religious
Rock: Alternative
Rock: Classic
Rock: Heavy Metal
Rock: Hard
Rock: Soft
Sound Tracks: Film
Sound Tracks: Theatre
Techno/Industrial
Vocals
World/International
RECORDS
General
Big Band/Swing
Blues
Children's
Classical
Country
Dance
Disco
Folk
Holiday
Instrumental
Jazz
Latin
New Age
New Artists
Opera
Picture
Pop
Rap/Hip-Hop
R&B/Soul
Reggae/Ska
Religious
Rock: Alternative
Rock: Classic
Rock: Heavy Metal
Rock: Hard

Rock: Soft
Sound Tracks: Film
Sound Tracks: Theatre
Techno/Industrial
Vocals
World/International
TAPES
General
Cassettes
8 Tracks
Reel to Reel
•**Movies**
VIDEOS
General
Action, Adventure
Cartoons
Children's
Classics
Comedy
Documentary
Foreign
Horror
Music
Mystery
Romance
Sci-Fi
DVD
Laserdiscs
PAL
8mm
16mm
35mm

COINS & STAMPS
•**Coins**
US
General
Cents
Nickels

Dimes
Quarters
Halves
Dollars
Errors
Collections, Lots
Mint, Proof Sets
Gold
Colonial
Commemorative
Currency
Certificates
Publications
Supplies
NON-US
General
Ancient, Medieval
Africa
Asia
Australia
Canada
Central America
England
France
Germany
Mexico
South America
Errors
Collections, Lots
Mint, Proof Sets
Commemorative
Gold
Currency
Certificates
Publications
Supplies
•**Exonumia**
•**Stamps**
US

General
19th Century: Used
19th Century: Unused
20th Century: Used
20th Century: Unused
Air Mail
Back of Book
Blocks, Sheets
Collection, Mixture
Covers
Duck Stamps
EFOs
First Day Covers
Possessions
Publications
Revenues
Supplies
Topical
WORLD
General
Africa
Asia
British Commonwealth
Central America
South America
Collection, Mixture
Covers
EFOs
Europe
First Day Covers
Publications
Supplies
Topical
•**Philately**
GENERAL

COLLECTIBLES
•**Advertising**
GENERAL

AIRLINES
General
American
Braniff
Delta
Eastern
Pan Am
Piedmont
TWA
United
AUTO
General
Buick
Chevrolet
Chrysler
Dodge
Ford
Pontiac
Bakery
Bus
CANDY
General
M&M
Cereal
Character
CIGARETTE
General
Joe Camel
Kool
Marlboro
Winston
CLOCKS
COFFEE
DAIRY
General
Borden's
DISPLAYS
DISTILLERY
General

Jack Daniel's
Jim Beam
Green River
Old Crow
DOLLS
DRUG STORE
FARM
General
John Deere
Allis Chalmers
Intl. Harvester
FOOD
FOREST SERVICE
GASOLINE
General
Citgo
Esso
Exxon
Gulf
Hess
Humble
Phillip 66
Shell
Mobil
Pennzoil
Texaco
Tydol
Quaker State
Sinclair
Standard Oil
Sunoco
HOUSEHOLD
LABELS
PREMIUMS
RADIO/PHONOGRAPH
General
RCA
Edison
RESTAURANT

General
Big Boy
SEED, FEED
SHOES
General
Red Goose
Buster Brown
Weatherbird
SIGNS
SOAP
SODA
General
Fountain
Canada Dry
Coca-Cola
Dr. Pepper
Moxie
Pepsi
7Up
Squirt
Hires Root Beer
SOUP
TELEPHONE
TINS
TIRES
TRAYS
TRUCK LINES
UTILITIES
General
Reddy Kilowatt
Handy Flame
Willie Wirehand
VICTORIAN TRADE CARDS
•Animals
GENERAL
BIRD
CAT
DOG
FANTASY

FARM
HORSE
REPTILE
ZOO
•**Animation Art**
GENERAL
HAND-PAINTED
PRODUCTION ART
SERICELS
•**Animation Characters**
GENERAL
HANNA-BARBERA
JAPANESE ANIMATION
KING FEATURES
WALTER LANTZ
WARNER BROS.
•**Art**
GENERAL
AMATEUR ART
ARTIST OFFERINGS
CALENDARS
DECORATOR/DESIGNER
PAINTING
POSTERS
PRINTS
SUPPLIES
•**Art: Fine**
PAINTINGS
DRAWINGS
SCULPTURES
MULTIPLE TECHNIQUES
•**Autographs**
GENERAL
ENTERTAINMENT
General
Movies
Space
Television
Recording Artists

POLITICAL
SCI-FI
•**Banks**
GENERAL
MECHANICAL
STILL
•**Barber Shop, Shaving**
•**Bears**
GENERAL
ACCESSORIES
ANTIQUE
ARTIST
BOYDS
General
Resin
CHAD VALLEY
CHERISHED TEDDIES
DEANS
MERRYTHOUGHT
MUFFY
RAIKES
STEIFF
•**Black Americana**
•**Breyer**
•**Bottles**
GENERAL
AVON
BITTERS
FLASKS
FRUIT JARS
HOUSEHOLD
INKS
MEDICINE AND CURES
MINERAL
POISONS
SODA
WHISKEY
•**Breweriana**
GENERAL

BOTTLES
CANS
COASTERS
OPENERS, CORKSCREWS
PAPER, LABELS
PRE-PROHIBITION
SIGNS, TINS
STEINS, DRINKWARE
TAP HANDLES, KNOBS
TRAYS
•**Casino**
GENERAL
CHIPS
•**Chalkware**
•**Circus, Carnival**
GENERAL
FAIRS
PROGRAMS AND POSTERS
SOUVENIRS
•**Clocks, Timepieces**
CLOCKS
CHARACTER WATCHES
POCKET WATCHES
WRIST WATCHES
OTHER TIMEPIECES
MISCELLANEOUS
•**Coin-Operated**
•**Collector Plates**
GENERAL
BRADFORD EXCHANGE
DANBURY MINT
FRANKLIN MINT
HAMILTON
KNOWLES
PRINCESS HOUSE
STATE PLATES
WEDGWOOD
•**Comic Books**
GENERAL

PRE-GOLDEN AGE
GOLDEN AGE
General
Superhero
Crime
Horror/Sci-Fi
Funny Animal
CLASSIC
SILVER AGE
General
Superhero
Horror/Sci-Fi
MODERN
General
1970–1980
1981–1990
1991–now
COMIC MAGAZINES
NEWSPAPER COMICS
COMIC FIGURINES
ORIGINAL COMIC ART
•**Contemporary**
•**Crafts**
GENERAL
CROSS STITCH
CROCHET
HANDCRAFTED ARTS
General
Artist Offerings
KNITTING
NEEDLEPOINT
SUPPLIES
General
Stamping
Patterns
TOLE PAINTING
•**Decorative**
GENERAL
AVON WORKS

DAVID WINTER
LILLIPUT LANE
LONGABERGER
HUMMEL
ENESCO
HARMONY KINGDOM
JOSEF
WADE
PRECIOUS MOMENTS
NORMAN ROCKWELL
ROBERT HARROP
WORLD STUDIOS

•Dept. 56
GENERAL
DICKENS' VILLAGE
HERITAGE VILLAGE
SNOW BABIES
SNOW VILLAGE

•Disneyana
CONTEMPORARY
General
Apparel, Accessories
Animation/Cels
Posters, Lithos
Books
Collector Clubs
Comics
Figures
Figurines
Holiday
Housewares
Jewelry
Limited Editions
Magic Kingdoms
Plush Toys
Pins, Buttons
Premiums
Records/Tapes/CDs
Toys, Games, Puzzles

Video/Laserdiscs
Watches
VINTAGE
General
Apparel/Accessories
Animation, Cels
Posters & Lithos
Books
Comics
Figures
Figurines
Holiday
Housewares
Jewelry
Pins, Buttons
Plush Toys
Premiums
Records
Toys, Games, Puzzles
Watches

•Ethnographic
•Firefighting
•Fraternal Groups
GENERAL
BOYS & GIRLS BRIGADE
BOY SCOUTS
GIRL SCOUTS
MASONIC
SALVATION ARMY
TRADE UNION

•Fishing
GENERAL
LURES

•Furniture
•Hallmark
GENERAL
KIDDIE CAR CLASSICS
MERRY MINIATURES
MINIATURE ORNAMENTS

SERIES ORNAMENTS

•Hawaiiana

GENERAL

ACCESSORIES

APPAREL

HULA

•Holiday, Seasonal

GENERAL

CHRISTMAS

General

Ornaments

Santa

Vintage

EASTER

HALLOWEEN

NEW YEAR

THANKSGIVING

VALENTINE

•Insulators

•Kitchenware

GENERAL

COOKWARE

General

Cast Iron

GRANITEWARE

COOKIE JARS

OPEN SALTS

SALT, PEPPER SHAKERS

TABLEWARE

General

Flatware

Hollow Ware

SMALL APPLIANCES

UTENSILS

•Knives

GENERAL

COMMEMORATIVE

POCKET

•Lamps

GENERAL

ELECTRIC

NON-ELECTRIC

PARTS

SHADES

•Limited Editions

•Lunchboxes

GENERAL

METAL

PLASTIC

•Magnets

•Maps/Atlas

GENERAL

ROAD MAPS

•Memorabilia

HISTORICAL

MAGIC

ROYAL

MOVIE

General

Gone with the Wind

Lobby Cards: General

Lobby Cards: Non-US

Posters: General

Posters: Non-US

Props, Wardrobe

Lithographs

Photos

ROCK-N-ROLL

General

Photos

Hard Rock Cafe

The Beatles

Elvis: General

Elvis: Buttons

Elvis: Clothing

Elvis: Concert/Tour

Elvis: Belongings

Elvis: Movie Items

Elvis: Music
Elvis: Novelties
Elvis: Photos
Elvis: Trading Cards
Grateful Dead
Kiss
Michael Jackson
Rolling Stones
The Who
TELEVISION
General
50s
60s
70s
80s
90s
THEATRE
WESTERN
OTHER
•**Metalware**
GENERAL
ALUMINUM
BRONZE
COPPER
PEWTER
SILVER
SILVER PLATE
•**Militaria**
GENERAL
ANCIENT
CIVIL WAR
PRE-WWI
WWI
WWII
KOREA
VIETNAM
SURPLUS
•**Music Boxes**
•**Native Americana**

GENERAL
ARTS, CRAFTS
ARTIFACTS
PRE-1940
•**Orientalia**
•**Paper**
GENERAL
EPHEMERA
MATCHBOOKS
MENUS
NEWSPAPERS
PLAYING CARDS
POSTCARDS
General
Animals
Artist Signed
Ethnic
Exposition
Greetings
Holiday
Military
Real Photo
State Views
Town Views
Transportation
Western
SCRAPBOOKS
•**Pez**
•**Phonographs**
•**Photographic Images**
GENERAL
DAGUERREO/AMBRO/TIN
CDV/CABINET
RISQUE
STEREOVIEW
VIEWMASTER
•**Pinbacks**
•**Police**
GENERAL

PATCHES
OBSOLETE BADGES
•**Political**
•**Promo Glasses**
•**Radio**
GENERAL
TRANSISTOR
TUBE
MANUALS
•**Religious**
GENERAL
CHRISTIANITY
EASTERN
JUDAISM
•**Science**
GENERAL
INSTRUMENTS
ROCK/FOSSIL/MINERAL
SPACE EXPLORATION
•**Science Fiction**
GENERAL
BABYLON 5
DR. WHO
GODZILLA
STAR WARS
STAR TREK
X-FILES
•**Sheet Music**
GENERAL
MILITARY/HISTORICAL
MOVIES/TV
NON-PIANO
RADIO
RAG
SONG BOOKS
THEATRE
TRANSPORTATION
•**Souvenirs**
•**Stoneware**

•**Telephone**
•**Textiles**
GENERAL
BEDSPREADS
DRAPERY
FABRIC
KITCHEN
LACE, CROCHET, DOILIES
LINENS
QUILTS
RUGS
SAMPLERS
TAPESTRY
•**Tobacciana**
GENERAL
ASHTRAYS
CIGAR
LIGHTERS
General
Zippo
PIPES
•**Tools**
•**Trading Cards**
COMIC
CREDIT/CHARGE CARDS
PHONE CARDS
MAGIC
GAMING
SCIENCE FICTION
Babylon 5
Star Trek
Star Wars
X-Files
OTHER NON-SPORTS
•**Trains, Railroadiana**
GENERAL
PAPER
•**Trains, RR Models**
GENERAL

AMERICAN FLYER
HORNBY
LIONEL
MARKLIN
MARX
OTHER TINPLATES
SCALES
HO, OO, TT
O
N, Z
Other
•**Transportation**
AUTOMOBILIA
AVIATION
BICYCLE
LICENSE PLATES
NAUTICAL
•**Umbrellas**
•**Vanity Items**
GENERAL
ACCESSORIES
COMPACTS
HATPINS
PERFUMES
•**Vintage**
GENERAL
CLOTHING
General
Accessories
Children's
Denim
Hats
Men
Purses
Shoes
Sports
Women
•**Vintage Sewing**
GENERAL

BUTTONS
MACHINE, ACCESSORY
PATTERNS
PIN CUSHIONS
THIMBLES
•**Weird Stuff**
GENERAL
SLIGHTLY UNUSUAL
REALLY WEIRD
TOTALLY BIZARRE
•**Western Americana**
•**World's Fair**
•**Writing Instruments**
GENERAL
PENS
PENCILS
DESKTOP ITEMS
INKWELLS
SETS
•**Miscellaneous**

COMPUTERS
•**Digital Cameras**
•**Hardware**
GENERAL
BOOKS
CPUS
DRIVES
CD ROM
IDE
SCSI
Floppy, Other
INPUT PERIPHERALS
MACINTOSH
MAINFRAMES
MEMORY
General
Ram
Sdram

MODEMS
MONITORS
MOTHERBOARDS
MULTIMEDIA
NETWORKING
PORTABLE
PRINTERS
General
Accessories
Supplies
PC SYSTEMS
SERVERS
TERMINALS
UNIX
VIDEO
VINTAGE

•**Software**
GENERAL
BOOKS
BUSINESS
CHILDREN'S
DESKTOP PUBLISHING
EDUCATIONAL
GAMES
General
Atari
Commodore
Sega
Sony
Nintendo
GAMES: INTERNET
Ultima Online
GRAPHICS, MULTIMEDIA
MACINTOSH
PROGRAMMING
REFERENCE
UTILITIES
General
Auction Utilities

•**Services**
GENERAL
INFORMATIONAL
General
Auction Services
WEB HOSTING

DOLLS, FIGURES

•**Dolls**
GENERAL
ANTIQUE
General
Bisque
Composition
ARTIST
CLOTH
General
Raggedy Ann, Andy
CLOTHES, ACCESSORIES
Antique, Vintage
Modern
EFFANBEE
FASHION (NON-BARBIE)
General
Gene
FURNITURE
HARD PLASTIC
HOUSE, MINIATURES
General
Vintage
IDEAL
MADAME ALEXANDER
MATTEL
MODERN
General
Cabbage Patch
Holly Hobbie
Rainbow Brite
Strawberry Shortcake

NANCY ANN
PAPER DOLLS
PATTERNS
VOGUE
General
Ginny
Ginnette
Jill, Jeff
•Figures
GENERAL
TROLLS
•Barbie
GENERAL
ACCESSORIES
VINTAGE BARBIE
VINTAGE ACCESSORIES

GREAT COLLECTIONS

JEWELRY, GEMSTONES
•Beads
GENERAL
SUPPLIES
•Gemstones
GENERAL
FACETED, CABOCHON
SPECIMEN, ROUGH
SETTINGS, TOOLS
PACKAGING, DISPLAY
•Jewelry
GENERAL
ANCIENT/ETHNOGRAPHIC
BEADED
General
Antique, Vintage
Contemporary, New
CARVED, CAMEO
CONTEMPORARY
COSTUME

General
Antique, Vintage
Bakelite, Plastics
Contemporary
Designer, Signed
FINE
GOLD
General
Antique, Vintage
Contemporary
Designer, Signed
SILVER
General
Antique, Vintage
Contemporary
Designer, Signed
VICTORIAN
VINTAGE
WATCHES

PHOTO & ELECTRONICS
•Consumer Electronics
GENERAL
AUDIO EQUIPMENT
General
Auto
Home
RADIO EQUIPMENT
General
CB
Ham
TELEPHONE
TEST EQUIPMENT
•Photo Equipment
GENERAL
ACCESSORIES
LENSES
LIGHTING, METERS
SUBMINIATURE

MEDIUM FORMAT
LARGE FORMAT
35MM
MOVIE
DARKROOM EQUIPMENT
VINTAGE, COLLECTIBLE
INSTRUCTION, MANUALS
•**Video Equipment**

POTTERY & GLASS
•**Glass**
GENERAL
ART GLASS
General
N. American
Bohemian
Czech
English
French
Irish
Italian
Scandinavian
CARNIVAL
CONTEMPORARY GLASS
General
Boyd
Crystal
Degenhart
Mosser
DEPRESSION
General
Anchor Hocking
Federal
Hazel Atlas
Indiana
Jeannette
Macbeth-Evans
U.S. Glass
40s, 50s, 60s

KITCHEN GLASSWARE
General
Accessories/Utensils
Butter Dishes
Cruets
Measuring Cups
Reamers
Swanky Swigs
EAPG
ELEGANT
General
Cambridge
Duncan Miller
Fostoria
Heisey
Imperial
Morgantown
New Martinsville
Paden City
Tiffin
Westmoreland
FENTON
FIRE KING
MILK
OPALESCENT
PAPERWEIGHTS
STAINED GLASS
SWAROVSKI
VASELINE
•**Pottery**
GENERAL
BAUER
BLUE RIDGE
BRITISH ART
BUFFALO
CALIFORNIA POTTERY
COLORADO POTTERY
DAKOTA POTTERY
DINNERWARE

EUROPEAN ART
FIESTA: CONTEMPORARY
FIESTA: VINTAGE
FRANCISCAN
FRANKOMA, GRACETONE
HALL
HAEGER
HEADVASES
HOMER LAUGHLIN
HULL
MAJOLICA
MCCOY
METLOX
MOORCROFT
NEWCOMB
OWENS
PFALTZGRAFF
RED WING, RUMRILL
ROOKWOOD
ROSEVILLE
ROYAL COPLEY
RUSSEL WRIGHT
SCANDINAVIAN ART
SHAWNEE
STAFFORDSHIRE
STANGL
TABLEWARES
TEA POTS, TEA SETS
UHL
WATT
WALL POCKETS
WELLER
VAN BRIGGLE
VERNON KILNS
•**Porcelain**
GENERAL
CHINTZ, SHELLEY
DECORATIVE
DINNERWARE

FIGURINES
FIGURINES: ANIMAL
FLOW BLUE
HAVILAND, LIMOGES
HUMMEL, GOEBEL
LEFTON
LENOX
LLADRO
NIPPON
NORITAKE
OCCUPIED JAPAN
PRECIOUS MOMENTS
ROYAL BAYREUTH
ROYAL DOULTON
RS PRUSSIA, RELATED
WEDGWOOD

SPORTS MEMORABILIA
•**Autographs: Sports**
GENERAL
BASEBALL
BASKETBALL
FOOTBALL
GOLF
HOCKEY
OLYMPIC
RACING
TENNIS
•**Memorabilia**
GENERAL
BASEBALL
BASKETBALL
BOXING
FOOTBALL
GOLF
HOCKEY
HORSE RACING
ICE SKATING
INDY 500

NASCAR
OLYMPIC
TENNIS
•Trading Cards
BASEBALL
General
Box
Lots
Packs
Rookies
Sets
Singles: Pre-1950
Singles: 1950–1980
Singles: 1981–now
BASKETBALL
General
Box
Lots
Packs
Rookies
Sets
Singles
FOOTBALL
General
Box
Lots
Packs
Rookies
Sets
Singles
HOCKEY
General
Box
Lots
Packs
Rookies
Sets
Singles
RACING

NASCAR
NHRA
OTHER SPORTS
•Minor League

TOYS, BEAN BAG PLUSH
•Action Figures
GENERAL
BABYLON 5
GI JOE
General
12 Inch
GODZILLA
MEGO
MOVIE
POWER RANGERS
STAR TREK
STAR WARS
SUPERHERO
TRANSFORMERS
SPORTS
General
Starting Lineup
Wrestling
•Bean Bag Plush
GENERAL
ACCESSORIES
General
Boxes, Displays
Clothes, Costumes
Tag Protectors
BAMMERS, BAMM BEANOS
General
Baseball
Football
COCA-COLA BEAN BAGS
DISNEY
General
Mickey and Minnie

Pooh and Friends
GRATEFUL DEAD
MEANIES
PLANET PLUSH
TY BEANIES
General
Bears
Holiday, Seasonal
TY OTHER PRODUCTS
General
Attic: General
Attic: Retired
Beanie Buddies
Pillow Pals: Current
Pillow Pals: Retired
Plush: Current
Plush: Retired
Sports Commemorative
TY RETIRED BEANIES
General
Bears
Holiday, Seasonal
TY TEENIE BEANIES
General
Beanies
Pins
TY TRADING CARDS
General
Cases
Boxes
Packs
Singles, Sets
WARNER BROS.
•**Diecast**
GENERAL
CORGI
DANBURY MINT
DINKY
ERTL

FRANKLIN MINT
HOT WHEELS
General
Red Line
JOHNNY LIGHTNING
LLEDO
MATCHBOX
General
Lesney
NASCAR
General
Action/Revell
Racing Champions
Winners Circle
NHRA
•**Fast Food**
GENERAL
MCDONALD'S
BURGER KING
WENDY'S
•**Fisher-Price**
•**Games**
GENERAL
BOARD GAMES
General
Horror/Monster
Movie/TV
Space
Sports
War Games
ELECTRONIC
ROLE PLAYING
VINTAGE
•**Electronic Pets**
GENERAL
FURBY
TAMAGOTCHI
•**Hobbies**
GENERAL

REMOTE CONTROL
- **Marbles**
  CONTEMPORARY
  VINTAGE
- **Modern**
  GENERAL
  BATTERY OPERATED
  WIND-UP
  VEHICLES
  LEGO
  SPACE TOYS
- **My Little Pony**
- **Peanuts Gang**
- **Plastic Models**
  GENERAL
  AIR
  AUTOMOTIVE
  MILITARY
  MONSTER
  SCIENCE FICTION
  SPACE
- **Plush**
  GENERAL
  BEARS
  CARE BEARS
  GARFIELD
- **Pokémon**
- **Slot Cars**
- **Teletubbies**
- **Toy Rings**
- **Toy Soldiers**
- **Wooden**
- **Vintage Tin**
  GENERAL
  WIND-UP
  FRICTION
- **Vintage Vehicles**
  GENERAL
  CONSTRUCTION

FARM TOYS
MOTORCYCLES
PRESSED STEEL
RUBBER
SLUSH
- **Vintage**
  GENERAL
  ANIMAL DRAWN
  BATTERY OPERATED
  CAP GUNS
  CAST IRON
  CELLULOID
  CHARACTER
  ERECTOR SETS
  PAPER TOYS
  PEDAL CARS
  PLAY SETS
  PULL TOYS
  PUPPETS
  PUZZLES
  RAMP WALKERS
  RIDE-ONS
  SPACE TOYS
  TOY PARTS
  TOY SOLDIERS

MISCELLANEOUS
- **General**
- **Baby Items**
- **Business, Office**
- **Clothing**
  GENERAL
  MEN
  General
  Accessories
  Big and Tall
  Boots, Shoes
  WOMEN
  General

Accessories
Evening Wear
Maternity
Plus Sizes
Shoes
Wedding
CHILDREN
General
Boys
Girls
Toddler
Infant
•**Equestrian Equipment**
•**Equipment**
GENERAL
CONSTRUCTION
FARM
INDUSTRIAL
RESTAURANT
SHOP
•**Adult Only**
GENERAL
ANIMATION
ART: NUDE
AUTOGRAPHS
BOOKS
MAGAZINES
CD
DVD
LASERDISC
PHOTOGRAPHIC
PIN-UPS
POSTCARDS
TRADING CARDS
VIDEO
•**Foodstuff**
•**Garden Items**
GENERAL
PLANTS/SEEDS

General
Indoor Plants
Flowers
Vegetables
GARDEN ACCESSORIES
PUBLICATIONS
•**Hardware Supplies**
•**Household**
GENERAL
BEAUTY
FITNESS
HEALTH
HOME FURNISHINGS
PET SUPPLIES
General
Bathroom Accessories
Canine
Feline
Reptile
Rodent
•**Metaphysical**
•**Musical Instruments**
GENERAL
BRASS
ELECTRONIC
EQUIPMENT
GUITARS
KEYBOARD, PIANO
PERCUSSION
STRING
WOODWIND
•**Real Estate**
•**Services**
GENERAL
INFORMATION SERVICES
SHIPPING
•**Sporting Goods**
GENERAL
ARCHERY

BASEBALL
BASKETBALL
BILLIARDS
BOATING
General
Jet Ski
Power
Sail
CAMPING
EXERCISE EQUIPMENT
FISHING
General
Lures
Reels
Rods
FOOTBALL
GOLF
General
Accessories
Drivers/Woods
Golf Balls
Irons

Putters
Sets
Wedges
HIKING
HUNTING
ROCK CLIMBING
SCUBA
SKATING
SKIING
SNOW BOARDING
•**Show Supplies**
•**Tools**
HAND
POWER
INDUSTRIAL
•**Tickets**
GENERAL
CONCERT
SPORTING EVENTS
THEATRE
•**Travel**

Page numbers in *italics* refer to illustrations.

About Me pages, 27–29, *28*
  contest for, 159
  for nonprofits, 167, 169, 170
Access, 253
accounts:
  questions about, 154
  setting up, 20–22
  viewing balance of, 246–47
accredited users, 29–30
AdGen, 101
Adults Only category, 41, 128
advertisements, 88, 128, 164
advice, unsolicited, 236
Agarpao, Chris, 10
alcohol, 41
American Society of Appraisers, 259
America Online (AOL), 94, 160–61, 247
Anderson, Jess, 96
animals, 40
Announcements board, 159
antiques, 39, 269
  definition of, 182
  malls and group shops, 215–16
  shows, 216–17
Antiques and the Arts Weekly (the Bee), 208
Antiques Road Show, 261
Antiques Trader Weekly, 209
AOL Café, 160
appraisals, 259–61
arbitration, 150
artifacts and historical items, prohibited, 39–40
artists, 79, 179
Arts and Crafts movement, 183
asking price, 226
Auction Assistant, 101
auction catalogs, 190, 203, 206
Auction Poster, 98, 101
auctions, 218–19
  canceling of, 116–17

capitalism and, 62
category featured, 100
for charity, 166–69
completed, 47, 190
Dutch, 25, 70–71
early ending of, 116
featured, 101
high-end, 55–56
interception of, 141
interference with, 140
keeping track of, 241–50
live, 203, 218–19, 231–33
nonperformance of, 141
non-reserve, 69, 82, 106–8
number of, 65
reserve, 69–70, 82, 88, 106–8, 118
time of, 60, 109–11
traditional vs. eBay, 14, 15
Auctionwatch, 93
Aunt Flossie, 157, 159
automated email, 30
automatic billing, 22–23
automotive categories, 39, 53, 56, 190, 269–70

bad behavior, 138–42
Balbo, C. J., 26
Balbo, Ersula, 26
Bannick, Matt, 158
bean bag plush toys, 39, 286–87
Beanie Babies, 184, 185, 196, 287
Best, Jayne, 156, 161–62
best price, 226
bidder searches, 49
bids, bidding, 9–10, 57–74
  canceling of, 116–17
  commitments involved in, 60
  email and, 57
  histories, 68–69
  increments in, 67–68
  at live auctions, 231–33

bids, bidding, (*cont.*)
  management of, 247
  minimum, 103–7
  nonpaying, 144
  on own auctions, 111
  process of, 57–60
  prohibited types of, 140
  proxy, 57, 61–63
  retractions in, 61, 140
  searches of, 48–49
  shill, 49, 140, 141
  sniping and, 63–65, 140, 232
  strategies for winning at, 61–69
  styles of, 65–67
  timing of, 65
  top amounts in, 68
Big Brothers/Big Sisters, 166
billing, automatic, 22–23
Billpoint, 110
boards, 155–64
  customer service, 158–59
  HTML on, 164
  peer-to-peer support, 159–61
  posting to, 157–58
boldface titles, 100
books, 39, 52, 270–72
  for collectors, 205–7
  Internet as source for, 205
  price guides, 207
  used, 205, 227
bootleg items, 142
brand names, 81, 83
Brian, the Category Guy, 38
business supplies, 53
Butterfield & Butterfield, 55, 203
buybacks, 220
Buyer Guide, 154
buyers, buying:
  deal closed by, 125–26
  email requests by, 115–16
  escrow services and, 128–30
  failed deals and, 148
  inquiries from, 151
  mistakes in, 237–38
  nonprofits and, 168
  remorse of, 112, 150
  sellers contacted by, 125–26
  successful, 223–38
buyer's premium, 233

cable modems, 19–20
Calendar, 159
cameras, digital, 97–98, 253
capital letters, 158

Carroll, Cherie, 227
cars, 39, 52, 56, 190, 269–70
Carter, Alexandra L., 3, 5, 126
Carter Cybernetics, 3
cash, 108–9
cashier's checks, 108
Cataloging by Columbus, 104
catalogs:
  auction, 190, 203, 206, 218
  exhibition, 205
  manufacturers', 205–6
categories, 3, 118, 192
  choosing of, 84–85
  featured auctions in, 102
  major, 38
  overview of, 269–90
  searching of, 37–39
  switching of, 115
category featured auctions, 102
Category-Specific boards, 161–62
certified checks, 108
CHAMPS/Project Team Work, 165
Chapel, 235
charges:
  by eBay, 23–25
  by i-Escrow, 130
charity, on eBay, 164–70
charity auctions, 166–69
chat rooms, 155–64
  policies for, 163–64
  as source of input, 71
  specific categories and, 161–62
checks, 108
Chen, Rebecca, 64
Christie's, 203
civility, 148, 149, 151
clothing, 52
Club99, 107
clubs, collectors', 219–20
coins, 39, 272–73
collectibles, 39, 273–81
  attribution and, 188–89
  checklist on value of, 183–89
  condition and, 184–86
  definition of, 182
  demand and, 183
  design and, 188–89
  grading systems for, 186
  historical significance and, 186–87
  material and, 189
  provenance and, 187
  quality and, 184
  rarity and, 183–84
  regional interest in, 182

restoration and, 186, 188
shows for, 217
sources of, 211–20
supply and, 183–84
uniqueness of, 181–82
value of, 181–97
vintage, 182
Collectibles and Platemakers Guild, 197
collecting, xv
accumulating vs., 176
beginnings of, 176–77
books for, 205–7
building and upgrading in, 180
buying mistakes in, 238
buying successfully in, 223–38
by children, 177
expertise in, 199–209
Internet help on, 207–8
as investment, 193–96
law of averages in, 234
motivations for, 173–76
parameters set in, 178–80
periodicals for, 208–9
personal choices in, 178
price in, 179–80
shopping etiquette in, 234–36
trading in, 236–38
collectingchannel.com, 177, 219
collections:
disposal and donation of, 261–62
insuring of, 255–59
inventory of, 251–55
refocusing of, 77
collectoronline.com, 219
collectors' clubs and newsletters, 190
collectors' series, 196–97
College Kids, 165
community customs, 30–35
Community Standards, 154
complaints, formal, 150
computer games, 52
computers, 19, 20, 39, 281–82
insuring of, 258
condition:
of items, 86
problems with, 150
and value of collectibles, 184–86
conditional returns, 112
conditions and terms of sale, for live
auctions, 233
consignment shops, 214
contact information:
false, missing, or omitted, 141
publishing of others', 142

contact terms, 73
cookies, 127–28
Cool Happenings, 159
copyright, violations of, 144–45
costs:
of boldface text, 102
of category featured auctions, 102
of featured auctions, 102
of Featured Gallery listing, 102
of Gallery, 100, 102
country of origin, 79
credit cards, 109, 110
fraud with, 11, 137, 148
credits, fee, 118–19
customer service boards, 158–59

Dahl, Dave, 120
Davis, Sammy, Jr., 50
dealers, 224
damaged items and, 231
sources for, 220
tax breaks for, 230
deals, disputed, 148–49
Diana, Princess of Wales, 187
Diana (eBay ambassador), 160, 204
digital cameras, 97–98
inventory and, 253, 255
Direct Support for New Users board,
158
documentation, 87
dolls, 39, 282–83
dots per inch (dpi), 97
DoubleClick, 128
downloading of files, 148
DSL (digital subscriber line), 19
due diligence, 71
Dungeon, 235
Dutch auctions, 25, 70–71

eBay:
community of, 6–8, 155–57
dispute resolution on, 137–52
formal complaints on, 137
founding of, xv–xvi, 6
four pillars of, 4–6
mastering of, 9–10
peak times on, 207
popularity of, 8
safety of, 11–12
site map of, 12–15, *14*, 265–67
value system of, 137, 164
volume of business on, 99, 127,
131
eBay addicts, 179

eBay a-go-go, 20
eBay Ambassadors, 5, 8, 13, 18, 50, 64, 96, 105, 126, 130, 139, 156, 160, 161, 175, 185, 204, 212, 221, 227, 243, 256
eBay Café 154, 157, 159, 160, 235, 258
eBay Customer Support Team, 157
eBay Foundation, 164–66
eBay International board, 161
eBay Life, 27, 159
eBay Magazine, 208
eBay power sellers, 8, 26, 120, 247
Echoes, 209
EEEC (Emergency eBay Evacuation Center), 235
electronics, 39, 283–84
email, 30, 57
email addresses, 146
    changing of, 154
    finding of, 127–28
Emergency Contact board, 161
Emerson, Ralph Waldo, 157
endangered species, 40
era collections, 179
escrow, 109, 152
    services for, 128–30, 138
Essentials of Book Collecting, 208
estate sales, 213
evaluating items, 71–72
exhibition catalogs, 205
expertise:
    developing of, 199–209
    marketplace and, 203
    research and, 203–9
    training your senses in, 200–3

factory collections, 179
family name, searching of, 53
Father Griff, 235
featured auctions, 102
Featured Gallery listing, 102
featured items, 102
Federal Express, 134, 135
fee credits, 118–19
feedback, 29, 31–35, *33*, 74
    basic rules of, 32
    on buyers, 136, 143
    negative, 34–35, 61, 117, 144, 150
    offenses in, 138–40
    positive, 34, 151
    responding to, 35, 246
    on sellers, 71, 143
    shill, 140
    solicitation or extortion of, 140
    star chart for, 34

user IDs and, 26–27
    viewing of, 246
Feedback Forum, 11, 149
fees:
    avoidance of, 88
    for Dutch auctions, 25
    final value, 24–25, 116, 118–19
    fixed, 25
    illegal avoidance of, 141
    insertion, 23–24, 116, 118
figures, 39, 282–83
firearms, 40
fireworks, 40
first bid, 103
Fisher Center, 166
flatbed scanners, 97
flea markets, 214–15
food, 54
For All Kids Foundation, Inc., 166
Forrest Gump, 230
Franck, Kaj, 184
fraud, 141
    credit cards and, 11, 137, 148
    insurance against, 142–44
Fraud Reporting System, 138, 143–44
Frequently Asked Questions (FAQs), 154–55
Friends, 160
Friends of Farm Drive, 165
FTP (file transfer protocol), 94
furniture, insuring of, 257–58

Gallery, 51–52
    cost of, 100, 102
    Featured, listing in, 102
    listing in, 102
    photos in, 100
garage sales, 213
garden items, 54
gemstones, 39, 283
General Support Q&A board, 158, 159
George Ann (user), 258
Gerdts, Bob, 105
Gibb, Mary Ellen, 9
Gibson, Mel, 166
gif, 98
gifts, 52, 101
Giving board, 169–70
glass, 39, 284–85
Glossary, 155
Great Collections, 39, 54–55, 283
Griffith, Jimmy (Uncle Griff), 103, 154, 157, 159

haggling, 224–31
hallmarks, 82
Handel Company Inc., 188
Hanks, Tom, 166
Hardesty, Dixie, 17, 18
hate speech, 163
help, 153–70
    on the boards, 155–70
    do-it-yourself, 154–55
Help link, 154–55
Help Overview, 154
heritage, 52
hijacking, 234–26
Hirsch, Jill, 185
Home Care Companions, 165
home furnishings, 52
hot ratings, 140
HTML, 89–90, 99–100, 160
    on the boards, 164
    for listings, 89–92
Huddleston, Dick, 243

icons, 26, 102
identity, misrepresentation of, 141
i-Escrow, 128–29, 152
illegal items, 142, 144–45
image hosting services, 93
Images/HTML board, 160
independent shops, 215
infringing items, 138, 144–45
Inn Dwelling, 165
insertion fees, 23–24, 116, 118
inspecting, at live auctions, 231–32
insurance, 138
    for collections, 255–59
    for computers, 258
    fraud, 142–44
    for furniture, 257–58
    homeowner's or renter's, 259
    for jewelry, 257
    non-scheduled items and, 258
    for paintings, 257
    revaluations and, 259
    scheduling in, 257–58
intellectual property, 145
Interactive Digital Software
    Association, 53
interference, with eBay's operations or
    site, 142
International Association of Appraisers,
    259
international shipping, 125
international users, boards for, 161
Internet, 17–20

codes and expressions on, 162–63
collecting sites on, 207–8, 219
credit card fraud and, 11, 137, 148
new and used books on, 205–7
photos on, 93–94
sales tax and, 52
shipper information on, 135
shipping supplies and, 132
Internet service provider (ISP), 93–94
inventory, 183, 251–55
    database of, 253, 255
    digital cameras and, 253, 254
    list of, 251–52, 255
    photos of, 253, 255
    software for, 253, 255
    spreadsheet for, 252, 254, 255
    videotaping of, 252, 254
ISDN (integrated services digital net-
    work), 19
iShip.com, 135
item descriptions, 118
    accuracy in, 151
    adding to, 114–15
    clichés in, 87–88
    photos in, 99–100
    successful, 85–87
item number, 126
items, locating of, 37–56

Janney (user), 258
JavaScript, 85, 163
jewelry, 39, 283
    insuring of, 257
jpeg, jpg, 98
Juvenile Diabetes Foundation, 166

Kaye, Elizabeth, 174
Keller, Maria, 139
key words, 44, 45, 83
Kimes, Curtis R., 212
King's Room, 235
Kitchen, Lorrie, 129
knives, switchblade, 41
Kodak, 93
Krause, 208
Kruse, Dean, 55–56
Kruse International, 53, 57

Lewis, Meriwether, 262
Lewis and Clark College, 262
libraries, donating collections to,
    262–63
limited editions, 197
Link Exchange, 128

links, 91–92
Lisa's Postcard Page, 208
listings:
  basics of, 80
  checklist for, 89
  choosing categories for, 84–85
  item descriptions in, *see* item
    descriptions
  latest, 45
  photos in, 92–100
  reviewing of, 113–14
  revisions of, 114–15
  rules for, 88–89
  simple, 85
  special options for, 101–2
  titles of, 78–79, 82–84
  using HTML in, 89–92
Lloyds of London, 142–43
lotteries, 88
Lucas, George, 166
lurkers, 162

MADD (Mothers Against Drunk
  Driving), 166
Mad Magazine Cover Site, 207–8
Madonna, 166
Magazine Antiques, 209
magazines and journals, 206
Maine Antiques Digest, 209
manufacturers' catalogs, 205–6
marks, 82
Martin, Dean, 50
Martin, Ricky, 166
material, 79, 82, 189
Max, Peter, 166
Meyer, Joy, 221
Microsoft Office, 250, 253
Microsoft Works, 250
Millbranth, Don, 9
Miller, Linda, 256
minimum price, lack of sale and, 118
Minnelli, Liza, 50
mint in box (MIB), 90, 156
miscellaneous category, 39, 288–90
misrepresentation, of identity, 141
Mister Lister, 113
modems, 19, 47
money orders, 108
Moser, David, 175
Mota, Ray, 50
movies, 39, 272
museums, donating collections to,
  262–63
music, 39, 243, 271–72

My eBay, 241–50
  AOL and, 247
  Bidder List on, 242
  completed auctions on, 242
  navigations with, 246–47
  preferences on, 241–46, 250
  Seller List on, 242
My Information, 154

National Association of Limited Edition
  Dealers, 197
Native American artifacts, 39–40
negotiating, 224–31
  buying in bulk and, 229
  factors in, 224–26
  groundwork for, 226
  mood breakers in, 230–31
  scenarios in, 228–30
New Features board, 158
new old stock, 89–90
new products, 52
New York Times, 174
nicknames, 22
nonpaying bidders, 144
nonprofit organizations, charity auctions by, 167–69
no reserve auctions, 69, 82, 106–8
notification, by email, 30
Nureyev, Rudolf, 174

object type collections, 178
obscenity, 142, 163
O'Donnell, Rosie, 166
Omidyar, Pam, xv, xvii
Omidyar, Pierre, xv–xvii, 6, 10, 148, 153,
  164
Onassis, Jacqueline Kennedy, 187
Online Traders Web Alliance, 107
On the Road eBay Tour, 217

pagers, for eBay, 20
paintings, insuring of, 257
Parents Helping Parents, Inc., 165
Parker, Ed, 13
passwords, 12, 21, 147, 154
patents, violations of, 144–45
patina, 186, 188
payments, 10, 108–9, 110
  methods of, 73
PBS, 261
periodicals, for collecting, 208–9
personal checks, 108
personal computers (PCs), 19
Personal Shopper, 49–51

pets, paraphernalia for, 53
photo equipment, 39, 283–84
Photopoint, 93
photos, 92–100
    accuracy of, 86
    adding to listing of, 99–100
    on computers, 95–98
    digital cameras and, 93, 97–98
    in Gallery, 100
    of goods, 94–95
    on Internet, 93–94
    permissions for, 95
    scanning of, 97
    tweaking and editing of, 98
    uploading of, 99
pickers, 220
Picture URL field, 99–100
pink shades, 26
pirated items, 142
pixels, 97
Pixhost, 93
police-related items, 40
Pongo, 93, 160
Pongo's Hints, 235
pop-up requests, 147
pornography, 163
pottery, 39, 284–85
Presley, Elvis, 13
price-based collecting, 179–80
price guides, 207
prices:
    asking, 226
    best, 226
    consultants for, 15
    cycles in, 192–93
    inquiring about, 226
    keeping tabs on, 190
    markups and, 190–92
    minimum, 103–6, 118
    mistakes and, 192
    profit margins and, 191–92
    of sold or on-hold pieces, 236
    value vs., 189–90
    wholesale, 237
Priority Mail, 134
privacy, 163
    eBay policy on, 138, 146–47
    protection of, 146–48
    user's role in protecting of, 147–48
production pieces, 188
profanity, 142, 163
Professional Coin Grading Service, 104
Professional Sports Authenticator, 104
profit margins, 120–21

prohibited items, 39–41, 138, 144–45
Project HELP (High Expectations
    Learning Program), 165
provenance, 86, 187
proxy bidding, 10, 57, 61–63, 247
pyrotechnic devices, 40

Q&A board, 154, 157
Queen's Roundroom, 235

racism, 142
real estate, 53
receipts, from nonprofits, 168
records, collectible, 243
refinishing, 186
registered users, 20–22
relisting, of items, 117–18
repairs, 150
resale number, 230
research, 203–9
    for live auctions, 232
reserve price auctions, 69–70, 82,
    87–88, 106–8, 118
resolution, of disputes, 148–51
restoration, 186
    cars and, 190
returns, 112–13
revaluations, 259
Rich's Archives at the Zoo, 235
Robinson, Ed, 247
Roosevelt, Franklin Delano, 186–87
Rosaaen, Rockin' Robin, 13
Roseville Pottery, 182
Roseville Pottery Exchange, 207
Rosie, 166
rules:
    for feedback, 32
    for listings, 88–89
    set by sellers, 72–74
runners-up list, for live auctions, 232
Rushton-Clem, Richard, 183

SafeHarbor, 11, 104, 130, 137–52
safety, of buying on eBay, 10–11
sales tax, 52, 230
satellite PC, 20
Saturdays, bidding on, 107
scanning, of photos or objects, 97
scheduling, insurance and, 257–58
scouts, 220
searches, 37–38
    of bidders, 49
    of completed auctions, 48
    customizing of, 41–44

searches, (*cont.*)
  for family name, 53
  Gallery, 51–52
  item numbers and, 47–48
  latest listings in, 45
  mistakes in, 47
  Personal Shopper, 49–51
  by region, 48
  of sellers, 49
  techniques for, 45–46, 47
  text-only, 47
  by title, 44–46
Seattle Film Works, 93
see my other auctions link, 92
Seller Guide, 154
sellers, selling:
  auction timing and, 109–11
  bidding on own auctions and, 111
  business practices for, 103–21
  buyers contacted by, 125–26
  categories and, 38, 41–43
  deal closed by, 125–36
  eBay businesses built by, 119–21
  escrow services and, 128–30
  failed deals and, 148
  final touches for, 113–14
  fraud in, 141
  items not sold by, 117–19
  lowest price set by, 103–6
  payment methods and terms set by,
    72–73, 108–9, 110
  questions for, 71–72
  refusal of bids by, 140
  responding to bidders by, 115–16
  return policy and, 112–13
  rules set by, 72–74
  sample email for, 126–27
  searches of, 48–49
  shipping and, 73, 111–12, 131–35
  strategies for, 117–18
  successful listings by, 77–102
  tracking down buyer's email by, 127
Sell Your Item form, *78*, 80–81
services, auctions of, 54
shills:
  bidding by, 49, 140, 141
  feedback by, 140
shipping, 111–12, 131–35
  costs of, 52, 73, 125–26, 135
  methods of, 73
  packing for, 131–33
  supplies for, 131–32, 134
shorthand, on Internet, 162–63

Sinatra, Frank, 50
Skoll, Jeff, xvi–xvii, 10
Sky Tel Page Recall, 20
sniping, 63–65, 140
  at live auctions, 232
software, off-the-shelf, 101
Song, Mary Lou, 38
Sotheby's, 203
sources, of dealers, 220
spam, 35–36, 142, 147
  nonprofits and, 168
specialized collectibles shows, 217
speed, on Internet, 17–20
sporting goods, 53–54
Sports Memorabilia (category), 39,
  285–86
spreadsheets, 248
  inventory on, 252, 254, 255
stamps, 39, 272–73
Starwood Hotels and Resorts, 166
Stickley, Gustave, 183
stocks and certificates, 40
strategies:
  for bidding, 61–69
  for selling, 117–18
Students Run LA, 165
Suggestion Box, 159
suspicious activities, 138–42
swap meets, 219
system-automated policies, 144

tag sales, 213
tax, sales, 52, 230
tax breaks, 230
tax deductibility, 167–68
taxes, donating collections and, 262
tax-exempt status, 167
theme collections, 178–79
threats, user-to-user, 142
thrift shops, 214
timing, of auctions, 109–11
titles, 78–79, 82–84, 117
  boldface text in, 101
  keywords in, 83
toys, 39, 286–88
Toy Story, 192
trademark violations, 144–45
trades, trading, 88, 236–38
TRUSTe Privacy Program, 146

Uncle Griff (Jimmy Griffith), 103, 154,
  157, 159
unconditional returns, 112

underage usage, 141
United Parcel Service (UPS), 125, 132,
   134, 135
United States Postal Service (USPS),
   132, 134, 135, 149
University Research Expedition
   Program (UREP), 165
uploading, 98
uppercase text, 158
user agreement, 21
user IDs, 22, 146, 155, 157–58, 242
   changing of, 26
   feedback ratings and, 27
   for nonprofits, 167
users:
   contact information for, 149
   new, 158
User-to-User eBay Q&A board, 160
User Verification, 138

vacations, 54
Verified Rights Owners (VeRO) program, 145
vintage collectibles, definition of, 182

violence, threats of, 163
viruses, computer, 148
Voice of the Customer program, 158
vulgar language, 142, 163

want ads, 88
weapons, 41
Web sites, 36, 99
   links to, 88
   see also About Me pages
WebTV, 85
Weird Stuff, 39, 177, 281
Welcome Wagon, 154
Wendlick, Roger, 262
Western Union, 108
Whitman, Meg, xvii
wholesale prices, 230
   estimating of, 237
World of Cast Iron Cookware, 208

Yahoo, arbitration page of, 149
Yellow Pages, 209

Zookeeper Twaze, 235

A very collectible card.

The new eBay™ Visa® card.

And the perfect way to round out your collection — with the convenient buying power of the new eBay Visa.

As an eBay Visa cardholder, you'll receive discounts on tradeshows, merchandise at the online eBay store and Krause publications — including the new eBay Magazine. Also, by putting your eBay Visa on file at eBay.com, you'll get a $10 credit* towards your eBay account. You'll get all of this at a low introductory 3.9% APR.**

To find out more and apply by phone call 1-800-613-0318. **ebaY.COM**

(The amazing place to buy, sell and collect.)